Praise for *Insane*

"I thoroughly enjoyed this book. Although this is a tragic topic and one that rightfully should embarrass all, Alisa Roth's *Insane* clearly and objectively lays out the extent and history of our abandonment of the mentally ill while setting forth thoughtful pathways forward. It is rare that I have seen anything written that truly captures the horror, inhumanity, and utter insanity of our society's approach to the treatment of the mentally ill like this book does. This book should be required reading for any person involved with the criminal justice system or legislatures."

—Thomas J. Dart, sheriff of Cook County, Illinois

INSANE

America's Criminal Treatment
of Mental Illness

―――――

ALISA ROTH

BASIC BOOKS

New York

For M, D, E, L, and H

Hachette Book Group supports the right to free expression and the value of copyright. The purpose of copyright is to encourage writers and artists to produce the creative works that enrich our culture.

The scanning, uploading, and distribution of this book without permission is a theft of the author's intellectual property. If you would like permission to use material from the book (other than for review purposes), please contact permissions@hbgusa.com. Thank you for your support of the author's rights.

Basic Books
Hachette Book Group
1290 Avenue of the Americas, New York, NY 10104

www.basicbooks.com

Printed in the United States of America

First Edition: April 2018

Published by Basic Books, an imprint of Perseus Books, LLC, a subsidiary of Hachette Book Group, Inc. The Basic Books name and logo is a trademark of the Hachette Book Group.

The publisher is not responsible for websites (or their content) that are not owned by the publisher.

Library of Congress Control Number: 2018933315

ISBNs: 978-0-465-09419-6 (hardcover), 978-0-465-09420-2 (ebook)

LSC-C

10 9 8 7 6 5 4 3 2 1

Contents

Contents

Introduction

Near the beginning of Ken Kesey's 1962 novel, *One Flew Over the Cuckoo's Nest*, the narrator recalls seeing a public relations man give a tour of the psychiatric hospital where the story is set. Boasting of how far things have come from the "old-fashioned cruelty" that used to reign in such places, he tells a group of visiting teachers, "What a *cheery* atmosphere, don't you agree?...Oh when I think back on the old days, on the filth, the bad food, even, yes, brutality, oh, I realize ladies that we have come a long way."[1]

As Kesey's novel makes devastatingly clear, however, this new-and-improved institution simply offers the same old abuse in a different package. The book centers around the struggle between Randle Mc-Murphy, a rebellious small-time criminal who feigns mental illness to avoid prison time—memorably played by Jack Nicholson in the 1975 film adaptation—and Nurse Ratched, the sadistic manager of the psych ward where he has been sent. McMurphy convinces the other patients to support him in an insurrection against Ratched's control; she eventually puts an end to it by having McMurphy lobotomized.

Few other works of fiction or nonfiction have so indelibly captured the horrors of psychiatric hospitals in the mid-twentieth century, from the lack of any real effort to cure patients to outright abuse of the kind the public relations man promised had disappeared; the over-medication of the patients; the forced inactivity; the humiliating and unsanitary conditions ("[one patient] stood so long in one spot the piss ate the floor and beams away under him").[2]

More than fifty years later, state psychiatric hospitals of this sort are, like lobotomies, long gone. Yet when we think that the hellish world Kesey captured belongs to another era, we are just as deluded as his fictional PR man. It's true that the *hospitals* have mostly disappeared: between 1950 and 2000 the number of people with serious mental illness living in psychiatric institutions dropped from almost half a million people to about fifty thousand.[3] But none of the rest of it has gone away, not the cruelty, the filth, the bad food, or the brutality. Nor, most importantly, has the large population of people with mental illness who are kept largely out of sight, their poor treatment invisible to most ordinary Americans.

The only real difference between Kesey's time and our own is that the mistreatment of people with mental illness now happens in jails and prisons. Today, the country's largest providers of psychiatric care are not hospitals at all, but rather the jails in Chicago, Los Angeles, and New York City. Across the country, correctional facilities are struggling with the reality that they have become the nation's de facto mental health care providers, although they are hopelessly ill-equipped for the job. They are now contending with tens of thousands of people with mental illness who, by some counts, make up as much as half of their populations.

Little acknowledged in public debate, this situation is readily apparent in almost every correctional facility in the country. In Michigan roughly half of all people in county jails have a mental illness, and nearly a quarter of people in state prisons do. In 2016 the state spent nearly $4 million on psychiatric medication for state prisoners.[4] In Iowa about a third of people in prison have a serious mental illness; another quarter have a chronic mental health diagnosis.[5] Meanwhile, nearly half of the people executed nationwide between 2000 and 2015 had been diagnosed with a mental illness and/or substance use disorder in their adult lives.[6] When a legal settlement required California to build a psychiatric unit on its death row at San Quentin, the forty beds were filled immediately. The mental health crisis is especially pronounced among women prisoners: one study by the US Bureau of Justice Statistics found that 75 percent of women incarcerated in jails and prisons had a mental illness, as compared with just over 60 and 55 percent of men, respectively.[7] A more recent study showed that 20 percent of women in jail and 30 percent in prison had experienced "serious psychological distress" in the month before the survey, compared with 14 percent and 26 percent of men, respectively.[8]

Although the overall number of people behind bars in the United States has decreased in recent years, the *proportion* of prisoners with mental illness has continued to go up. In 2010, about 30 percent of people at New York's Rikers Island jail had a mental illness; in 2014, the figure rose to 40 percent, and by 2017, it had gone up to 43 percent.[9] Studies of the most frequently arrested people in New York, Los Angeles, and elsewhere have found that they are far more likely than others to have mental illness, to require antipsychotic medications while incarcerated, and to have a substance use problem.

That there are so many people with mental illness locked in our jails and prisons is but one piece of the crisis. Along with race and poverty, mental illness has become a salient feature of mass incarceration, one that must be accounted for in any discussion about criminal justice reform. Mental illness affects every aspect of the criminal justice system, from policing to the courts to prisons and beyond. Nor are the effects limited to the criminal justice system; many people with mental illness cycle back and forth between jail or prison and living in the community. The racial inequity of the criminal justice system has been widely noted: it is estimated that one out of every three African American men and one of every six Hispanic men born in 2001 will be arrested in their lifetimes.[10] But for Americans with serious mental illness, it is estimated that as many as one in two will be arrested at some point in their lives.[11] It's not just arrests. One in four of the nearly one thousand fatal police shootings in 2016 involved a person with mental illness, according to a study by the *Washington Post*. The *Post* estimated that mental illness was a factor in a quarter of fatal police shootings in 2017, too.[12]

People with mental illness are among the most disadvantaged members of our society, and when they end up in the criminal justice system, they tend to fare worse than others. People with mental illness are less likely to make bail and more likely to face longer sentences.[13] They are more likely to end up in solitary confinement, less likely to make parole, and more likely to commit suicide.[14] Yet jail and prison have become, for many people, their primary means of getting mental health care. Their experiences offer an especially eye-opening view of a criminal justice system that today houses more than two million people and costs us hundreds of billions of dollars a year.

Diagnosing and treating mental illness is complicated. Unlike physical diseases like diabetes or cancer, there is no definitive test, and our assumptions about what constitutes "craziness" have continued to shift over the centuries. In biblical times and still today in some cultures, seeing visions or hearing voices is an indication of holiness, not madness. I spoke to the mother of a man with severe mental illness who recalled telling her son that the voice he heard couldn't be Jesus because Jesus would never say such awful things. Others might consider it a sign of mental illness to hear Jesus saying anything, good or bad. Even medical understanding of sanity is ever-changing: as recently as 1973, the *Diagnostic and Statistical Manual of Mental Disorders*—the preeminent guide to psychiatric diagnosis and treatment—listed homosexuality as a disease. (It was not until 1987 that homosexuality was completely removed from the DSM.)

Beyond the difficulties of diagnosis, finding an effective way to treat serious diseases such as bipolar disorder or schizophrenia is often a matter of trial and error. Sometimes, a medication regimen stops working. Many psychotropic medications have severe side effects. The likelihood of side effects emerging increases the longer a person takes these medicines; sometimes the side effects are so bothersome that patients decide to quit taking them.

In *One Flew Over the Cuckoo's Nest*, Kesey describes the two kinds of patients in the hospital as Acutes ("because the doctors figure them still sick enough to be fixed") and Chronics (who are "in for good, the staff concedes").[15] When Kristopher Rodriguez, a thirty-one-year-old man from Florida, first went into the criminal justice system, it seemed like he would have been classified as an Acute; now nearly a decade later, he would almost certainly qualify as a Chronic. A tall, strapping

boy whose friends called him Dino, as in "dinosaur," he was diagnosed with schizophrenia when he was around fourteen. His mother,
Gemma Pena, had come home from work one night to find that he
had disconnected the hot-water heater, convinced that the CIA was
using it to spy on him. At first she thought his behavior was simply
evidence of grief over his grandmother's death a few months earlier;
Rodriguez had been especially close to her. But when he continued to
act strangely, saying he was hearing voices, Pena called the police and
had him hospitalized against his will.

It was the first of perhaps a dozen times that she had him "Baker
Acted," as it is known in Florida. (The Baker Act was named for
Maxine Baker, a member of the Florida state legislature who pushed
for the 1971 law that today governs involuntary commitments in the
state.) The next few years were a blur of doctors' appointments, drug
use, homelessness, arrests, and voluntary and involuntary hospitalizations, a history that his mother has documented in four overstuffed
shopping bags she keeps hidden away in her rented efficiency apartment in Hialeah, a Miami suburb that has a large Cuban population.

The papers and mementos she spreads on the neatly made double
bed include photos of her son as a dark-haired baby with fat cheeks
and dark eyes, the remnants of his baseball card collection, certificates
of achievement from the taekwondo class he took in middle school,
the footprint the hospital took when he was born, letters from mental health clinics following up on missed appointments, worn snap-
shots of him as a twelve-year-old in his Navy Cadets uniform, and
old prescription bottles, some with medication to manage his mental
illness still inside: Abilify, Clozaril, Benzotropine. When a hurricane
threatened to flood her ground floor apartment recently, she put all
the documents into plastic bins, which she wrapped in plastic bags and
set on the high bar table in her kitchen alcove. "I had to save my son's
records," she said. "That was my main concern."

She keeps them all as if sheer existence of this detritus, this catalog
of his long-ago accomplishments might somehow propel him back on
track. She hopes the medical records will help him re-qualify for Social Security Disability when he gets out of prison. The pills she keeps

as evidence in case he ever decides to join one of the lawsuits alleging that the medication leads to compulsive gambling and other problems.

The dusty artifacts, infused with cigarette smoke, also serve as evidence of her devotion to what could be called the Kristopher Project, the frustrating and years-long effort to manage his illness: all the times she went to court to have him committed to the psychiatric hospital, the pillbox she bought and filled in a vain attempt to help him take his medication, and scraps of paper scrawled with phone numbers of doctors, lawyers, and social workers. Pena, who trained as a medical technician and currently works as an administrative assistant in the maternity clinic at a hospital near her home, attributes her tenacity to maternal love. "I decided to be a mother," she says frequently. "God gives us choices, and I chose to be a mother."

Rodriguez is currently serving a ten-year sentence in a Florida state prison for trying to rob somebody at gunpoint in 2008, when he was twenty-two. He spent five years in jail before he took the plea bargain; people with mental illness often spend far longer in jail waiting for their cases to be resolved. During his time in jail, he was sick enough that he had to be hospitalized three separate times—twice for psychiatric crises and once because he was so psychotic that he mutilated his genitals. His mother said the second psychiatric hospitalization was the last time she saw him lucid.

Nevertheless, after he accepted a plea bargain, he was transferred to prison. His first few months there, he lived in general population. (One wonders how Florida's department of corrections was not notified of the extent of his illness before he arrived.) After a few months of occasional run-ins with prison staff, he was moved to a unit for prisoners with mental illness. About a year ago his condition deteriorated to such an extent that he was moved to the Lake Correctional Institution, a prison northwest of Orlando that is equipped with an inpatient psychiatric unit. Even so, his mother says, her son remains severely psychotic, an assessment apparently shared by the Florida Department of Corrections, which regularly denies Pena visits on the basis that Rodriguez is too sick to see her.

Pena says that she writes her son regularly but that it's been years since he's written back. She sent him pictures of herself and his brothers and nieces, but he tore them up. When she does get to visit him, the son who used to take pride in being a natty dresser smells terrible and is often visibly dirty, as if he hasn't bathed in weeks, even though she regularly puts money into his commissary account so that he can buy toiletries. (Prisoners who want basic items, from potato chips to a radio to toothpaste and shampoo, have to use the money in their commissary accounts, usually provided by family and friends.) During their last visit he got so agitated, yelling and pounding his fists on the table, that the corrections officers handcuffed and shackled him, and took him away strapped into a wheelchair. His medical records show that his medication compliance has been spotty; sometimes Rodriguez refuses to take it, and other times it hasn't been available because the supplier didn't deliver it to the prison.

For years now, Rodriguez has been stuck in this sad limbo: according to the state, he is well enough to stay incarcerated but far too sick to live in the general prison population or even to get regular visits from his mother. Lawyers who have examined his case say his story is typical. Florida's prisons have been the subject of repeated investigations for their treatment of prisoners with mental illness; so have jails and prisons in other states, including California, Illinois, and Alabama. Indeed, jails and prisons across the country are filled with thousands of people like Kristopher Rodriguez.

Tom Dart, the sheriff of Cook County, Illinois, which encompasses the greater Chicago area, says there is a fundamental mismatch between the legions of people with mental illness who inhabit jails and prisons and the services that those jails and prisons are able to provide. So critical is the problem that in 2015, Dart appointed a clinical psychologist to run the Cook County Jail, one of the largest in the country, which he oversees. (It's far more typical for wardens to rise through the ranks of corrections officers or other law enforcement.) "It would be no different if you were to populate college calculus classes with … preschool kids," he told me. "You would imagine, the professor doesn't know how to deal with it, it's the wrong population for this class, but you keep filling the class with four-year-olds."

When I first started reporting on mental illness in the criminal justice system, I believed the oft-heard explanation that this crisis was the result of closing the state psychiatric hospitals: beginning in the 1960s, we took people out of asylums, and because there was no place else for them to go, they moved, more or less directly, into jails and prisons. But I quickly discovered that the story was far more complicated. The severe neglect of community mental health care in the United States has certainly contributed to the extraordinary number of people with mental illness behind bars. But far worse than that, I came to realize, we have re-created much of the same dysfunction that pervaded the asylums of the nineteenth and twentieth centuries and the very abuses we sought to end by shutting them down. Overcrowding is common, oversight is poor, and abuse is widespread. There is also a more fundamental problem than the sheer *number* of people with mental illness who get arrested and end up in jails and prisons, or the ways they are treated when they get there. In many cases, they shouldn't be there at all.

The patchwork of institutions and entities—cops, courts, and correctional facilities—that together make up our criminal justice system is deeply fragmented and bureaucratic. Throughout our history we have struggled to figure out what transgressions should be considered crimes: for a brief period within my grandparents' lifetimes, it was against the law to drink a glass of wine; within my parents' lifetimes, interracial marriage was illegal. In my adult life, I have watched marijuana become legal in state after state. Over the last forty years, the War on Drugs, in combination with aggressive policing tactics like broken windows—cracking down on small crimes to deter people from committing larger ones—drove millions of people into the criminal justice system. And mandatory sentencing laws kept them there for longer and longer periods. State after state has looked to redefine crimes, in part as a way to manage overcrowding in prisons: in 2010, for example, South Carolina raised from $1,000 to $2,000 the threshold at which theft was considered a felony so that fewer people would go to prison for the crime, one of at least thirty-five states to make similar

changes since 2001.[16] Where marijuana use was once a punishable offense, seven states and DC have now legalized it for recreational use.[17]
And several states have begun to view possession of smaller amounts
of drugs as misdemeanors, not felonies.

There is still little consensus about the rationale for incarceration:
is it deterrence, rehabilitation, or retribution? Given the dramatic
overrepresentation in our jails and prisons of people of color and low-
income people, it could be argued that the reality has as much to do
with oppression and social control as it does with any coherent theory
of punishment. Regardless, we have created a system that has left the
United States with by far the highest per capita incarceration rate of
any large nation in the world.

It's important to acknowledge how often race, poverty, and mental
illness overlap in the criminal justice system, creating a mutually rein-
forcing downward spiral. But of all the gross imbalances of our current
approach to criminal justice, perhaps no group has been hurt as much
as people with mental illness. Once they are caught in the criminal
justice system, they are far less able to cope with its demands and are
at much higher risk for exploitation and abuse. This book seeks to understand why we are shunting some of the most vulnerable people in
America into jails and prisons—and why have they been so mistreated
when they get there.

In examining the complicated forces behind this crisis, I hope to
spur action to end the abuses and to bring more compassion and common sense into the way we approach mental illness in our society. In
the course of my research, I have found that people in one jurisdiction
or even one area of the criminal justice system are often unaware of
what their counterparts in other places or other parts of the system
are doing. This book is addressed to the general reader. But I hope
that the links made here will encourage practitioners of both law and
medicine and others who are involved with mental illness and criminal
justice to see that any true reform will require coordination and engagement on many levels and, ultimately, in many places.

We will hear stories of unbearable cruelty, abuse, and neglect.
We will also see countless kind acts and unlikely heroes—including

corrections officers and judges, attorneys and doctors, family members and social workers—who have, like Kesey and nineteenth-century reformer Dorothea Dix, made the mistreatment of people with mental illness their cause. And we'll see the courage and determination of people who, despite varying degrees of "sanity," struggle to fight the system and improve their lives.

The first part of the book, "Ensnared," shows how and why people with mental illness are so easily swept into the criminal justice system. It begins with the story of Bryan Sanderson, a former firefighter and amateur comedian whose bipolar disorder ruins his career, destroys his marriage, and lands him in the criminal justice system, where, untreated and increasingly psychotic, he is driven to unspeakable acts of self-harm; he now devotes his time to teaching police how to deal with people with mental illness. This section also visits the special mental health units at the Los Angeles County Jail, showing the dark reality of care at one of the nation's largest jails and the extraordinary challenges faced by the medical and security personnel who work there. A third chapter then looks back at the history of mental health care and criminal justice in this country, showing the extent to which the problems we confront today have been with us since the establishment of the first jails and hospitals in the colonial era.

The second part of the book, "Locked Up," looks at how jails and prisons have taken on the job of providing mental health care. It explores the difficulties of providing quality care in this setting and the abuses—both official and unofficial—that can result. The tragic story of Jamie Wallace, a young man incarcerated in the Alabama prison system—which some have called the worst in the country—shows how the combination of mental illness and a dysfunctional system can be deadly.

The third part, "Breaking Free," shows how difficult it is for people with mental illness to get out of the system once they are in it. It looks at the ways that mental illness puts people at a disadvantage in interactions with both law enforcement and the courts, as well as some nationwide efforts to keep people out of the jail and prison to begin with, by disrupting the structures seen in the first two parts of the

book. Much of this is examined through the story of Kyle Muhammad, a man who has tried over and over again to stay on the right side
of the law. His mother has, more than once, called the police on him
to ensure his safety despite the risk of his getting caught in the criminal justice system again.

Our understanding of mental illness has come a long way over
the past two centuries. Thanks to brain scans, we now know that the
brains of some people with bipolar disorder respond differently to
lithium than others.[18] Researchers have found genes that are linked
to an increased likelihood of developing schizophrenia, so in the future we may be able to help people mitigate their risk of developing
these illnesses, much as we already can with things such as diabetes,
heart disease, and many cancers.[19] The pharmaceuticals we have today,
while imperfect, are much more effective at treating symptoms of the
diseases than earlier ones, and they are a far cry from early, often cruel
treatments such as lobotomies or water immersion—a therapy that involved suspending patients in tubs of water for days on end.

Yet in so many other ways, we continue to treat people with mental
illness almost exactly as we did before electricity was invented, before
women had the right to vote, and before the abolition of slavery. We
still lock sick people away from the rest of society. We still keep many
of them in solitary confinement. We still fail to provide adequate treatment for them. And we have known almost since the beginning that
all of this is wrong. It's wrong because it doesn't cure mental illness
or prevent people with mental illness from committing crimes when
they get out. And it's wrong because locking up vulnerable people in
inhumane conditions is fundamentally immoral.

That we know all this but continue to relegate sick people to our
courts, our jails, and our prisons shows how irrational—how insane—
our approach to both mental health care and criminal justice remains.

Author's Note

REPORTING ON THE CRISIS OF mental health illness in our prisons and jails has taken me deep into two of the most closed worlds—mental health care and criminal justice—in the United States. In addition to official rules that limit information flow—HIPAA and sealed court records, among others—the stigma of both mental illness and a criminal record is very real. As a journalist, I have struggled to reconcile my deep-seated belief in open records and information sharing with a desire not to harm people or expose them to unnecessary discrimination.

Wherever possible, I have sought to use in my accounts the real names and identifying characteristics of those interviewed. Unless otherwise noted, I have identified public officials, jail and prison employees, and law enforcement officers by their real names. In some cases I have chosen to refer to a person who only appears once or twice by a generic reference—"a physician who works in a jail," for example—rather than by naming her. Unless otherwise noted, this is simply to avoid bogging down the stories with extraneous detail.

For the prisoners and former prisoners themselves, I have approached the question on a case-by-case basis. Bryan Sanderson and Brian Nelson have both generously agreed to let me use their real names. The person I call Kyle Muhammad shared his stories and his records with me in exchange for anonymity, which I have granted him. Jamie Wallace is dead, but many details of his life and his case are in the public record; other information has been provided to me by his family members and friends. The generous access I was given to the commitment hearings at Bellevue Hospital and at the restoration-to-competency classes at the Fulton County Jail was in both cases contingent on my maintaining the anonymity of the participants.

Some situations were less clear-cut: during my time at the Los Angeles County Jail, for example, I learned the names of a number of the people being held there. With that information I was often able to use public records to learn more details of their cases. However, because they did not know why I was there and they were not given an opportunity to object to my presence, I have chosen not to identify them by their real names. Finally, in the Epilogue my own connection to the story meant that I have been privy to many more details than I would have been otherwise, and I chose not to use the real name of the person I refer to as "Matthew," or that of "Mr. Johnson," out of respect for this family. In none of these cases have I changed identifying details beyond the name; where there is information about a crime or a person that might compromise the person's privacy, I have simply omitted it.

My research draws on extensive interviews with subjects, family members, and experts; personal medical, jail, and prison records; court and other public documents; and newspaper articles, books, and other source materials. Medical, court, and jail records provide a wealth of information but are not infallible. Likewise, people's memories—and the version of the memories they choose to share—are not always accurate. Wherever possible, I have sought to cross-reference and corroborate stories, and the accounts I present here are, to the best of my understanding, accurate. In cases where I have been unable to confirm details—such as the precise order of events in Jamie Wallace's time in prison—I have tried to make that clear.

In a few places, I have drawn on interviews I did for outlets, including *Marketplace* and NPR. This includes the interviews at the Cook County Jail (Introduction and Chapter 4), with corrections officers (Chapter 5), and with Ray Echevarria (Chapter 6). I first interviewed Brian Nelson (Chapter 6) in a project for the ACLU.

A brief note about terminology: in common parlance we tend to use the words *jail* and *prison* interchangeably. However, there are important differences. Jails are run at a local, usually county, level, overseen by a warden or deputy with significant autonomy. They are designed primarily to hold people who haven't yet been convicted of any crime. That is, defendants are held there from the time they are arrested until they are bailed out or, if they cannot make bail, until they are tried or accept a plea bargain and are convicted or released. Jails are also used to hold people who have been sentenced to short terms, usually less than one year. Prisons, on the other hand, are run by the state (or federal) government, part of a larger system of institutions. It is here that people serve out longer sentences *after* they have been convicted of a crime.

The difference is significant for several reasons. The average stay in jail is short, with the result that jail populations tend to be very transient. For people with mental illness, this means that a jail is an especially unstable and disorienting social environment. Medically, it can be difficult or impossible to receive an accurate diagnosis in such settings, let alone an effective course of treatment. If a person is intoxicated when he is arrested, it can take several days just for the drug to clear his system. Jails are sometimes compared to emergency rooms: necessary gateways to the system but largely unprepared to deal with longer stays. Yet people with mental illness, whose cases often take far longer than others to get through the court system, may be stuck in jail for prolonged periods; some defendants end up staying in jail for years before their cases are resolved.

By contrast, in prisons the population consists of people who are serving a specific sentence, which usually means far less turnover and greater stability. These facilities are far from therapeutic and may sometimes be as susceptible to medical neglect and abuse as jails; ultimately, their mission is punishment, not medical care. Nonetheless, they provide a setting in which, ideally, some kind of consistent longer-term treatment can be offered.

Wherever it makes sense, I have distinguished between jails and prisons. If it is an issue that relates to incarceration more generally, I have tried to specify that as well.

Mental illness is a broad term used to describe many different disorders and many degrees of illness. Just as the common cold, measles, and AIDS are all infectious diseases, mental illness encompasses everything from anxiety to schizophrenia. The three that come up most frequently in this book are major depression, schizophrenia, and bipolar disorder (previously known as manic depression). The terms and characteristics will likely be familiar to many readers, but for clarity I include a brief summary here.

Major depression is a mood disorder characterized by feelings of great sadness or emptiness. A person with major depression often loses interest in daily activities, has changes in appetite and sleep, may have difficulty concentrating or making decisions, or has recurring thoughts of death and/or suicide.[1] Just under 7 percent of Americans—about 16 million people—have major depression.[2]

Bipolar disorder is characterized by episodes of mania and may also include cycles of depression. In a manic episode, people experience an "abnormally and persistently elevated, expansive or irritable mood... and persistently increased goal-directed activity or energy." They may need less sleep, be more talkative than usual, and engage in "activities that have a high potential for painful consequences," such as excessive spending or risky sexual behavior.[3] About 2.6 percent, or just over 6 million Americans, have bipolar disorder.[4]

Schizophrenia—a condition that appears in just over 1 percent of the population—or about 2.4 million adults—is a disorder characterized by symptoms including delusions (fixed beliefs about something that is not true), hallucinations (sensing something that is not there— for example, hearing voices or seeing things), disorganized thinking or behavior (the person may switch from one topic to another, for example, or do strange things that seem disconnected from reality, like wearing heavy coats in summer), and so-called negative symptoms, which includes things like diminished facial expressions or speaking without affect.[5]

Many jails and prisons identify major depression, bipolar disorder, and schizophrenia as "serious mental illnesses" while referring to other also potentially debilitating conditions (such as post-traumatic stress disorder) as just "mental illness." In their statistics, some differentiate between the two. For example, Rikers Island says that 43 percent of its residents have a mental illness while 11 percent have a *serious* mental illness.[6]

There are numerous terms—many still in use today—for both people with mental illness and those who have been involved with the criminal justice system that are considered deeply offensive. Others, words or phrases such as "the mentally ill" or "inmates," are still much in use but are seen by the people themselves as derogatory. In an effort to respect the wishes of those with "lived experience," I refer to my subjects as "people with mental illness" or a "person with schizophrenia." I refer to people in jail or prison (or those who were formerly in jail or prison) as people or, where necessary to distinguish them from others, as incarcerated people or prisoners. (Some will argue that "prisoner" is not technically accurate for someone who is in jail, but to avoid unnecessary contortions, I am using this term for any person who is being held in a penal institution.)

There are numerous terms for the people who are responsible for the care of prisoners, terms that vary from institution to institution and jurisdiction to jurisdiction. Again for purposes of consistency, I have chosen to call all of them corrections officers. When the difference between, say, a corrections officer and a sheriff's deputy is relevant, I have tried to clarify that.

Finally, readers will note that I give far more attention to men than women prisoners in my book. Women are the fastest-growing group of prisoners, and incarcerated women are disproportionately more likely to have a mental illness than are incarcerated men. I have tried to address this in Chapter 5. However, women still make up only a tiny fraction of incarcerated people—including the subset of incarcerated people with mental illness—so much of the challenge of remedying the current crisis concerns the male population.

PART I

ENSNARED: HOW WE GOT HERE

1

Jail Is the Only Safe Place

ON MARCH 26, 2006, THE sheriff's department in Spartanburg, South Carolina, received a call from the Fairfield Inn near Interstate 85, just outside of town. It was 7:30 A.M. A hotel guest had encountered a naked man in the elevator.

Three sheriff's deputies went to the fifth floor of the motel to intercept the man. "When the elevator arrived, the door opened and we observed men's clothing on the elevator floor and a heavy set white male standing nude in the elevator holding a green shirt over his genital area," one of the deputies later wrote in his report. "As I stepped into the elevator, the male dropped the shirt and was standing completely nude. The suspect was taken into custody and identified as Bryan Allan Sanderson."

When the elevator returned to the ground floor, a hotel worker brought the deputies a sheet, which they attempted to wrap around Sanderson as an elderly couple looked on. They put him in the back of the squad car and took him to jail. He was charged with indecent exposure. For Sanderson, it was the beginning of a long, unfortunate story, one that ultimately changed his life forever.

Sanderson's behavior on the morning he got arrested was certainly odd, and it was probably frightening, or at least startling, to the hotel guest he encountered in the elevator. But it was hardly threatening. Nor was there anything about his rather ordinary background to suggest he was a danger to society. Yet the police and later the judge treated him as if he were. Even if few other people face such devastating consequences as Sanderson did, his story shows how easily someone with mental illness can get pulled into the criminal justice system.

Sanderson had been a firefighter for nearly two decades. He had started a handyman business in 1999. He had been married twice, and he and his second wife, a nurse, had recently moved into a custom-built five-bedroom house in Williamsburg, Virginia. Her children lived with them, and his son joined them on weekends. There was a brand-new Cadillac Escalade in the two-car garage. They went on cruises and took trips to Disneyland. Sanderson also had a history of mental illness. At the time of his arrest, he was manic and for weeks had been hearing voices in his head. He had been getting progressively sicker, and his life was beginning to unravel.

As happens with so many people, being in jail made his symptoms worse. He smeared feces around his cell and threatened officers and other prisoners, so the deputies put him into solitary confinement. In solitary he continued to stir up trouble, throwing his food instead of eating it. The only time he was let out of his cell was for the occasional shower. On those days he was handcuffed and escorted by several officers. Sometimes he attacked the officers who came to his cell. No one seemed to notice or care that he was severely manic. Some of the officers even taunted him.

In South Carolina, indecent exposure is a misdemeanor punishable by up to three years in prison. Five and a half months after Sanderson was arrested at the hotel, he finally appeared before a judge and accepted a plea for time served—that is, the time he'd already spent in jail counted as his punishment. He says the judge gave him forty-eight hours to leave South Carolina. He did. But as a result of that ordeal, and what came after it, Sanderson lost his family, his livelihood, and his comfortable middle-class life. Today he lives alone in a two-bedroom bungalow, dependent on disability payments and the kindness of friends and family.

I FIRST MET BRYAN SANDERSON in the church in Williamsburg where he runs a support group for people with mental illness. One of his friends had told me to look for him, but the truth is, he's hard to miss. He's medium height but extremely overweight. His walk is hesitant and lumbering, not surprising for somebody still learning to navigate with a white cane. He has round cheeks and a neatly trimmed brown mustache; he seemed to say hello to every person who walked by that evening. He invited me to come to his house the next day.

He opened the door when he heard my car in the driveway. He says that since he became blind, his hearing has sharpened to the point where he could hear "a mouse pass gas." We sat at his kitchen table, which was dwarfed by his bulk. Years ago, when he was still a fire-fighter, Sanderson performed amateur stand-up comedy in clubs all over Virginia and North Carolina, inspired by his day job with the Williamsburg Fire Department. "I would tell 911 stories, twist 'em," he said.

Even though the closest he gets to performing these days is the oc-casional training session he does for local police departments, teaching cops how to manage encounters with people with mental illness, you can hear the old comedian in the way Sanderson tells his story. There's a kind of glibness and timing of carefully calibrated pauses that make it sound like he's delivering a monologue. Even though they're dark, or maybe because they are, the punch lines are funnier than his only actual performance I've seen.

That performance took place in January 2001. Sanderson, then thirty-four, was competing for the title of "America's Funniest Fire-fighter" on the television talk show *The View*. Sanderson wore a heavy yellow firefighter's coat that made him look even larger and a big, vi-sored helmet.

"Have you seen this Degree deodorant?" he asked in his last joke of the short set. "It's body-heat activated." After a pause, "I should have paid attention to that. I went into a house fire the other day, and my armpits exploded." Sanderson ended up losing the contest that day to a firefighter from Queens, New York, but he didn't mind much. He was thrilled just to be there.

At the time, everything seemed to be going right for him. Sanderson, who had moved to Williamsburg in junior high school, had many friends in town, especially among his fellow firefighters and the city's police officers. Not long after his appearance on *The View*, he was able to quit his job at the fire department. He wanted to focus on his handyman business, Sanderson Services. He ran the company out of a small house he rented in town; most of his employees were current or former firefighters.

Barely a year later, though, and with no warning, Sanderson got depressed: "It looked on paper like there was no reason for that, [but] I started thinking I would be better off dead." Sanderson worried about what killing himself would do to his family. As a firefighter, he'd responded to suicides many times: "It would piss me off because family members could find them." He decided to try anyway. One weekend, he drove to a house he was renovating, climbed a ladder in the carport, and tied a rope around one of the rafters. He had put the noose around his neck when he saw movement in the yard next door. "If you ever see somebody almost commit suicide, it's awful," he said. "I was afraid I was going to mess it up." He didn't want to "sort-of" kill himself and end up in a wheelchair with a feeding tube. Or maybe he wasn't as suicidal as he thought. He rocked the ladder onto two legs a couple of times, but he just couldn't work up the courage to kick it out from under himself.

Sanderson climbed down the ladder and left it there. He felt like a failure. He got into his car and drove to the deserted end of a dirt road. He took a piece of dryer-vent hose, put it over the tailpipe, and ran it into the car. He sat there for a few minutes with the engine running, hoping the carbon monoxide would kill him. But he got hot sitting in the car. It's ridiculous, he says now, for a firefighter to be whining because "it's too damn hot to kill himself." He finally gave up and drove home.

The next day, he was driving on the highway when he burst into tears. Still crying, he called his wife. He ended up an inpatient at the local psychiatric hospital, where most of the other patients seemed to be detoxing from substance use rather than recovering from suicide attempts or depression. Every morning, the psychiatrist came around to check on him. "I should have gotten an Oscar," Sanderson said, because he would always respond with "I feel good." After three days the hospital sent him home with a thirty-day supply of sleeping pills, tranquilizers, and antidepressants. He was far from well.

Although Sanderson credits his acting skills for the quick discharge, the brief hospitalization is typical. If it had been an involuntary commitment—and Sanderson no longer remembers if it was—seventy-two hours is the longest the hospital could have kept him without having a court hearing to prove that he was a danger to himself or others. If it had been voluntary, he might have stayed longer, but insurance payments for mental health care are often capped, and bed space, even in private facilities, is in high demand. The result is that people are often released before the medication they've been given kicks in, before they're well enough to be on their own, or, sometimes, even before a clear diagnosis has been confirmed.

If a patient says he feels well, it can be hard for a clinician to prove otherwise. And suicidal patients can sometimes legitimately be treated on an outpatient basis. On his third night home, Sanderson couldn't sleep; he lay awake watching the clock. Around three or four in the morning, he took out the pills he'd been given, looked in the mirror, then swallowed them all. He put the bottles back in the medicine cabinet and went back to bed.

Soon after, he went upstairs to the TV room. The walk upstairs was difficult because the pills were already starting to take effect. Before she left for work, his wife came to check on Sanderson and found him passed out in the TV room. She called 911. This time he stayed in the psychiatric hospital for eleven days and left with an official diagnosis of depression. "It doesn't take a rocket scientist to figure *that* out," he said.

But it wasn't just depression; it was bipolar disorder. Sanderson's initial depression soon turned to mania, which he says his wife recognized when she saw how much he was spending on his business. Sanderson's mother says she remembers him talking excessively. She also says he was obsessed with an idea for an invention he had—something that would keep birds out of dryer vents—and spent a lot of money on patent attorneys.

His wife took him to a psychiatrist, who diagnosed him correctly and prescribed lithium. It helped, but the side effects bothered him, and eventually he quit taking it. This is common. The side effects of many psychotropic drugs, which include weight gain, sluggishness, and sexual dysfunction, are bothersome, and patients often quit taking them once they start to feel better. (This is true of medications generally; once a patient starts to feel better, he often decides to quit taking them.)

A year later, the mania returned, his marriage fell apart, and he moved into the small house he used for his business. For no apparent reason, he had hundreds of Christian T-shirts printed up, white with a black-and-yellow logo—like the one from the television show *Fear Factor*—that read "Faith Factor." There was a Bible verse underneath. He began visiting online dating sites and met a woman who ran a bar in San Antonio. It was around this time that he first heard the voice. He was lying in bed when heard it say, "Take your shirts to Texas." It was a man's voice, and it spoke to him calmly, almost in a monotone. "I thought God was talking to me," Sanderson says. "Man, God is talking to me!" The next day, he boxed up all the shirts and sent them to the woman.

Soon after that, Sanderson decided he, too, needed to go to Texas. So he put a bunch of tools into the camper, which he'd bought on the spur of the moment after driving past a dealership that was having a sale. He hooked the camper up to his gray F250 pickup truck—also bought on a whim, from a cop friend who was going through a divorce and needed the cash—and headed for San Antonio. (Sanderson says that he bought both vehicles on credit and that he never made a payment on either loan. Years later, he found out from a credit report that the camper had been repossessed. The truck eventually disappeared in San Antonio.)

He was heading southwest toward San Antonio when just off Interstate 110 in Baton Rouge, three enormous crucifixes rose out of the landscape, marking the spot where a mega-church was to be built. Sanderson pulled off the highway and sat under the crosses, reading the Bible. He noticed the members of a church group who had stopped there to pray. This was in the months after Hurricane Katrina, and they were planning to buy food to distribute to victims of the storm.

The voice spoke to Sanderson again: "Give them a check for $500." So Sanderson waved down one of the pastors and wrote a check. By this point, Sanderson had no money in his bank account. "The check wasn't worth a darn," he said. "It had to have bounced. But I was convinced I was hearing from God. If God's going to tell me to write a check, he's going to put money in there somehow."

The group happened to be from a church called the City of Refuge, based in San Antonio. San Antonio! The pastor invited Sanderson to visit. A few days later, Sanderson showed up at the church, which was in a shopping center away from downtown, and put the last of his money—ten dollars or so—in the collection plate. A blond woman was at the pulpit talking and called him up to the front of the church. "I'm here, the Lord led me here," he said. "I'm down to the last dollar." The congregation members pulled out their wallets, and Sanderson left with $200.

One of the people at the service was a homeless man named Kelly. He introduced Sanderson to his friends, a couple who was also homeless. *If I were homeless,* Sanderson thought, *I'd want to have a place to live.* An apartment complex down the street from the church was offering a hundred-dollar move-in special, so Sanderson rented a two-bedroom apartment for Kelly and his friends. (Apparently, he could still get credit at this point, even if he didn't have any cash left.) He bought them pizza. They used his truck to bring over furniture from somebody's storage unit; he even dragged the mattress from his camper into the apartment and slept there for a few nights.

By this point, Sanderson's mother, Yvonne Roberts, had realized he was manic. Over the phone, she tried to convince him that the whole San Antonio plan was a bad idea. "I'm not sure this is what you are supposed to be doing," his mother recalls telling him. "He kept saying it was God who told him to do this," asking her "Who am I to argue with God?"

After several days with his new friends, Sanderson decided to go home. A pawnshop paid him $450 for his tools and toolbox, and he used the money to buy a plane ticket back to Virginia. He had Kelly drive him to the airport, leaving the camper and the truck with him. "I don't even know if he had a license!" Sanderson says now. He later reported to the San Antonio police that the truck had been stolen; it was never found.

As soon as he got home, Sanderson packed whatever tools he had left into his red Jeep Cherokee and headed back toward San Antonio with vague plans to open a homeless shelter. It didn't matter that he had no experience with or interest in providing services to the homeless, or that he was out of money. The voice told him to do it, and he had to obey it. "When you're in psychosis," he says, "there's something about your sickness that you think this voice knows everything."

He stopped at a Walmart in North Carolina to buy some things for "his" homeless shelter: a television and some CDs. He had nearly made it to the South Carolina border when the voice told him to "take the next exit, get a hotel, get some sleep." He had barely slept in days, so it seemed like a good idea.

The hotel was on the outskirts of Spartanburg, just off the interstate. He holed up in a room there for a few days, leaving only to eat at the Denny's next door or to find pawnshops where he could sell more tools. On the third morning, he decided he was ready to go on, so around 7 A.M. he dragged his duffle bag into the hallway and shut the door behind him. As soon as it shut, he realized he'd forgotten something. He put the key card back into the lock to open it again, but it didn't work. He tried again: "The more times I got the red [light on the card slot], the more times I got pissed off." It's a response that anyone who's ever been thwarted by a finicky key card can relate to. Except for what happened next.

"I took all my clothes off," he said. "Every stitch, pushed the [elevator] button, and threw everything in." He caught a glimpse of his reflection in the shiny brass doors, grabbed a T-shirt from the floor to cover himself, and began riding the elevator from the first to the fifth floor and back again. Over and over and over.

After a while, the elevator stopped on the third floor, and a petite African American woman got on. "You would think she would take the other elevator," he jokes. "I looked at her and said 'hello.' She didn't respond." Pause. "There are some stuck-up people in South Carolina." He had already pushed the button for the first floor, and the elevator headed down again. "I'm full service that way," he says. The woman reported him to the front desk clerk, who called the sheriff's deputies.

"None of the bail guys wanted to talk to me," he says. "I don't know how bail bonds work, but apparently a naked guy from out of state is a bad idea."

This was Sanderson's first arrest. When the deputies handcuffed him, he got terrified and angry. He tried to fight back, which made him seem unruly and dangerous. The same thing happened in jail: Sanderson was deluded and frightened, and he had loud outbursts that made him seem dangerous. In both cases the officers took his behavior as reason enough to treat him more harshly, treatment that in turn aggravated his response.

On some level, this conflict between people with mental illness in the criminal justice system and those who run the system seems inevitable. The criminal justice system is built around a punitive, authority-based approach. Jails and prisons have many rules about how prisoners are supposed to behave, rules that are often, or seem to be, capricious. It's partly about keeping everybody safe in what can be a dangerous and volatile environment. But it's also sometimes control for the sake of control. Depending on how they're being enforced, the rules can be hard for anybody to follow—standing in precisely the right place at exactly the right time, for example. For a person with symptoms of mental illness, it can be nearly impossible to obey the rules. To corrections officers trying to maintain order, though, that may come across as insubordination, not a response to fear or confusion: as the officers escalate their own response, the prisoner is simply less likely to do what he is told.

"There is an inherent tension between the security mission of prisons and mental health considerations," writes Jamie Fellner, an attorney who has studied the abuse of people with mental illness in the criminal justice system. "The formal and informal rules and codes of conduct in prison reflect staff concerns about security [and] safety.... Coordinating the needs of the mentally ill with those rules and goals is nearly impossible."[1] It's not just the needs of people with mental illness but also their abilities; a person in a severe manic episode may be unable to control his or her behavior, regardless of the consequences.

In Sanderson's case, the consequence of his behavior was that he was put into the "hole"—solitary confinement—almost immediately: "Now I'm in the hole. I don't understand jails, how they work. They do head counts four, five times a day. I'm supposed to stand by the bed [for the head count]. I don't stand up. I lose [recreation time]. I'm never getting out."

Solitary confinement, which is meted out as punishment at the discretion of the jail or prison staff, is known to exacerbate mental illness and even cause it. Breaking rules in solitary confinement is typically punished with more time in solitary, so people often end up there for extended periods.

Another reason that incarceration is so damaging to people like Sanderson is that corrections officers often lack awareness about people's cases specifically and about mental illness more generally. As far as Sanderson can remember, he received no medical evaluation, no mental health care, and no medication, even though he had previously been hospitalized twice.[2]

Through all of Sanderson's fights, confusion, and subsequent punishments, the voice in his head kept talking to him. Before he went to jail, it had been like an annoying coach, giving orders that were sometimes outlandish but more or less harmless. Now it turned into a villain, sinister and threatening. Instead of appearing occasionally, it was talking to him almost nonstop: "It's telling me [this is] not a jail. It's a CIA training facility. 'They're going to kill you. They're going to find your family and kill your family.'"

His mother said Sanderson would tell her the president had been warning him that three serial killers disguised as corrections officers were in the jail and were plotting to kill him. Their plot, he reported, was to use cyanide, which they were flushing through the toilets. Another voice appeared, this one of a former customer who had (in reality) died. It was more encouraging than the first one: "We're watching you from heaven. We're proud of you; you're doing a good job."

Then the auditory hallucinations were joined by visual ones. Seeing things that aren't there is far less common than hearing voices. But Sanderson saw police and firefighters he had worked with in Williamsburg. He saw his ten-year-old son jumping up and down on the third tier of the jail: "You might say that one cop looks like another, or like a firefighter, but you can't tell me I don't know what my son looks like." He later learned that the jail had only two tiers. He had hallucinated not only his son but also an entire floor of a building.

After he attacked a sheriff's deputy, the jail finally sent him, in handcuffs, waist chains, and shackles, to the state psychiatric hospital in Columbia, South Carolina. A doctor there confirmed his earlier diagnosis of bipolar disorder. This time, the doctor determined that it was bipolar with psychotic features, meaning he was so manic he had become psychotic. He put Sanderson back on lithium. He didn't have access to Sanderson's medical records, though, and Sanderson was unable to provide any details about his previous treatment. So the doctor ended up putting him on what amounted to only about half the dose he had been on earlier. As Sanderson describes it, this made him only half-sane.

When he was finally released from jail, his mother bought him a plane ticket back to Virginia and picked him up at the airport in Richmond. As she said, "I didn't recognize him. He had lost so much weight." He literally had nothing: no house, no job, no money. She checked him into a motel in town—"It was code for 'Your crazy ass ain't staying in my house,'" he said—bought him toiletries and food, and gave him money to eat in the restaurant across the street. She showed him the want ads in the newspaper so he could start looking for a job.

That night, he lay on the bed in the motel room, terrified. He was still sure the CIA was after him. The motel had an exterior walkway, and every time he heard somebody go past the door, he was sure that somebody from the agency was finally coming to get him. He was desperate to see his son but was terrified that a visit would tip off the agents to his son's whereabouts. The only place Sanderson would be safe was back in jail. So he hatched a plan: he would rob a bank and make sure he got caught.

The idea came from an experience he'd had years earlier when, as a firefighter, he'd helped catch a pair of armed bank robbers. The one who had a gun was given a seventeen-year prison sentence. "In my mind, psychotic as I was," he said, "I thought, if he got seventeen years for *one* robbery, if I rob *two* banks, maybe they'll give me life."

He got dressed in a Hawaiian shirt and jeans and retrieved from his old office a minivan he'd retrofitted into a work vehicle. A ladder was still attached to the roof, and the big letters on the side read "Sanderson Services: Trustworthy Help Around the Home." His phone number was there, too. He now sees the comedic potential in this detail. "Not an ideal escape vehicle," he said the first time he told me the story. Another time, when I called him back to follow up on something, he made a different crack: "You're robbing a bank [in a van] with your name and phone number on it, to make sure they get hold of you if they have any questions."

He didn't have a gun, but on an invoice from his metal contractor clipboard he wrote a note to the teller at the SunTrust Bank: "Give me 10k. I have a gun." (He did somehow have the presence of mind to tear off the top of the invoice, where his name and phone number were printed, before handing it to her.) In some circumstances, *saying* you have a gun means you can be charged with having a weapon whether you do or not.

After five or six tries, Sanderson worked up the nerve to give the note to the teller, who quickly handed him a stack of fifty- and one-hundred-dollar bills totaling just under four thousand dollars. Sanderson didn't even have a bag to put them in. The teller knew it wasn't the full amount and turned to get more bills, but Sanderson had what he wanted: "That's enough. Thank you." ("Momma would've been proud," he said later.)

At a Bank of America across town, he gave the teller a copy of the first note: "I was trying to streamline the process." Then, cash in hand, he headed for the highway to drive himself to jail. The police stopped him, guns drawn, and asked where he was coming from. "I'm coming from both banks," he answered honestly.

This time after he got arrested, a psychiatrist *did* examine him and upped his lithium dose. He stayed for weeks, waking up every morning, thinking, "Thank God I'm in jail." Then suddenly, he says, the medication kicked in, and his head cleared. It was, he says, like he had been lost in a cornfield and suddenly reached the edge, where he got his bearings again. "Oh my God," he realized, "I'm in trouble."

He was evaluated by two more psychologists, one paid for by his mother and one by the state. A judge finally found him not guilty by reason of insanity, which meant he was acquitted of the criminal charges, but instead of serving prison time he would be committed to a psychiatric hospital until a judge decided he was sane enough to be released safely. Contrary to popular belief, this is an extremely rare finding.

SANDERSON DIDN'T STAY AT THE hospital for very long. At the right dose, his medications brought his symptoms under control, and he was released seven months later. He moved out, first to a group home and then to his own apartment. It might have been better, in retrospect, for him to have remained in the hospital or at least under some supervision.

At the time, though, it all seemed for the good. It was the beginning of getting his life back on track. He saw his son. He got a job as a peer specialist at the psychiatric hospital where he had been a patient, using his own experience to help others deal with their illnesses. He refocused his business on cleaning lint out of dryer vents.

Then he went off his medication again. After about a year, the voice in Sanderson's head came back. It spoke in the same monotone as before, warning him that his neighbor, with whom he had had a previous altercation, was building bombs in his basement apartment. "It is absolutely critical," the voice said, "to search the neighbor's apartment, to keep him from blowing something up." The impulse to protect or save people is a running theme in Sanderson's life. There's the firefighter job and the rescue delusions. One friend called it a savior complex. Another person called it just showy gestures. Whatever the case, he knew he had to save the world from his neighbor's bomb. He started going through the neighbor's garbage. Then one day when his neighbor was at work, Sanderson broke into his apartment.

In the refrigerator he found several sticks of butter. Plastic explosives! He took them outside. In the backyard he found a large trash can full of gardening soil. Clearly the makings of a fertilizer bomb! He called the police, who quickly determined that they were actually just butter and soil. He was charged with breaking and entering, which is a felony. But the officer was an acquaintance from his firefighter days and convinced him to come in for a psychiatric evaluation.

At the behavioral health facility, the mental health technician took him into an exam room to do the intake interview. She was a young woman with dark hair that went past her shoulders. As is standard safety protocol, she sat in the seat closest to the door. Sanderson sat in a chair with his back to the wall, desk between them.

Sanderson was answering her questions when the voice in his head interrupted: "That woman is the daughter of Benjamin Netanyahu, the Israeli prime minister." Sanderson leaned his head back against the wall and closed his eyes. "Well, he's got a pretty daughter," he thought. Suddenly, the voice changed its story: "No! That's Satan's daughter!" When Sanderson opened his eyes, the woman's face was spinning, her eyes two glowing red dots, like a demon in a horror movie: "It was the scariest thing I ever saw."

Terrified, Sanderson leaped up and sprinted for the door. The tech stood up as he went past her, either to run or to try to stop him. "I saw a demon coming out of the chair," Sanderson says, "so I punched the demon."

The tech later told police that she hadn't initially felt threatened by Sanderson. But when she asked him to sign the admission papers, he got upset and tried to leave. She convinced him to stay and, now concerned about his behavior, asked a colleague to join them in the office. (This, too, is standard safety protocol if a tech or doctor feels threatened.) Sanderson said he was hungry, so the third person left to get him a sandwich. At that moment, Sanderson stood up and punched the tech in the mouth.

The next thing he remembered, he was sitting on a bench on the hospital grounds, shoes and socks off, rubbing his feet. A police officer he knew was there, one with whom he had taught training sessions about how cops should handle people with mental illness. Sanderson was disoriented: was this part of a role-play in a training session? The officer asked Sanderson why he was having a bad night. "Because no one is perfect," he answered.

In many states, assaulting a health care worker is a felony; few make an exception for an assailant who has a mental illness or other impairment. The laws have come from very reasonable demands that nurses and other health care providers have made for workplace safety.[3] But there's room for interpretation. Something benign and even understandable such as resisting a shot of forced medication can be seen as an assault. Sanderson could have been charged with felony assault, which carries a minimum punishment of a year in prison. Instead, he was charged only with misdemeanor assault and battery. The police took him to jail anyway.

In an effort to manage the crisis of mental illness in the criminal justice system, jurisdictions have begun examining different inflection points, places where the trajectory of a person's engagement with the system could have gone differently.[4] The police officer's decision to take Sanderson to jail that day would prove to change the course of his life completely.

Sanderson spent the next four days locked in a cell on the jail's medical unit. Officers were supposed to check on him at ten-minute intervals, but he was oblivious to his surroundings. He would "wake up" periodically and realize his clothes were off. That there was water on the floor. Or that his bed was turned upside down. Several days later, he woke up naked on the floor of his cell. His head was next to the door. He had no idea how he had gotten there. But the voice was still in his head. It told him he was a sinner: "You've got to blind yourself."

Still lying on the damp floor of his cell, Sanderson took his left index finger and shoved it deep into his left eye socket. Then he stopped and yelled, "I can't do this. I can't do this." He saw the metal door of his cell and began bashing his head against it. He later told the doctor he had read a passage in the Bible telling him to pluck out his eye.[5]

His mother came to see him in the hospital. She found him with "both eyes bandaged. Both hands handcuffed to the side of the bed, and two big jailers on either side." He was completely out of his mind, laughing and giggling. He told her he planned to buy a hotel in town and turn it into a homeless shelter. He had no memory of scraping the pupil off his left eye, or of plucking out the right one.

He also has no memory of that visit. The next thing he remembers was hearing a woman's voice saying, "I'm going to put some ointment in your eyes." He was in the hospital, and she was a nurse. He remembers feeling the cream on his face, but everything was dark. "Am I blind?" he asked her. He was.

The psychiatrist who examined him in the hospital said Sanderson could not tell him why he had been in jail. He didn't appear either manic or depressed at this point, the doctor wrote, noting that there are "occasions where the psychosis leads up to an act like this and then it seems to cause some kind of release and the intensity of the psychosis decreases." He would follow Sanderson's behavior in the hospital, the psychiatrist wrote, "but I do not see any reason he cannot go back to the jail with psychiatric follow-up there, and of course under close observation once he is medically cleared." I called the psychiatrist, who still works at the hospital. I wanted to ask him what he thought would be accomplished by sending Sanderson back to jail at that point, but he did not return my call.

After a few days in the hospital and a few more in the state psychiatric facility, he was transferred to jail—to the same unit where he had blinded himself. Soon after, he was released to his mother. The state eventually dropped the charges.

IN PICTURES FROM BEFORE THE incident, Sanderson's eyes are an expressive dark liquid brown. Today, his right eye is a prosthetic. His left eye is his own, but it is vacant, unseeing. He keeps his driver's license in a plastic lockbox in the closet. There are no sidewalks on the road in front of his house, and the cars drive by fast enough that it would be foolhardy for him to walk on it. Besides, he's still figuring out how to navigate with his white cane. His house is too far outside the city limits to make him eligible for paratransit—transportation services for people with disabilities—so unless his mother or a friend comes to get him, he is effectively under permanent house arrest.

On the wooden coffee table in his tiny living room is the Bible he can no longer read. On the wooden bookshelves are photographs of him and his mother and his son, pictures he can no longer see.

He lives off disability payments, supplementing them with occasional gigs training police in how to interact with people who have a mental illness. He spends most of his time in an armchair in his crowded second bedroom, listening to a radio station that reads a different Bible verse every fifteen minutes.

He is remarkably hopeful for a man who has been through all that he has. He makes jokes about being retired. He's optimistic, probably irrationally so, that he can regain the sight in his remaining eye. He says he's been to five different ophthalmologists: "I'm waiting on my miracle. If you're going to believe, you'd better dream big...."

On Tuesdays a friend takes him to the local Lutheran church, the one where I met him that first day, where he runs a support group for people with mental illness. Most of its members are patients at

Eastern State Hospital. Sometimes John Hinckley, Jr., the man who shot President Ronald Reagan in 1981, shows up; he lives in town with his elderly mother.

Sometimes Sanderson thinks about how different his life would be if he had been given the right amount of lithium by the doctor in South Carolina or if he had gotten treatment instead of jail after he punched the psych tech: "At any rate, you can't change things. Mom always says you can't unscramble eggs. So I just keep looking to the future, and I try not to look back too much."

On Wednesdays, when his mother brings him fried chicken and V8 juice, she secretly checks to make sure he's taking his medicine: "I think he's stable, but he fooled me before. I stay aware. The dog bites you the first time, it's the dog's fault. Bites you the second time, it's your fault."

2

The Largest Psych Ward in America

"You should see it when we open the door," one of the deputies says, matter-of-factly. He's talking about the almost overpowering stench of feces coming out of the tray slot he has just opened.

A tray slot resembles an oversized, locked mail slot in the middle of a cell door. Through it, prisoners are handed their food trays, pills, and toilet paper. But it's really much more than that; it's a way to access the cell without opening the door. If a person is believed to be dangerous or volatile, corrections officers will reach into the food slot to handcuff him before opening the cell door. A nurse or other clinician will reach through the tray slot to take a prisoner's temperature, or she may have the prisoner reach an arm out to have his blood pressure checked. In some places, mental health professionals administer "therapy" by talking through the tray slot. Worse, corrections officers sometimes use the food slot to discharge pepper spray into the cell to make a suicidal person quit cutting himself, to stop a fight between cellmates, or to force a recalcitrant person to come out. Or, as in this case, it's simply a way to talk to somebody, to be heard over the general din without having to open the door.

I'm on a mental health unit in the Twin Towers Correctional Facility at the Los Angeles County Jail, one of the biggest providers of psychiatric care in the country. The jail generally, and units like this one more specifically, offer an ideal vantage point from which to observe the challenges faced by people with mental illness who end up in the criminal justice system and, conversely, the challenges faced by a criminal justice system that is overwhelmed by the large numbers of people with mental illness who have ended up in its care. The scale of the situation is magnified by the size of the LA County Jail, which is one of the biggest in the country. But the problems seen here, large numbers of very sick people in a penal institution that struggles to provide care with far too few resources, are found in just about every jail and prison across the country.

Jails and prisons are dehumanizing places: the uniforms that strip people of their individuality, the endless rules, the gruff way that many, though certainly not all, officers address prisoners. The sense of us and them, that divide between the prisoners and the officers or really the prisoners and the rest of us, is especially pronounced on mental health units like this one, where many people are either openly aggressive—growling, snarling, yelling, banging on doors—or completely unresponsive. Even the very legitimate caution with which the deputies approach the cells adds to the sense that these people are something other than human, creatures to be feared.

On any given day, around sixteen thousand people are locked up in the LA County Jail, a sprawling institution made up of seven buildings spread across the county. (The number fluctuates daily; it has in recent memory gone as high as twenty thousand.) The majority of them are housed in two main buildings, though, the Twin Towers and the Men's Central Jail. The towers—squat, off-white fortresses—and Men's Central sit on the east side of the city, between the train tracks and the river, in an out-of-the-way stretch still untouched by the spreading gentrification of downtown. The buildings are just a few streets away from skid row, about fifty square blocks that police say account for roughly half of all crime in the area. Skid row's population is similar to the jail's, in both size and makeup: both are predominantly poor, with high rates of both mental illness and substance use. Los Angeles has periodically been accused of operating a revolving door between skid row and the jail, sweeping up people for minor crimes; hospitals have also been accused of dumping homeless patients there.[1]

As in other places, many people get out of the LA County Jail very quickly, within a matter of days or even hours. But others, particularly those with mental illness, may be there for months or even years. There are many reasons for this, among them the fact that people with mental illness are less likely to make bail—according to one study done in New York City, only 12 percent of those with mental illness versus 21 percent of those without. And for those 12 percent who do manage to make bail, it takes much longer—forty-eight days versus nine days for those without mental illness.[2] A person who doesn't get bailed out has to stay in jail until his case is resolved. That could mean until the case is dismissed or until he is acquitted. Or it could mean until he is convicted or, more likely, accepts a plea bargain. Those convicted of misdemeanors serve their sentences in jail, while most people convicted of felonies are sent to state prison. One exception to this is that starting in 2011, California began transferring some people to local jails to serve out their sentences in order to try to manage overcrowding in the state prisons. That means that unlike most other people in jail, some people in LA County and other California jails have actually been convicted of more serious felonies.

Outside of Los Angeles, the jail is best known for occasionally housing celebrities like O. J. Simpson and Robert Downey, Jr. But far more common than celebrity prisoners are those with mental illness. About 25 percent of the men here need mental health care; most of those are too sick to live in the general jail population and are instead housed in special units in the Twin Towers, a hulking structure that is less tower than fortress. There are far fewer women in the LA County Jail, but as is true elsewhere, a far higher percentage of them require mental health care—about 40 percent. For the very sickest people, men and women, there is an inpatient unit, which despite having recently been expanded to fifty-five beds is perpetually full.

Various mental health units are divided over several floors of both towers, while the inpatient hospital unit is housed in a third building, which can be accessed from inside the jail via a ramp hallway from Tower Two. From the inside, the "towers," which are connected by two interior hallways, are nearly indistinguishable from each other.

Like Dante's Purgatory or the Buddhist Jigoku hell, prisoners are moved from floor to floor as their condition improves or, more often, deteriorates. Unlike those mythical places, though, where an upward trajectory always connotes betterment, here neither the direction nor levels of movement are so clearly defined.

Take the High Observation ("High Obs") units, which occupy four and a half floors of Tower One. These are for people who clinicians or deputies believe cannot safely share a cell with another person. Many of them are not even allowed to wear the regular jail uniform—baggy pants and shirts similar to surgeons' scrubs—or to have regular blankets, for fear they will use them to hang themselves. Instead, they wear suicide gowns. Sometimes called "turtle suits," these heavy shapeless smocks are made of a quilted cloth that is supposed to be indestructible—picture the blankets that movers use to protect furniture—so they can't be torn or tied into a noose.

Most of them are allowed out of their cells only in handcuffs—and some only in handcuffs *and* leg shackles—but the requirements are irrelevant for many of them because they refuse to come out of their cells at all. In the jail classification system, these people are considered outpatients, but in a civilian context, this seems like an odd distinction: all the patients live here. But the High Obs units are simply jail cells where mental health care is administered in the same way that other medical treatment is delivered in the jail. There is no individual therapy offered in the jail. Mental health care consists primarily of medication and medication management.

The hospital unit, on the other hand, officially called the Forensic Inpatient Unit and universally known by its acronym, FIP, is licensed as an acute psychiatric ward, much like any inpatient acute psychiatric ward in the outside world. Prisoners who are sent to FIP are inpatients, and they may be committed there involuntarily. As in the outside world, there is also more demand for inpatient-level care than there are available beds. Dr. Mark Ghaly is in charge of community health programs for the Los Angeles County Department of Health Services, the agency that took over medical care in the jail system in 2016. In that role he supervises the person in charge of correctional medicine; he is also working on projects to divert people with mental illness out of the jail. "If you took an average psychiatrist for a walk through High Obs," he said, "and asked him 'Where do these patients belong?' He would tell you a good portion belong in inpatient beds. A lot of people who should be getting inpatient hospitalization aren't." To be clear, this is not to say that all of those patients require institutionalization or even *long-term* hospitalization. They may simply need the kind of intensive treatment that is available only in an inpatient setting. It's also worth noting that for many, getting proper mental health care along the way might well have prevented them from deteriorating to this point. In this, the LA County Jail is far from unique. "It's the embarrassment of the way we've done mental health in this country in the last two decades," Ghaly said.

One of those people who probably needs inpatient treatment is the man with the ghastly-smelling cell. The deputies bang on his cell door and shout offers of a shower or "rec"—recreation—time through the tray slot. He does not respond at all. Photocopied papers in a plastic sleeve attached to the outside of the door show a mug shot of an African American man. But peering through the scratched glass of the door, it's impossible to see the face, let alone recognize it; the man's entire body, as far as I can tell, is wrapped in a dark-blue blanket cocoon on the lower bunk. What I can see, though, even in the dim fluorescent lighting, is where the smell is coming from: the cell is covered in feces. Rubbed on the edge of the top bunk. On the floor. Smeared in deliberate circles on the wall. Used as paste to affix sheets of paper towel to the wall in a neat eye-level row, like artworks hung in a gallery. There's something particularly disturbing about how intentional the behavior is; this is not simply an accident by someone who didn't make it to the toilet in time.

Nor is it an isolated incident. Cells here are defaced with feces often enough that in a 2014 letter about conditions in LA County Jail, the US Department of Justice wrote, "Mental health line staff complained that many of the cells are very dirty and that steam cleaners were not routinely being used to clean feces-smeared cells."[3] The jail has been under the scrutiny of the Department of Justice, the ACLU, and others for decades, in part because of its care and treatment of prisoners with mental illness. The jail has been under new leadership since 2013, and even critics concede that the situation, though not perfect, is far better.

Corrections officers and other officials from across the country have similar scatological stories. Some are far more disgusting: the man who regularly reached into his pants, defecated onto his own hand, then threw it at whomever opened his cell door. The one who ate it, with a chaser of toilet water, straight out of his stainless-steel toilet. The corrections officers' union in New York City regularly tweets out tallies of members "splashed w/ possible blood-urine-feces."

It's tempting to see such stories as evidence for the idea that people with mental illness, especially those who have committed or are accused of committing crimes, are dirty, disgusting, and best kept locked up and out of sight. In reality, these episodes tell us something quite different. They show what too often happens to people with serious mental illness given minimal treatment in the pathogenic (disease-causing) environment of correctional facilities. Scatolia, the clinical term for playing with feces, is rarely seen in the outside world but is widely described among people with mental illness who are confined to jails and prisons. It's behavior that indicates just how sick and how desperate many of these people are.

Nonetheless, diagnosing mental illness in people in jail can be tricky. Prisoners sometimes fake it as a way to be removed from the often chaotic and dangerous general population or just in an effort to get what they hope will be a better housing assignment. As one doctor who worked in jails for many years told me, "Everybody in correctional health has half an eye to 'Is this person trying to get something over on me?'" Even for seasoned mental health professionals, it can sometimes be hard to tell the difference between a person who is truly ill and one who is looking to game the system. And in the deprived environments of correctional facilities, people do sometimes go to great lengths to get something they want. At the Cook County Jail in Chicago, I met a "jumper," a man who had jumped off the second tier of the jail, the social worker said, so that he would get sent to the county hospital. Even in the locked prison unit there, she said, the rules are more lax, the food is better, and there's more of it. Corrections officers and even doctors say healthy but predatory prisoners sometimes try to get moved to special units specifically to prey on people with mental illness. Despite a reputation for being dangerous, people with mental illness are much more likely to be victims than perpetrators, whether of physical abuse or psychological abuse, or of being coerced out of money or food.[4]

Health care professionals and corrections officers are often quick to accuse prisoners of malingering, or faking it. I've heard many stories of people with long-standing diagnoses of mental illness being told they aren't sick and getting taken off their medications as a result; I've seen medical records where symptoms are interpreted as separate from mental illness, so insomnia is given as the primary diagnosis, rather than a symptom of bipolar disorder, or weight loss is interpreted as a gastrointestinal problem.

But it is also hard to account for many of these extreme behaviors—mutilating one's own genitals, blinding oneself, eating feces, or, frankly, just being able to bear the smell of a tiny cell that has been covered in it—unless as some form of madness. They are actions no sane person would willingly take. Even the DOJ's letter is a bizarre commentary on the state of things: the complaint from mental health workers was only that the cells aren't being cleaned well or often enough, not that they are *regularly* being defaced with feces.

The very fluidity of mental illness complicates matters, as does the lack of reliable statistics on the number of people with mental illness who end up in the criminal justice system. Still, regardless of the precise numbers, and despite a handful (or even more) of fakers, two things are clear: there are far too many people with severe mental illness in the criminal justice system, and they receive far too little appropriate treatment while they are there.

One afternoon at Twin Towers, I was talking to Lieutenant Mike Burse, a career sheriff's deputy who was, when I first met him in 2015, in charge of overseeing the jail's mental health units; he now works in internal affairs at the LA County Sheriff's Department. He looks like a caricature of a good cop—strong, chiseled jaw, perfectly pressed

uniform shirt that shows off almost comically large biceps. Burse's office on the top floor of Tower Two was decorated with posters of old
Los Angeles, a toy sheriff's car, and family photos, including several of
his son, who's a police officer in one of the Los Angeles suburbs. His
window looks out onto the Hollywood sign, Dodgers Stadium, and
palm trees silhouetted against a perfectly blue southern California sky.
It's a stark contrast with the cramped and dingy quarters downstairs
where the prisoners are housed.

We were in the middle of a long, rambling conversation about policing and the Bible when I noticed the banging. It was the kind of
metallic clanking that steam radiators make when the heat comes on.
But the LA County Jail has no radiators—it doesn't get cold enough to
need them—and besides, it was late spring, and the air-conditioning
was on. Somebody's trying to escape, I joked. "Oh yeah," Burse said,
"we're above 172 [one of the High Obs units]. They drum all the
time. If they're good drummers, it's fine. When they're bad, it drives
me crazy."

Then he went back to talking about the Bible. His favorite book is
Ecclesiastes because it says that no matter "how good you are, no matter how evil, you both end up in the same place, six feet under the dust
you were formed from," he said. "Life is vanity, chasing the wind. I
keep thinking, 'What makes me better than the guy in that jail cell?'"

It reminded me how, earlier that day, Burse told me about a deputy
he'd had who couldn't deal with a particular prisoner, a man who'd
been accused of sexually abusing a child or something similarly awful.
Burse had found her another post until she could be reassigned permanently because, he said, the most important thing in this job was
to treat all the prisoners the same way: not because they hadn't been
convicted yet or even because they were sick, but because that was a
deputy's job.

The jail, he says, is doing the best it can with the mandate and resources it has been given. Still, he said one day, as we walked past a cell
where a man in a suicide gown lay sleeping on top of another suicide
gown he had spread on the floor, "This is wrong. If you are mentally
ill, this is a horrible place."

SOME OF THE MOST OBVIOUSLY sick people here are on the High Observation Units. To get there, you ride a large stainless-steel elevator, less rickety than some jail elevators I've ridden, which opens into a small sally port. Sally ports are often used to control movement between different parts of jails and prisons. They function something like a lock on a canal, but for people instead of boats: you walk through one door, which has to close behind you before the next one opens to release you. They're often controlled remotely, which is disconcerting, for even if you are a visitor, your movements are controlled and happen only at the mercy of the jail staff. Health care workers often talk about being guests in the house of corrections, meaning that they depend on the cooperation of security staff to do their work; walking through sally ports reminds me how that is true, even for something as basic as moving around the workplace.

The sally port opens into a large open space known as the staging area. As jail spaces go, the staging areas are light and airy, thanks to the "outdoor" recreation areas that flank them on either side. These are kind of like screened-in porches, a way for people to get fresh air and sunshine without actually going outdoors. Three walls are solid, and the fourth, aligned with the exterior wall of the building, is made of fencing and is open to the air.

Walk through the staging area past the outdoor recreation spaces, and you come to a door that leads to the living spaces. Each living space is divided into two sides, labeled with three-digit numbers that identify their location. So Unit 172 is in the first tower on the seventh floor on the second side. Each side is then subdivided into three pods, A, B, and C on one side and D, E, and F on the other. The three pods sit side by side, facing what is called the indoor recreation area but what is really just a large space with fluorescent lighting that serves as an office for the deputies. There are computers here that deputies use to look up information about the prisoners, along with phones and coffeemakers. It's also in this space where much of the mental health care, including appointments with the psychiatrist or other clinicians, takes place.

Above the "desks" with their computers and coffeemakers is a glass-enclosed officers' booth from which an officer can—with the help of security cameras—keep an eye on both sides of the floor and, in case of emergency, call for backup. I stood in one and found I had a hard time seeing into each pod. With so many screens for the security cameras, keeping track of them was difficult.

Each pod has two tiers or levels; there are eight cells on each tier, for a total of sixteen cells per pod. A metal staircase runs to the second tier, and a narrow catwalk runs in front of the upper cells, an industrial version of an old-style road motel. There are gun-slit windows in the cells that let in so little sunlight you don't really notice it. Inside each cell is a metal bunk bed—because the people on High Obs have been found too sick to be double-celled, only one bunk is occupied. In a 2015 report the Sheriff's Department noted that this requirement has put additional strain on the jail system as a whole: "This made the second bed in these multi-person cells unavailable for use. The loss of bed space caused crowding in general population housing areas."[5] Some people collect garbage on the empty bunk, crumpled paper bags or empty milk cartons sometimes arranged in neat rows and sometimes just tossed there. At the end of the bed closer to the door is a stainless-steel toilet-sink combination. The cells all face a large common area known as the pod day room, which is mostly filled with spider tables, round stainless-steel tables with attached stools. (The seats are supported by individual legs that are attached to the table "body," hence the name.) The cell doors and the catwalk's banister and railings are painted a different color on each floor—dull versions of blue and gray and purple—which do little to either reduce the institutional feel or to help distinguish them one from the other.

The pods have a surprising amount of glass in them. The cell doors are mostly windows, although they're so scratched and dirty that it can be difficult to see through them clearly. They are also not very strong. The deputies say people who are angry or psychotic often manage to kick the plexiglass out of its frame. Even the shower and the toilet are enclosed in glass rooms, with only thin strips of frosted glass providing a modicum of privacy.

Each pod is enclosed by a double-storied glass wall that allows a deputy standing on the floor of the indoor recreation area or in the security booth to see into all three units simultaneously. It makes the place feel like a zoo exhibit, especially when—as often happens on these units—the prisoners act bizarrely: lying on the tables, holding animated conversations with interlocutors nobody else can see or hear, or rolling around on the floor. The public displays of peculiar behavior help elide the fact that these are real people, people like Bryan Sanderson, whose lives somehow got derailed.

In a recent letter to the jail, the US Department of Justice criticized how little time people on some of the High Observation Units spend outside their cells, saying it is "inadequate."[6] The goal is to have ten hours of group therapy and ten hours of free out-of-cell time each week, for a total of twenty hours out of cell, which, when you think about it, is still not very much. Officers carefully document when a prisoner leaves his cell, for how long, and if, when he's out, he takes a shower or goes to "rec" time. And when somebody refuses to come out, as often happens, the officers document that as well.

What the letter fails to mention are the dispiriting options for how to spend out-of-cell time. A prisoner may be brought to the pod's common area to sit at one of the spider tables, where his nondominant hand is cuffed to the table. The Department of Justice criticized this as well, saying that the decision about whether a particular prisoner needs that level of restraint should be made on an individual basis.[7]

There is little to do there but sit or—for the saner and more social among them—to chat with fellow prisoners who may or may not be able to hold up their side of the conversation. Sometimes, there are drawing materials, but the deputies have to be careful to collect all the pens and pencils at the end because prisoners could use them to hurt themselves or somebody else. Walking around is basically impossible because of the handcuffs, although some people wander like a chained dog as far as their tethers allow, sometimes climbing up on the tables or lying down on the floor.

Alternatively, prisoners may go to the euphemistically named "small management yards." These are cages within the outdoor recreation areas, similar to the pens at a dog kennel, where prisoners who don't get along with others can safely have time "outdoors." The cages are approximately twenty-four feet long and five-and-a-half feet wide— big enough for a man to lie down in but narrow enough that a man doing karate kicks will rattle the metal fencing and short enough that running at anything faster than a jog would risk hitting the end. There are five cages lined up next to one another in the rec space. As in other parts of the jail, there is a television mounted on the wall that runs constantly.

The other outdoor recreation area is a basketball court, where people may be brought, either alone or, if their behavior merits it, in small groups. One story has it that a few years ago a severely psychotic man who had been brought to the basketball court for rec took off his clothes, then tore three old-fashioned pay phones out of the cinderblock walls. Three pay-phone–shaped rectangles are still visible in the paint. The man proceeded to shoot baskets with the phones and, according to two witnesses I talked to, actually made one. When he started climbing the wire cage wall, medical staff had to give him a shot of medication to calm him down.

Prisoners whose mental illness is less severe—but who are, make no mistake, still quite sick—live in the so-called service areas in Tower Two. They're laid out the same way as the High Obs floors, but because the people in the service areas are less sick than those on High Obs, they are free to spend time unshackled in the pod's common area. And because the jail is overcrowded, some people in the service areas actually live in the common areas, sleeping on bunk beds that have been set up in the floor space around the spider tables.

In this strange, upside-down world, the absolutely sickest patients are, by some measure, the luckiest. They are the ones who are in bad enough shape to earn a coveted spot in FIP. This unit has recently been expanded to fifty-five beds, making it the second-largest inpatient psychiatric unit in Los Angeles County. (For comparison, the largest, LAC+USC Medical Center—also one of the largest public hospitals in the country—has around seventy beds for acute psychiatric patients.)

Like other parts of the jail, FIP is guarded by deputies, and the rooms are locked cells, but it still feels more like a clinic. It's quieter and cleaner than the rest of the jail, and the food is said to be better. In the restricted environment of jails and prisons, getting even slightly better food can be a very big deal. Patients here are more likely to be on medication, either because clinical staff convinced them to take it or because, as a licensed acute psychiatric clinic, the doctors here can, with proper approval, medicate over objection. That is, they can force very sick patients to take medication to alleviate their symptoms. Either way, the result is that some patients here appear healthier than those housed in other areas of the jail.

Even so, people here are still obviously very sick. Mike Burse, the lieutenant who used to be responsible for mental health, walked me through the unit. We saw a man lying on his cell floor near the door, who shouted at us, "You the law? I don't take no mental health meds." Then we passed a man, a blanket wrapped around his shoulders, holding the bottom of a plastic cup to his lips, "playing" it like a trumpet. Then past a man with wild white hair and beard. His mattress was on the floor, the bed frame covered in paper bags and other garbage. Burse shook his head. "We can't fix these people," he said.

Competition for the fifty-five slots is high, so "getting FIP'ed" is like winning the clinical lottery. There's a FIP watch list, a perpetual waiting list of eighty to a hundred High Obs prisoners who are in line to go to FIP when a space opens up. At 8:30 every morning, mental health staff, psychologists, custody staff, and people from the medical department meet to orchestrate the decision of who gets into FIP. It's a decision that could affect a prisoner's well-being for months or even years to come. The mental health staff bring a list of people they think are well enough to be discharged from the FIP to make room for others, and the deputies report which people under their watch on the regular mental health units are sick enough to go to FIP. Think about that for a minute: these are law enforcement officers—whose academy training mainly focused on things like arrests and safe use of weapons—making recommendations to psychologists about which patients are doing well and which need more treatment.

On the Monday I watched the meeting, it was personal.

"He spat in my fucking face," says one deputy, a petite woman with blond hair pulled into a tight bun. She sounds close to tears. She's still waiting, she says, to find out whether the prisoner in question is HIV-positive or not.

"He should be in the clinic," says another deputy. "He should not be on the floor." Others concur, saying he's "ridiculously hostile and assaultive."

"I wish I had better answers," one psychologist, a short rotund man in black pants, says mildly.

"That sucks," said the other psychologist at the meeting, a reddish-haired man with sideburns and square glasses. "I'd be beside myself if he had spat on me." He sounds sleepy.

A lieutenant offers to have the psychiatric nurses weigh in, and the conversation moves on to the waiting list. There are five people the team has agreed are sick enough to get FIP'ed when spots finally open: "Castillo is number one, if he's here. Noguera is the clearest guy who has no issues," the short psychologist said. "Morton is on the list. He went to the [LAC+USC Medical Center] last week, came back, and his cell is already flooded; there are clothes in his toilet." Morton is seventy-five years old.

Sometimes people agree to go to FIP. Even in jail, though, there are rules that govern treating somebody against his will. So more often than not, getting FIP'ed ends up being an involuntarily commitment, known in California as a 5150, after the section of the welfare and institutions code that governs involuntary hospitalizations. (Among California law enforcement officers, 5150 is often used as a noun to describe somebody who needs to be hospitalized, and in street slang, it's been adopted to simply mean "crazy.") A 5150 in jail works like this: if the person is not responsive, then deputies go into the cell, handcuff him, and then put him on a gurney to go upstairs to the clinic. If the person is awake, a nurse or other clinician may talk to him and try to convince him to come voluntarily, but if he won't, then deputies have to do an extraction. They put on protective equipment that is basically riot gear—knee and elbow pads, helmets, and large plastic shields. They may start by releasing pepper spray into the cell to try to encourage the person to "cuff up" (get handcuffed) and come out. If the person doesn't come out, then the deputies come into the cell, where they use their shields to get the person up against the wall or onto the floor, where they can restrain him for transport to FIP. (This is not unique to LA County. Cell extractions are a common way to get people, with or without mental illness, out of their cells for any number of reasons.) "We try to always use the absolute least amount of force that we have to," Burse said. "We do it in a way that they're putting the least amount of harm on the inmate and the least amount of risk on themselves."

Nonetheless, in Burse's view, FIP transfers should be done by medical orderlies, which the jail doesn't have: "We are using police tactics and police weapons and calling it a use of force. It's not different than if I went out and tackled a guy who just robbed a liquor store. We're applying those same policies for a guy who is so mentally ill he's going to die if I don't get him to a mental hospital right now." Medically speaking, that may be a bit of a stretch, since mental illness in and of itself tends not to be fatal. But the metaphor is accurate. Legally speaking, the extractions are treated as uses of force, with each incident requiring extensive documentation and investigation. LA County's legacy of abuse against prisoners has made the jail officials more cautious about uses of force than those at other institutions, but this tension between medicine and corrections is consistent in institutions across the country. (In LA County, at least, doctors have to sign off on some cell extractions.)

There are numerous videos of cell extractions, and they resemble nothing so much as a commando raid or a home invasion. What Burse doesn't say is that even when everything goes right, being the target of an extraction is a frightening experience, all the more so for a person who is psychotic and/or paranoid.

Numerous professional associations have come up with guidelines for proper care of prisoners with mental illness. The American Psychiatric Association calls for treatment in jail that is equivalent to what *should be available* in the civilian society.[8] The emphasis is theirs, acknowledgment that the treatment available in many communities in the United States is rarely what it should be. In this respect the situation at the LA County Jail and others replicates the outside world too well: intensive treatment is reserved for the sickest of the sick, and who gets treated becomes a game of figuring out who is most desperate for basic care.

JAILS AND PRISONS HAVE A particular odor, a mix of dirty laundry, unwashed people, and excrement. This is exacerbated, even in institutions lucky enough to have air-conditioning, by the sheer masses of humanity crammed into close spaces. In some places, it's a cumulative staleness that hangs in the air. In others, it's a nearly unbearable stench that hits you as soon as the front door opens. Invariably, though, there is an intensity to the atmosphere that makes it feel like it will stick in your hair and clothes after you leave, like the residue of alcohol and cigarette smoke after a night in a bar.

As jails go, Twin Towers doesn't smell especially bad until you get up close to the cells, which on High Obs, at least, the deputies have to do quite frequently. In front of the cells, it ranges from strong to barely tolerable when the doors are closed and far worse when they're open. The pungency depends in part on how often the occupant is willing to submit to a shower and how many old milk cartons he is saving in his cell (a common practice) and whether his particular demons compel him to smear the walls with feces or other things. On this floor, the deputies brave the stench every thirty minutes for regular prisoners and every fifteen minutes for suicidal ones, walking past the cells with a handheld device that looks like a smartphone. They check for signs of life from the person inside. Sometimes they have to bang on the door until the person inside stirs; others save the deputies the trouble because they stand guard constantly, shouting, snarling, or just staring. Once the officers have confirmed the well-being of their charge, they scan a QR code affixed to each cell door. It's high-tech proof that they checked and that the person inside is OK, if being OK is defined as still alive and not engaged in any obvious act of self-harm.

Deputy Jorge Zavala is a medium-sized man with short black hair and black plastic-frame glasses. He has spent, by choice, eight of the ten years he has been with the Sheriff's Department working High Obs. It's more challenging, he says, than working with the general population, where the work is more about security and crowd control: "Being here, you feel more like a [health care] worker. We do so much to help [the prisoners]." Besides talking to them, that means making sure that they're taking their medication and reporting to doctors when they don't, or when they exhibit worrying behaviors.

A flat orange tool, like a bottle opener or a key chain, hung from a loop on his pressed green uniform pants. I asked him about it, and he flipped it open to reveal a small hooked blade. It was a knife designed for "cutting down"—that is, rescuing people who have tried to hang themselves. His explanation was so brief and so matter-of-fact that I later discovered I hadn't even bothered to transcribe it fully in my notebook. It was like asking a carpenter about the tool hanging from his belt: "Oh, yeah, it's a hammer. I use it to bang in nails."

Suicide is the leading cause of death in jail—it's far more common in both jail and prison than in the outside world—and hanging is the most common method. One of the biggest jobs at the LA County Jail, as elsewhere, is to try to prevent it in the first place. Prevention methods include surveillance cameras, suicide-proof gowns and bedding, ligature-resistant beds and showerheads, and regular suicide checks.

Nonetheless, those efforts fail often enough that cut-down tools are as much a part of the deputies' tool kits as handcuffs. Similar to what EMTs and police use to cut through a seat belt quickly in an emergency, the cut-down tool's sharp, shielded blade can slice easily through a sheet or T-shirt that has been tied into a noose, but its hooked shape makes it hard to use as a weapon if somebody gets hold of it. Zavala said he has used his cut-down tool a couple of times over the years.

Besides cutting down prisoners who manage to fashion some kind of noose, deputies must make sure that they don't have access to materials they could use to harm themselves. That includes a surprisingly wide range of things: pencils, plastic bags, mattresses, even toilet paper. Even so, people are remarkably resourceful. A paper affixed to one cell door reads "No eggs or cereal bowls." Inside, a short Latino man with bushy black hair, dressed in a suicide gown, holds up his forearms to show thick, red stripes, raw scars from wounds self-inflicted with shells from hard-boiled eggs and broken bits of plastic dishes.

Twice a day, there are meetings—the FIP meeting and another one—for deputies to debrief with clinicians about the prisoners. (They also meet informally throughout the day.) "We describe the behavior, how they're doing," Zavala told me. "They'll ask questions: 'Is he doing this?' 'Is he eating?' 'Is he talking to himself?' 'Is he sleeping?'" What the clinicians don't do is tell the deputies the patients' diagnoses. The deputies aren't supposed to know that because to be privy to such information would violate HIPAA rules. Passed in 1996, the Health Insurance Portability and Accountability Act (HIPAA) was intended, in part, to protect the privacy of people's health care records. In everyday life, that keeps employers, say, from finding out that you have HIV or family members from learning that you were treated for major depression. Those notions of privacy might make sense in a civilian world of appointments in doctors' offices or clinics, where there are computers and rooms for storing medical records and private exam spaces for seeing patients. In this environment, though, the rules seem ridiculous, if not downright dangerous.

Crucial medical information, which could have a direct bearing on how a prisoner is treated, is not disclosed to the officers who are responsible for their safety. Some legal arguments would allow corrections officers to be privy to people's health care information, but I have not encountered a jail or prison that has agreed to interpret the HIPAA rules in such a way as to allow that.[9] Yet at the same time, prisoners are also subjected to extraordinary invasions of privacy because of space constraints and security concerns. It's the worst of all possible scenarios. Medical information that could help deputies understand a person's behavior is kept secret, but the actual medical care—meetings with a psychiatrist or therapist, for example—is conducted in the open, which, among other things, could make the patients less likely to be honest and forthcoming.

Here, many of the psychiatric exams are held in the indoor recreation area, the same space where deputies make and drink coffee, work on the computer, and keep an eye on people. Even from across the room, and above the general din, it's hard to avoid hearing the psychiatrist telling the man in front of him "you have a history of schizophrenia, cutting yourself all the time." It struck me as both ironic and disingenuous when a psychologist scolded me after he realized I'd been sitting with a social worker as she performed mental health evaluations on the prisoners. When she heard his complaint, she shrugged: "Like we have any privacy here."

Although deputies may officially know nothing about the specifics of a person's condition, the deputies and everybody else can *see* which prisoners have been diagnosed with a mental illness, for those in general population wear beige uniforms, and the ones with mental illness are made to wear royal-blue scrub-style pants and a bright-yellow shirt. And the suicidal ones are made to wear dark-blue suicide gowns.

Zavala and other deputies told me that even without specialized medical training or access to the patient medical records, they feel that working here has made them pretty good diagnosticians. New rules mandate that recent graduates of the academy who come to work in the jail must receive forty hours of training in working with people with mental illness. But older deputies tell me they have not received any special training.

Regardless, many of the people here are so obviously sick that it doesn't take much to realize something is wrong. There is the large, muscled man who spends hours doing sit-ups, naked. At first, a deputy said, his tattoos and vigorous exercise routine made them think he was a gang member. But then they heard him talking, saying things like "Hey, if the Marines would come, will the Navy kill all the Air Force guys?"

There's the pudgy man with pale skin and greasy strawberry-blond hair, eyes staring into the distance as he paces around the spider table like a chained dog. He's yelling: "Calvin Jones doesn't see me! I'm complaining. I'm complaining. I'm complaining. I see all the colors. Tan, brown...." Later, in what could arguably be a moment of sanity, he sings out "I don't wanna be in this place no more."

There's the man with angry dark eyes and a wild mess of black hair who incessantly screams obscenities and threats through his cell door. He's torn bright-green jail-issued underpants to bits to make elaborate jewelry, which he wears around his neck and wrists. And there's another man, with neatly combed dark hair and a thick Magnum PI–style mustache, who, in response to a question about where he lives when he's not in jail, cheerfully told the psychiatrist that he rents a house in Los Angeles from his friend, the "honorable FBI director, James Comey." He even gave her a phone number for his "landlord." Minutes later, Comey's "tenant" got angry and agitated, trying to get up from the stool where he was shackled, shouting at anyone who will listen: 'I'm not no fucking mental patient. I know my constitutional right.... I'm not going to sit in this jail until 2022."

These people are obviously not well. And treating them requires significant medical training. The question for the deputies, the *de facto* frontline care providers, is what their role should really be. Knowing that a brain disease is at the root of the offensive or bizarre behavior can help them respond appropriately, with sympathy rather than aggression. Ultimately, though, these are people who need active treatment in order to get well, something that the LA County Jail and others around the country struggle to provide. It's places like this where the tension between the priorities of mental health care and corrections is most visible: thousands of desperately sick people receiving minimal treatment for their mental health problems, being cared for by people with little training for that aspect of the job, and all this at great expense—simply because they have been charged with a crime.

However, it's not just a lack of access to treatment. Some of the people with mental illness at the LA County Jail have been charged with misdemeanors, often the kinds of low-level quality-of-life crimes committed by homeless people and especially people who are both homeless and have a mental illness. The man who reported living in a house owned by the FBI director was arrested in a traffic stop gone wrong. As with much in the criminal justice system, race also plays a part: African Americans and Hispanics are more likely to be arrested than whites. But according to at least one study, in both local jails and state prisons a slightly higher percentage of white people (71 percent and 62 percent, respectively) were found to have a mental illness than blacks (63 and 55 percent) or Hispanics (51 and 46 percent).[10] This could have to do with racial differences in diagnosis or in the willingness to seek treatment. One lawyer also suggested to me that it was a matter of numbers: whites are so much less likely to get arrested that when they do, there are usually "extenuating" circumstances. At the same time, outside of jails and prisons, in civilian life, there are also racial components to psychiatry: for example, poor people and African Americans are more likely than wealthier white people to be diagnosed as having schizophrenia and other psychotic disorders, and cultural and financial barriers sometimes keep them from seeking mental health care.[11] In other contexts, people with mental illness and access to adequate, appropriate medical care are able to live productive, dignified lives. For the people I saw at Twin Towers, though, circumstances have conspired to leave them in a vicious cycle of poor treatment, addiction, and incarceration.

Of course, as in other jails and prisons, some of the people with mental illness are here for truly serious crimes, the kind that make doing a Google search of their names like reading the tabloids on a bad news day. That man in the clinic with the wild hair and beard holding a food tray in front of his face was accused of brutally stabbing a tourist in front of the man's young children. (In a happy ending fit for the tabloids, the man survived, thanks to the quick work of two police officers visiting from out of town, who happened to be walking by.) One wonders how adequate mental health care could have changed the trajectory of this man's life; newspapers reported that he had been in and out of state psychiatric hospitals for years. Or there's a spacey young man with a thin goatee who almost slides off his chair several times during his meeting with the social worker. Wearing a blue suicide gown, he keeps his dull dark eyes downcast as he talks. He was charged with killing both his father and uncle, and has been in jail for seven years waiting for his case to proceed.

At least in this stage of the criminal justice system, we don't have a very good way of differentiating between the severity of the different illnesses or the severity of the crimes. So the man who was stopped for a traffic violation is essentially treated the same way as the one who tried to kill the tourist. The result is that they are both stuck here, neither getting well nor in many cases getting justice. In Los Angeles, as elsewhere, the competing demands of medical care and jail security mean that Zavala and his coworkers guard them like the accused criminals they are in the eyes of the law and simultaneously treat them like the severely ill psychiatric patients their doctors say they are, all with neither specialized training nor even enough information to make informed decisions about their care. It's a setup that seems destined for failure.

In the noise and chaos of the jail, the many people who spend their days sitting or sleeping curled up near the door on the floor of their cells seem benign and barely worth notice. Surrounded by other, more violent or aggressive cases, their quiet suffering often fails to attract attention until their condition becomes acute and they require urgent care. But several deputies told me that like the towels and T-shirts many wear wrapped around their heads, hiding by the door or under the bed is a quiet sign of their madness, a response to the paranoia that plagues so many of them or an effort to drown out the voices in their heads. One described their attempts at camouflage as "survival instincts."

While dealing with an unpredictable population, the deputies also have to rely on survival instincts. "One day I get shit thrown on me or get spit on," said one deputy, "and then the next day, it's 'Hey, how're you doing?'"

To try to anticipate any attacks that may be directed their way, the deputies affix red, yellow, purple, and green magnets, the size and shape of bumper stickers, to the outside of the cell doors as a warning about the person inside: "volatile" reads one; "gasser" reads another. Gassers are people who launch a slurry of feces, urine, blood, semen, or other fluids through open tray slots or sometimes, with the help of old milk cartons (the small ones found in school cafeterias), through the crack around the cell door. Deputies will tape the crack around habitual gassers' doors or occasionally encase the entire cell front in a sheet of plastic, like a house undergoing treatment for termites.

Getting gassed is the act of having that nauseating slurry launched at you, and every deputy has a spitting story or a gassing one or both. Jorge Zavala says he's lucky to have only been gassed once, but when it happened, it came as a total surprise: "This inmate who gassed me didn't have anything against me," he said. "I used to talk to him all the time." Zavala was delivering meals on the top tier of one of the pods; the prisoner had rigged the tray slot so it wasn't locked. "He had a cola bottle full of feces," Zavala said. It got him on the side of his face and in his ear, on his torso and on his clothes. "It was disgusting. I could taste it."

Even though they are already incarcerated, prisoners can be criminally charged with assault for gassing or spitting, and assaulting an officer in this way can add years to a sentence. The assault is treated simply as another crime for which the person may receive a new charge, added onto the previous one. In California, people have been punished with as many as five additional years in prison for gassing officers.

Some people require individualized signs. On the door of cell number 14 in the A Pod, below magnets reading "UNPREDICTABLE" and "SPITTER," is a note printed out on printer paper: "Inmate Gomez spat at deputies on 4/19/16." Other signs warn that a cell's inhabitant has to lie on his bed when food or pills are delivered, as protection against hijacking, which is what deputies call it when the person sticks his arm or other object through the tray slot so that it can't be closed and locked.

It's hard to know if all these security measures—the signs, the handcuffs, the general precautions—are truly necessary in every case or merely the result of the one-size-fits-all approach that is required to run a large county jail. In any case the problem is not just that the system can't differentiate between people whose crimes are minor and people whose crimes are serious; it also doesn't do a very good job of separating the sick and dangerous from the just plain sick or even from those who might simply be responding psychologically to the prison environment.

It's challenging, a deputy tells me as we walk along the cells trying to convince people to come out for out-of-cell time, because you're supposed to get people out, but you also have to protect yourself. "If you pull him out, and he punches you, then you have to use your hands," he says, but when that happens, the supervisors ask, "Why did you pull him out?"

"Everybody's different, with different kinds of problems," another deputy, named Michael Caulfield, tells me. A short white man with ruddy skin and a paunch, he has been working this floor for fifteen years; he says his knowledge of mental illness and how to deal with it is entirely self-taught: "One day they're fine, and one day they're not. You can't take anything personal. If you take it personal, all these guys would be locked in."

Case in point is Joseph Henderson, a small, light-skinned African American man who carries around paper bags filled with garbage that he refers to as his property. "You have to be careful not to throw it away," one of the deputies said. Henderson was charged with a misdemeanor weapons possession involving a knife. He was found incompetent to stand trial and has been waiting for a spot to open up in an in-jail restoration-to-competency program, which will hopefully make him sane enough for his case to proceed. He looks harmless, a slightly stooped middle-aged man in jail scrubs, but the deputies say that in reality, he's extremely volatile. I watched a psychiatrist talk to him from several feet away, deputy at her side, even though he was handcuffed to his seat.

Others appear so harmless—vulnerable, even—that it's hard to imagine what crime they could have committed, let alone what possible danger they could present in jail or out of it: people like the man the deputies referred to as Precious. I never learned his real name or why he got arrested. He was an elderly white man, diminutive and frail with rheumy eyes and fuzzy white hair. He was so unsteady on his feet, shuffling around in his plastic jail slippers, that when he came out of his cell for "rec" time, the deputies had to help him navigate the stairs down from the second tier.

The whole situation is frustrating for the deputies, none of whom ever imagined they were going into mental health work. "We're not the Department of Mental Health; we're not psychiatrists," says Alejandro Fernandez, a tall deputy who works in the Twin Towers and plays soccer in his spare time. "We as deputies, we know how to arrest people. We know how to put people in jail. We don't know how to take care of people with mental illness." This disconnect between the job description and the reality of life at the jail is particularly stark in Los Angeles. Unlike some places, where being a corrections officer is an end unto itself, in Los Angeles the job is left to sheriff's deputies, the same law enforcement officers who are responsible for, among other duties, policing unincorporated Los Angeles County. Until recently, a rotation in the county jail was often just a first stop out of the academy before the deputies hit the street.

The use of conventional correctional methods to address complicated medical situations involving mental illness pervades the jail system and creates not just bureaucratic hassles but also real dangers to both prisoners and deputies. In its 2014 letter the US Department of Justice recounted the story of a man with a long history of mental illness who had committed suicide in the jail. Despite that history and the fact that the arresting officer had flagged the man as suicidal, he ended up being housed in a regular, nonmental health cell: "[The Sheriff's Department and the mental health authorities] have separate policies and procedures.... Further it is unclear who has the authority to enforce this mental health policy, given that the arresting or transporting officers do not report to the mental health staff."[12] A 2017 report from the monitor assigned to the jail as a result of a 2015 settlement between the county and the Department of Justice suggests that suicide-prevention protocols and communication between correctional and medical staff have improved in the intervening years. (The county health department has since taken over jail medical care.) However, the incident shows how the disconnect between medical and correctional staff—a common issue in jails and prisons—can have dire consequences.

The deputies I observed on the mental health unit in Los Angeles treated the prisoners with kindness and care, even when they were difficult or unpleasant. (Of course, it is possible, likely even, that my presence meant they were on exemplary behavior. However, I was there for many hours over the course of several days without a media relations person or other intermediary to watch their conduct.) When a prisoner started yelling at Alejandro Fernandez, the deputy tried to talk to him reasonably, then simply walked away quietly and let another deputy take over. "The way I see it, we're dealing with a bunch of little kids," he said. "They want what they want. And who can blame them? If it's reasonable, I try to accommodate them." Even this sympathetic response, though, betrays his misunderstanding of his charges' conditions; they may be sick, but they are adults with complicated emotional and medical needs, not merely children in adult bodies.

Another time, an old man with thinning hair, several missing teeth, and a shuffling walk—another person whose presence in the jail is hard to comprehend—was walking across the pod when he accidentally defecated on the floor. The deputy with him called for a trustee— a prison-worker whose jobs range from cleaning cells to working in the kitchen—to wipe up the mess, then gently escorted the man to the shower.

However, in its 2014 letter the Department of Justice noted that it had received reports of deputies verbally abusing prisoners at the LA County Jail.[13] And abuse, both verbal and physical, of people with mental illness is a common complaint in jails and prisons. Only twice did I witness behavior in the LA County Jail that struck me as overly rough. I once watched two deputies shouting repeatedly at a man through a cell door that he was going to be put in solitary confinement. Mike Burse and another deputy who were with me said the man likely didn't have a mental illness and had somehow negotiated his way onto the floor. The other time wasn't on a mental health unit. It took place in a hallway somewhere near the intake area, where people are first processed after their arrest: a young Latino man was sitting on a toilet, his lower half barely protected from view—at least from where I was standing—by a low cinder-block wall. Directly in front of him were six or eight deputies, talking. The man asked for some toilet paper, and one of the deputies began to berate him. "Did you have permission to take a shit?" the deputy shouted repeatedly, before eventually bringing the man a handful of paper towels.

MOST ADMISSIONS TO THE MENTAL health units happen on the seventh floor of the Twin Towers. There a psychiatrist and a social worker set up shop in the open area between the security booth and the pods, the same space where the deputies were chatting about the big fight that broke out among prisoners in general population the night before. It was these admissions exams I was observing when I was reprimanded for violating the prisoners' privacy.

The social worker, whom I will call Mary Mason because she did not have authorization to speak to me, sits at a faux wood desk, black laptop open in front of her. On the other side of the desk is a stainless-steel stool, its single leg bolted to the ground. Deputies bring people over one at a time, handcuffing them to the stool in front of her desk. It's an arrangement that ostensibly ensures Mason's safety but makes it so the prisoner can neither stand up completely nor even sit up straight.

Her job, she explains, is to do an initial screen, trying to decide who can be housed with others, who needs a single cell, who needs to see the psychiatrist, who's just faking it. She looks up their histories, often painfully brief, to try to figure out "Why are they up here? What are they trying to gain by being up here?" This worry about being manipulated points to a critical difference between correctional medical care and community-based care; in community-based medicine, health care workers generally assume that their patients are telling the truth about their symptoms.

Depending where a person is arrested, he may be brought directly to the LA County Jail, or he may spend the night in a lockup somewhere in the far reaches of the county. If the arresting officer or the deputy who booked the person flags him, as Mason said, as "gravely disabled, a danger to themselves or others," he may come directly to the mental health floor from booking. Others she sees have been living in general population for hours, days, or even weeks when an officer found they were suicidal, homicidal, or just acting strangely. "You're allowed to act weird," Mason said, "but sometimes the deputies say they're too weird, get 'em out of here"—that is, out of general population.

Prisoners who request mental health care are often sent here for evaluation. The mental health floors are all at Twin Towers, so somebody who is worried about being transferred to another jail in a different part of the county may ask to be transferred to the mental health floors as a way to stay in downtown Los Angeles. Others come looking for a "safe" place; there was talk that morning that some of the people involved in the previous night's fight might appear for psychiatric exams.

Mason's first patient of the morning is a thin Latino man with black hair, patchy beard, and a missing upper tooth. "What brings you here?" she asks.

He says the voices in his head were telling him to hurt himself. "I'm not sure why," he says. "I was told I was schizophrenic, out there on the streets." His record shows he's taking two medications used to treat psychosis; he tells her he doesn't like them.

Some people are already on medication when they get arrested. Others have been prescribed medication but aren't taking it when they get picked up; sometimes not taking their medication leads to the behavior that gets them arrested. Many get their prescriptions only when they arrive at jail.

"You're going to have to wait for your medication adjustment," Mason tells the man. "You're going to have to go on the waiting list; you'll have to wait. Coming up here doesn't mean a med adjustment. There are so many of you guys and not enough staff. Does that make sense? I know it's not ideal."

Mason told me later it can take two weeks or longer to get a medication adjustment because there simply aren't enough psychiatrists available to see patients and write the prescriptions. She says many people will claim to be suicidal because they think they'll get medications sooner. Historically, it has even been complicated for a person who was already taking medication when he arrived at the jail. He might have been given a different one when he got there, or it may have taken awhile to get the prescription to him. Since the county health department took over medical care in the jail, one of the things the new administrators are trying to change is access to medication. "It's a huge deal," says Dr. Ghaly, "because people with mental illness become unstable in places like jail, and they lose stability faster when they lose their meds. So we've set as an objective, anybody who we know is on meds, get them on them." Now, if a person comes into the jail and says he has been on Wellbutrin, for example, the jail aims to get him restarted on it right away.

While Mason talks, the deputies continue to bring in more patients, chaining them to a long metal bench with their backs to her. Meanwhile, inside the pod, behind the plate-glass wall, a trustee walks the catwalk in front of the cells, tucking lengths of toilet paper into the handles on the cell doors. From there, it will get handed to the prisoners as needed. "You hear people calling for their toilet paper," Mason said, because it's too dangerous for them to have it inside the cell. Over the years, people have occasionally used toilet paper or paper towels to suffocate themselves.

It's but one of the many features of this pod, visible even from a distance, that indicate the special nature of its population. In a cell in the A Pod, a man with an Afro, his suicide gown half off, stands staring out his cell door, waving endlessly at somebody or something only he can see. In the B Pod, a man in a cell on the second tier stands naked, openly masturbating in front of his cell door. Nobody tries to stop him; nobody even really seems to notice. When I comment, Mason says, "He does it all the time." In a place where there is excrement on cell walls, where people are shackled to tables and exercise in cages, public masturbation barely registers.

Across the room from Mason is the psychiatrist, an Asian man in cargo pants and a polo shirt. His desk faces the room; his back is to the pod. In front of him, a man with dark hair, wearing the blue-and-yellow jail scrubs that ID him as a prisoner with mental illness, is handcuffed to the stool. He can't stand up and is slightly off-kilter when seated. "I have not really slept a night's sleep since December of last year," the man said. (It's late April.)

"What's wrong with you?" the psychiatrist asked.

"I'm suffering from happiness, sir," the patient answered with the exuberance of a wedding MC. "I don't have a mental illness. I have mental happiness."

Whatever his official diagnosis, the options for this man's treatment in the jail are limited. There is no individual therapy available. The occasional visits with therapists and psychiatrists are primarily for the purpose of checking that medication is working. There is, ostensibly, group therapy, but at least on the surface the options appear to be of little clinical value. Once I observed "relaxation therapy": people were shackled to the spider tables while the movie *Space Jam*—"one of our intellectual movies," the social worker joked—played at top volume. Another time, I saw a social worker setting up for the "socialization group," where another group of people, again shackled to the tables, were rewarded with cookies and tea or coffee simply for coming out of their cells.

The psychiatrist will likely offer the happy man medication, but it's unlikely that he will be *forced* to take it. Forced medication of psychiatric patients is a complicated and fraught issue, both in and out of jail or prison.

Some patients say being forced to take medication is a violation of their civil liberties. But the question of whether to insist that a psychiatric patient take medication is a complicated one: mental illness itself is often defined by a break with reality, so it can be hard to know whether the patient should really be entrusted with that decision. This is especially true for patients with paranoia—who often believe that the medication is an attempt to poison them—or for people who lack insight into their illness and don't understand that they need medication. Sometimes, a patient needs medication to become sane enough to realize that he needs the medication. Not taking medication can also make a person's illness worse, and left untreated, mental illness can lead to dangerous behavior or even suicide.

The Department of Justice has criticized Los Angeles for not medicating more people over objection. Not doing so, the department warns, means the jail is effectively writing off the patients who won't take the medication: "It is important to note that prisoners might initially refuse psychiatric medication, but later agree to take it at the urging of the treatment team."[14] Except in an emergency, medicating over objection is a cumbersome process, one reason that jails are often loath to take it on. But it's often possible, given time and patience, to convince patients to take their medication just by talking to them or, in some cases, offering incentives like food or phone time. At the same time, psychotropic medications come with heavy, sometimes dangerous, side effects. Some patients don't want to take them because side effects such as sluggishness and fatigue make them vulnerable while in jail or prison. Patients' rights advocates and civil libertarians have argued that a patient must be allowed to make the decision for himself or herself, regardless of where the person is. It's a calculus that becomes more complicated when a person is not only compromised mentally but also incarcerated.

While the psychiatrist talks to the man suffering from "mental happiness," the deputies bring more prisoners out of their cells and shackle them to the spider tables in the pod behind him to wait for their turn to talk to the doctor. At one, an older African American man with a beard, the hair on the top of his head sticking up, moved himself carefully onto the floor. Hand still cuffed to the seat, he lay on the floor next to the table, rolling around on his back. Periodically, he lifted his hips and belly off the ground; sometimes he yelled incomprehensibly. When a deputy brought him some food, he rolled over on his knees and, sandwich on the floor, used his teeth to tear open the plastic packaging. He ate in that position, like an animal, without using his hands. He was eventually escorted out to the psychiatrist's desk, and after a deputy offered him extra food, he agreed to be medicated and was taken away to get a shot.

Although forced medication is usually permitted on an emergency basis, in a nonemergency situation forcing someone to take medication requires petitioning a judge, usually with supporting testimony from several people. *Washington v. Harper*, a 1990 US Supreme Court case, sets the minimum standard for forced medication in jails, saying that a prisoner may be medicated over objection only if he is a danger to himself or others and/or gravely disabled. Except on FIP, somebody in the LA County Jail who doesn't want to take psychotropic medication is unlikely to be forced to do so.

Even when the jail doctors decide to medicate somebody over objection, it's complicated by the interplay between medical needs and security concerns. The medicine is given as an injection. The deputies almost always put the person in four-point restraints while he gets the shot so that if he struggles, he can't hurt himself or anybody else. Four-point restraints are a narrow metal bed fitted with wide leather straps at each corner. The straps buckle tightly around each wrist and each ankle, leaving the patient spread-eagled on the bed. As when they restrain a patient as part of an involuntary commitment to FIP, deputies are required to report the use of restraints as a use of force incident.

Physical restraints like this have been almost completely phased out in civilian psychiatric facilities. In Oklahoma I joined a tour to view antique psychiatric equipment that had been used in the old state hospital—things like water baths and electroshock machines. A psychologist was showing the museum pieces to a group of medical aides who were training to work at the current state hospital. She pointed out the restraint bed: such equipment has become so rare today, she said, that when a patient on her unit had recently needed to be restrained, nobody was sure how to do it correctly.

One afternoon, I accompanied a couple of deputies to retrieve a prisoner from the bus depot behind the jail. The depot is like a Greyhound station for the dozens of Sheriff's Department buses that deliver prisoners from county lockups each morning and take them to and from court appearances every day. That morning in court, a man named Mark Kloster had lashed out at a bailiff. He was taken out of the courtroom and put into a transport chair, a kind of wheelchair used to transport prisoners who are unruly or believed to be dangerous. He was African American, tall with droopy eyes and matted hair that stuck up on top. He was dressed in the blue-and-yellow jail scrubs and thick white athletic socks with no shoes; in his lap, he clutched a bag lunch. His long, gangly arms and legs and his torso were held immobile with black cloth straps.

He ignored the deputies as they wheeled him across the driveway, even when they tilted his chair way back to get up over the curb; he seemed not to hear any of their questions about how he was or what had happened. When they wheeled him into the elevator with his face to the back wall—all prisoners are required to ride the elevator that way for security reasons—he suddenly snapped to attention. "Am I going to A Pod? Can I go back to my room in A Pod?" he asked anxiously. He sounded like a business traveler checking into his regular hotel and asking for his favorite room. "They're excited to come back, to see we're still here," said Michael Caulfield, the deputy. "It's an extremely complicated problem."

A complicated problem of a completely different nature is how to get a volatile person into his cell without hurting him *and* without putting the deputies at risk. Kloster's favorite cell in the A pod was not available, so they found another one, this time on the ground level so they wouldn't have to take the restraint chair up the steps.

Because his sandwich and other food were wrapped in plastic—forbidden in the cell because it could be used to asphyxiate himself or somebody else—a deputy had to convince Kloster to surrender his lunch. There was a brief negotiation, and he finally agreed. The deputy unwrapped the lunch and set it in the cell sink for him.

Then, as dictated by protocol and safety rules, the operation got more complicated. First, the deputies cleared the area around the cell. They brought people who had been sitting at the spider tables to their cells. They asked a medical team that was meeting with a patient in the indoor recreation area to move to a different spot. And they walked me to the observation booth, where I was allowed to watch through the one-way glass.

Battleground thus prepared, six deputies gathered around Kloster's chair. A deputy in training stood at the ready with a can of pepper spray the size of a small fire extinguisher. One deputy opened the cell door. Another released Kloster's legs from their restraints as a third tilted the chair toward the open door, effectively dumping him into the cell. The deputy quickly shut and locked the door behind him.

The whole scene was one more strange incident that in this peculiar world took on a disconcerting sense of normalcy. The deputies were ready for battle, but even the negotiation over giving up the sandwich was perfectly pleasant, almost friendly. Kloster may have been—justifiably—terrified, but he was compliant. Still, there was an undercurrent of fear in the whole process, an unspoken sense that this man was truly dangerous, that the situation could, and realistically might, spin out of control. It was as if Kloster were a tiger, a dangerous creature brought in from the wild that could lash out unexpectedly and had to be wrangled into a cage.

It's possible that Kloster was dangerous. His most recent arrest had been on a felony charge, and he'd been arrested several other times over the last few years, each time, interestingly, ending up in the state psychiatric hospital. The deputies knew that he'd been violent in court that morning. And their jobs, after all, are to keep order in the jail and to keep the prisoners and themselves safe. But treating somebody as a threat, as somebody who should be feared, may in turn push him to respond in kind. The protocols that deputies are made to follow may be so scary to the person that he responds by trying to protect himself.

This assumption that there is a real potential for danger defines the way we frequently deal with people with mental illness. Police have told me it's part of what's behind cops' quickness to arrest, to respond with force, and even—and this happens with astounding frequency— to shoot. Judges suggest that it's one reason they are hesitant to set reasonable bail; prosecutors' concede that it's one reason they are unwilling to negotiate better plea bargains; parole boards exhibit unwillingness to let out people with mental health issues.

Unfortunately, it's nothing new. It's been with us since the earliest days.

3

The Asylum Fallacy

IN THE 1930S A BRITISH psychiatrist named Lionel Penrose examined the ways that societies confine people in prisons and in psychiatric institutions, and he concluded that there was a connection: "As a general rule, if the prison services are extensive, the asylum population is relatively small and the reverse also tend to be true. The size of the prison population, furthermore, is closely related to the extent of ascertained crime in a country."[1] Today, the "Penrose Hypothesis"—the idea that there has historically been an inverse relationship between the populations of asylums and prisons—is seen by most experts as an oversimplification. But something remarkably close to it is still frequently used to explain our current crisis of mental illness in the criminal justice system.

As the number of people with mental illness in our jails and prisons has reached alarming levels, a story has emerged to explain how the crisis developed. Policy makers, mental health care professionals, and the press each tell this story in slightly different ways, but the broad contours are generally the same. The story begins with the failure of the state hospitals and the promise of community-based care. This led states to begin downsizing the hospitals and later closing them, which left hundreds of thousands of people without access to regular mental health care. Without proper treatment, their illness drove them to behavior that got them arrested until, over time, with ever-larger numbers of people with mental illness falling into the criminal justice system, jails and prisons became the new asylums.

Looking at the raw numbers, the story seems to make sense. In 1950, around 450,000 people with mental illness lived in health care facilities, including psychiatric institutions and nursing homes. By 2000, the number had dropped to about 170,000. (Some discussions of this period suggest higher numbers of people living in institutions but do not account for the fact that many who lived in hospitals in the 1950s had brain disorders, such as dementia or epilepsy, which do not meet today's definition of serious mental illness.[2]) This period of deinstitutionalization coincides with the explosive growth of prisons and the beginning of the era of mass incarceration. Between 1971 and 2004, the prison population in the United States went from about 200,000 to 1.4 million, a 600 percent increase. Over the same period, jail populations went from about 130,000 to more than 700,000.[3] A combination of factors, including the War on Drugs, the expansion of mandatory sentencing laws, and the rise in broken windows policing drove much of that growth, but if the standard story is to be believed, the shift of people out of state hospitals contributed to that growth as well. There is even physical evidence to support the theory. In the 1980s and 1990s, many states, finding themselves with empty asylums and in need of new prison beds, literally converted the old hospital buildings into prisons.[4]

Thus, we blame the crisis of mental illness in jails and prisons that we face today on the failure of the mental health care system in the second half of the twentieth century. This story is seductively straightforward: there is a population of people with mental illness who require care, and without enough clinics and hospitals to provide that care, this population will end up incarcerated. What's more, the story comes with an easy policy solution: increase access to mental health care, and the problem of people with mental illness in the criminal justice system will go away.

The trouble is, much of the story is wrong.

It is indisputable that the history of asylums is closely linked to the history of criminal justice. The modern asylum movement began in the 1850s, as a response to the problem of mental illness in jails. The reformer Dorothea Dix, horrified by the number of people with mental illness she found behind bars and, even more, by the appalling conditions in which they were kept, wrote vivid accounts of what she had witnessed, drawing national attention to the problem. Her exposure of this mistreatment and neglect prompted state legislatures to build public hospitals to *care* for these people instead. But the asylums were rarely funded properly, and in the twentieth century they became severely overcrowded, leading eventually to terrible conditions of their own.

One could interpret this history as further confirmation of the story we tell ourselves about the shift from asylum to prison: the asylums were developed to care for people with mental illness who had been warehoused and mistreated in jail. So it would make sense that when the asylums closed, those people ended up back in jail. But history shows something else. Throughout US history we have had trouble figuring out how best to care for people with mental illness, and we have had a sizable population of people with mental illness who end up in our jails and prisons. Although historical records and statistics provide only an approximate view, it is clear that our jails and prisons have always served to some extent as clinics or hospitals for people with mental illness, from the earliest days of colonial America through the era of the asylums in the late nineteenth and early twentieth centuries, and right up to the present. This was true even during the heyday of the state hospitals in the mid-twentieth century, when, it is estimated, only about 1 percent of the total population with a serious mental illness was incarcerated. That about 5 percent of the total population of people with mental illness is now in jail or prison can be attributed to the overall rise in incarceration.[5] This speaks to the fact that the overrepresentation of mental illness in the criminal justice system is partly a story of mass incarceration.

Moreover, it's far from clear that the same people who had been in the state hospitals later became the core of the jail and prison population with mental illness. Researchers Richard Frank and Sherry Glied point out that the residents of state psychiatric hospitals were largely elderly, female, and white. By contrast, people in jails and prisons are mostly young, male, and not white. Hospital patients overwhelmingly had a diagnosis of schizophrenia; people with mental illness in jails and prisons show a range of diseases that is much closer to the range found in the general public. Public policy professors Stephen Raphael and Michael A. Stoll estimate that deinstitutionalization (from hospitals) accounted for only between 4 percent and 7 percent of the overall rise in incarceration.[6] Another study proposes that people who were released from hospitals did end up in the criminal justice system, but in jails, not prisons. Researchers found that large numbers of state hospital patients reported having been arrested, though few had spent time in prison. This theory is further supported by evidence that many of the crimes committed by people with mental illness are minor and thus do not lead to prison time.[7]

To fully comprehend the causes of the current crisis, we have to understand the extent to which the problem of deficient psychiatric care facilities and the problem of mental illness in prisons and jails have, from the outset, unfolded in tandem. It's not that one caused the other. Rather, *both* problems have been fundamentally shaped by many of the same forces: lack of resources, lack of effective political interest, and, above all, a lack of understanding of the actual needs of those who are sick. Since the earliest days of the republic, policies and practice have also been overwhelmingly shaped by the belief that people with mental illness are dangerous and pose serious threats to the social order, and thus need to be isolated—in regular hospitals, psychiatric facilities, or, if necessary, jails or prisons.

SHOULD MENTAL ILLNESS BE TREATED within the regular health care system, or should it be treated in specialized facilities? This debate, which lies in the background of much current discussion about mental health policy, had already begun in the colonial era.

In 1751 Benjamin Franklin asked the Pennsylvania Assembly for money to set up the first hospital in America. Franklin proposed raising two thousand pounds from private citizens, to be matched by a four-thousand-pound contribution by the assembly.[8] The proposed facility was to be a general hospital, but it would include a separate ward for treating mental illness. In his petition to the assembly, Franklin noted the growing number of people with mental illness in the colony and invoked the (perceived) threat that they posed: "That with the Numbers of People the Number of Lunaticks, or Persons distemper'd in Mind, and deprived of their rational Faculties, hath greatly increased in this Province. That some of them going at large, are a Terror to their Neighbours, who are daily apprehensive of the Violences they may commit."[9]

Franklin went on to say that "it has been found, by the Experience of many Years, that above two Thirds of the mad People [treated at Bedlam Hospital in London] have been perfectly cured." In a later account of the hospital's founding—a kind of annual report produced in 1754 by the hospital's managers—it was noted that before the hospital was built, the only place to accommodate people with mental illness had been the House of Correction, and "that House was by no Means fitted for such Purposes."[10]

In 1752 the Pennsylvania Hospital opened in Philadelphia in a house rented from a judge. Four of the first six patients were psychiatric cases. By the 1780s, about half the hospital's patients were psychiatric cases.

Despite Franklin's hope for patients with mental illness, the conditions they initially faced in the new hospital were quite grim. They lived in cold and smelly basement cells that were "damp and unwholesome." They were often put in restraints: hand irons, leg locks, and straitjackets. Wealthier patients could pay ten dollars per week for a private room and, sometimes, a private servant. (This last foreshadowed a future where more money often means better treatment or, at least, better conditions.) The psychiatric patients were considered curiosities by the public, who would come to ogle them, and the hospital eventually posted a sign saying that those who wished to look should pay four pence to offset the hassle.[11]

A decade and a half later, Virginia Governor Francis Fauquier began pursuing an alternative idea for treating people with mental illness:

a stand-alone hospital. In 1766 the Assembly agreed to build the hospital. When it had done nothing a year later, Fauquier again asked the General Assembly to support the construction of a psychiatric hospital in Williamsburg. It would be the first institution of its kind in the colonies. In explaining his rationale, Fauquier told the assembly that to guarantee public safety, he regularly had to put people with mental illness in jail: "I am as it were compelled to the daily commission of an illegal act, by confining without my authority, a poor lunatic, who, if set at liberty, would be mischievous to society."[12] With no place else to house them, other colonies, including Connecticut, New York, and Massachusetts, also regularly jailed people with mental illness.[13]

The Publick Hospital for Persons of Insane and Disordered Mind finally opened in Williamsburg, Virginia, in 1773, in a building Thomas Jefferson disdainfully described as a "rude, misshapen" pile resembling an oversized kiln for baking clay. The first "keeper" or director was a man named James Galt, a goldsmith by trade and a member of a prominent Williamsburg family. Galt had previously spent five years in charge of the city's jail.[14] His hiring was perhaps the earliest example of the overlap between the administration of penal institutions and psychiatric ones. It's an overlap that continues today: in 2014 a clinical psychologist took over as head of the Cook County Jail in Chicago.

Today you can visit a historical reconstruction of the Publick Hospital—the original burned down in the 1880s—on the edge of colonial Williamsburg. Inside, a few of the twenty-four original rooms have been set up to show visitors what it looked like when the hospital was in operation. There is an elegant simplicity to the rough-hewn wood floors, the whitewashed brick walls, even the wrought-iron chains that were used to shackle patients to the walls. In the hallway outside is a display of equipment that has been used to treat mental illness over the years: a wooden restraint chair, a straitjacket, an "electrostimulus device." As I left the exhibit, another visitor asked the woman selling tickets why the patients were kept chained up. Before the ticket seller could answer, the woman's teenage son replied, "They were mentally ill." The ticket seller nodded: "They were mentally ill."

The Publick Hospital took only people who were acutely psychotic or who were seen as dangerous to society; alcoholics and the chronically ill were not permitted. If a patient's family had the means, they were expected to pay for their own care; in practice, the government ended up providing free care to most patients.[15] The care provided at the Publick Hospital was primitive and included submersion in cold water, bleeding, and the frequent use of restraints, including manacles and, later, straitjackets.[16] Still, in its early years the hospital had few patients. Most people with mental illness continued to live with family; in some cases, communities provided money to make that possible.[17]

Around the time of the Revolution the hospital ran into financial trouble, and after the war ended, it closed. Foreshadowing what happened when the state psychiatric hospitals were closed two hundred years later, the remaining patients from the Publick Hospital were released into the community; with nowhere else to go, at least one ended up in jail.[18] The hospital reopened in 1786; its descendant survives as the Eastern State Hospital, where the firefighter Bryan Sanderson was treated some two hundred years later.[19]

The stories of these early hospitals highlight questions that have recurred throughout our history and that still resonate today. Who should bear the cost of caring for people with mental illness? Where should people with chronic, as opposed to acute, mental illness be treated? And should we treat mental illness in specialized psychiatric hospitals, as was attempted in colonial Williamsburg, or within general hospitals, as Benjamin Franklin had advocated?

As IT HAPPENED, THESE EARLY experiments with psychiatric care coincided with another major innovation in American social policy: the rise of the modern prison. In 1787 a friend of Benjamin Franklin and fellow signer of the Declaration of Independence, Benjamin Rush, hosted at Franklin's house a meeting of the Philadelphia Society for Alleviating the Miseries of Public Prisons. A Pennsylvania physician, Rush was a social reformer who specialized in caring for the poor;

Rush was also one of the founders of modern psychiatry—he published the first psychiatric textbook in the United States, *Observations and Inquiries upon the Diseases of the Mind,* in 1812 and was involved in the development of the earliest mental hospitals.[20]

At that time, punishment was not the prime motive for imprisonment. People were locked up either before their trials or until the punishment—fines or whippings, stocks or cages, banishment or execution—could be carried out. There was no thought that punishment would teach the person himself a lesson, but rather it would serve as a warning to others to deter them from committing the same crime.[21]

In the 1780s, Rush and his fellow reformers proposed a completely new model of punishment, one that would use imprisonment as a way to encourage rehabilitation. At that time, the jail on Philadelphia's Walnut Street was a dysfunctional place where newly arrived prisoners were expected, among other things, to buy their fellow prisoners a round of drinks from the taproom run by the warden. Undeterred by the challenge, Rush's organization decided to transform it into what would become the prototype for the world's first penitentiary, Eastern State.

In 1829, several decades after Rush's project to reform the jail was successfully launched, Eastern State was built just outside Philadelphia with the explicit aim of producing "regret and penitence in the criminal's heart." The early Philadelphia prison reformers believed people who committed crimes weren't bad, but rather had been failed by various social institutions in the past: family, church, school, and the like. This is a concept that we have begun to come back around to—understanding, for example, the role that childhood abuse or other early trauma can play in both the development of mental illness and the likelihood that a person will commit a crime.

The right prison, the idea went, could make up for that. Early corporal punishments had targeted prisoners' bodies. This new model targeted their minds. It replaced debauchery and drink with hard work and contemplative isolation, all in a pristine institutional setting.[22]

At the time it was built, Eastern State was the most expensive building in America. Designed by British-born architect John Haviland, it consisted of seven cell blocks that radiated out from a central rotunda. The exterior was a daunting Gothic façade; the interior had barrel-vaulted hallways and tall windows.

The individual cells were centrally heated and had flush toilets (this in a time when even the White House had neither). The cells were lit by skylights, and each had an adjacent walled yard where the prisoner could spend time outdoors. The prison was organized around the belief that extreme solitude would aid prisoners' rehabilitation, the precursor to the solitary confinement that is widely used in the United States today. Prisoners were supposed to stay mostly in their cells and to occupy themselves with manual labor, such as shoemaking or spinning, and with religious introspection, by reading the Bible. When they left their cells, they were hooded, both to keep them from getting distracted and from having any contact with the guards. Since that time, the underlying approach to punishment through incarceration has remained remarkably consistent. It is an approach that has had far-reaching consequences for prisoners, particularly people with mental illness.[23]

IN THE DECADES AFTER THE Revolution, the problem of mental illness in US jails became a recurring theme. People with mental illness who lacked family support ended up in poorhouses in large numbers. This placed a heavy burden on these institutions, which were similar to homeless shelters—places where poor people could live at the government's expense. Others ended up in jail. Both institutions tried to avoid responsibility for people with mental illness, so much so that by the turn of the nineteenth century, Massachusetts and other states had passed laws that *required* welfare and penal institutions to accept people with mental illness.[24] Nineteenth-century jailers were no more inclined to take on this responsibility than were their twenty-first-century counterparts. "It is a source of great complaint with the sheriffs and jailers that they must receive such persons, because they have found no suitable accommodations for them," wrote minister-turned-prison-reformer Reverend Louis Dwight.

Dwight had begun visiting jails in Massachusetts in the 1820s to bring Bibles to the people there. What had started as a religious mission became a public health one. He was appalled by the conditions he found, especially among those with mental illness: "The ventilation was so incomplete that more than one person, on entering them, has found the air so fetid as to produce nausea, and almost vomiting. The old straw on which they were laid, and their filthy garments, were such as to make their insanity more hopeless; and, at one time, it was not considered within the province of the physician's department to examine particularly the condition of the lunatics. In these circumstances, any improvement of their minds could hardly be expected."[25] He found people who had been held in cells for years; in the winter, he noted, it was unbearably cold.

It is startling how little has changed since Dwight made these observations nearly two centuries ago. His description of fetid air reminded me of a cell I stepped into in the Cook County Jail one day, where the stench was so strong that it triggered my gag reflex. Prisoners with mental illness are regularly held in solitary confinement for years. And in a twenty-first-century variation of keeping prisoners in extreme temperature conditions, many states still refuse to air-condition their prisons, even though excessive heat is extremely dangerous for people who take psychotropic medications.

Some of the first concerted efforts to find alternatives to jails as a place to care for people with mental illness came from private citizens. Around the same time as Dwight was calling attention to the abusive conditions of early-nineteenth-century jails, philanthropists in cities such as Boston and Philadelphia began building private psychiatric hospitals. Boston got a mental hospital—the private facility now known as McLean Hospital—before it got a general one. These institutions were ostensibly intended to serve people from all income levels. Nonetheless, from the outset, administrators were reluctant to accept too many poor or otherwise undesirable patients: their funders did not want their institutions to become charity hospitals.[26] To combat the image of being a charity institution, McLean Hospital refused to take nonpaying patients but did agree to allow poor people to pay on a sliding scale.[27] If they couldn't afford even that, the towns where the patients lived were expected to foot the bill. However, the model proved unsustainable, and less than five years after it was founded, McLean was $20,000 in debt.

At that point the state of Massachusetts stepped in and built a public psychiatric hospital in Worcester, some forty-five miles away. Poor people were sent there instead, leaving McLean for the wealthy.[28] By the mid-1830s, McLean served mostly "an improved class of sufferers," which "has rendered the classification, especially of convalescents, far less embarrassing and difficult."[29] McLean would eventually provide care and respite for such notables as the poets Sylvia Plath and Robert Lowell and the mathematician and Nobel laureate John Nash.

These private hospitals were far nicer than their public counterparts. Margaret Fuller, a columnist for the *New York Tribune,* visited the Bloomingdale asylum in New York in the 1840s: "[Bloomingdale] is a house of refuge, where those too deeply wounded or disturbed in body or spirit to keep up that semblance or degree of sanity which the conduct of affairs in the world at large demands may be soothed by gentle care, intelligent sympathy, and a judicious attention to their physical welfare, into health, or at least, into tranquility."[30] At Bloomingdale, the "shades of character and feeling were nicely kept up, decorum of manners preserved, and the insane showed in every way that they felt no violent separation betwixt them and the rest of the world, and might easily return to it."[31]

Around the same time that private philanthropists were turning their attention to care for the wealthy, Dorothea Dix took up the cause of care for the poor. In 1841 she agreed to teach a religious class in a Massachusetts jail, and much like Dwight a decade earlier, she was outraged by what she found—people with mental illness being held with criminals and being kept "in cages, closets, cellars, stalls, pens! Chained, naked, beaten with rods, and lashed into obedience!"[32] Dix began visiting jails and poorhouses from Massachusetts to Indiana and found similarly wretched conditions almost everywhere. The problem was not just that people were being abused; the prisons were fundamentally unsuited to dealing with people with mental illness: "Jails and Houses of Correction cannot be so managed as to render them suitable places of confinement for [people with mental illness], and who, never having violated the law, should not be ranked with felons, or confined within the same walls with them. Jails and Overseers of Houses of Correction, whenever well qualified for the management of criminals, do not usually possess those peculiar qualifications required in those to whom should be entrusted the care of lunatics."[33]

In 1843 Dix started traveling to state legislatures to convince them to build what would be more than thirty public hospitals, institutions that were intended to offer at least the possibility of a cure or, barring that, a safe and welcoming asylum—in its most literal sense of the word—for people with mental illness.[34] Some of these hospitals had more ambitious therapeutic aims and provided treatment, however misguided by today's standards. But others were merely custodial, no better than a "well-kept prison," as one person described the public hospital in western Virginia.[35] Charles Dickens was appalled by what he saw when he visited the asylum on Blackwell's Island (now Roosevelt Island) in New York City in 1842:

> [E]verything had a lounging, listless, madhouse air, which was very painful. The moping idiot, cowering down with long disheveled hair; the gibbering maniac, with his hideous and pointed finger; the vacant eye, the fierce wild face, the gloomy picking of the hands and lips, and munching of the nails: there they were all, without disguise, in naked ugliness and horror. In the dining-room, a bare, dull, dreary place, with nothing for the eye to rest on but the empty walls, was a woman locked up alone. She was bent, they told me, on committing suicide. If anything could have strengthened her in her resolution, it would certainly have been the insupportable monotony of such an existence.[36]

Some of the early hospitals, on the other hand, occupied large campuses complete with working farms and other industrial operations.

I saw vestiges of the old campus at the Griffin Memorial Hospital in Norman, Oklahoma, about twenty miles south of Oklahoma City. The hospital was made up mostly of low-rise brick buildings with filigreed wrought-iron balconies. Like the prisoners in early jails and prisons, patients at these hospitals were expected to work; the asylums were like plantations, communities unto themselves, with much of the work at them done by the patients.[37] In Norman, patients grew vegetables and raised pigs, chickens, and dairy cows to feed the thousands of patients and the hundred or so staff members who lived there. The site also had an industrial laundry, a bakery, a catfish farm, a dental clinic, and even a cemetery.

The work was said to be therapeutic, but as the narrator in the semiautobiographical 1946 novel *The Snake Pit* points out, it was also free labor. Committed to a psychiatric hospital after a breakdown, she complains to her husband about how hard it is for her, with her brain addled by electroshock treatments, to perform the menial jobs that are presented as occupational therapy. He tells her not to worry because it's just therapy, not a real job. "[I]t is interesting to me," she answers, "that most of their occupational therapy gets work done that they would have to hire out otherwise."[38]

Taken together, these hospitals provided the makings of a mental health care system. Much thought went into the planning of some of the individual asylums, but remarkably little planning went into their creation and collective mission. Thus, there was little consideration of how they would work as a system.[39] Hospitals were often built far from the urban centers where they were most needed. Like the Publick Hospital in Williamsburg, most asylums started out by caring for only patients with acute disorders. Such patients would come, get treated, and go home, ostensibly cured. Later, states realized that people with chronic mental illness also needed care and either expanded the existing hospitals or built new ones for this purpose.[40]

Because the alternative was often the poorhouse, the bar for treatment at the hospitals was set low.[41] And as hospitals grew rapidly, even ones that had started out with real therapeutic models—and many did—were forced to abandon them when the number of patients

simply grew too large. The public hospital in Worcester, Massachusetts, opened in 1833 with 120 beds; thirteen years later it had nearly
400 beds.[42]

Still, it's important to remember that even in 1950, when institutionalization of people with mental illness was at its highest levels, only
about a third of people with serious mental illness lived in psychiatric
hospitals or other institutions. The majority—roughly 60 percent—
still lived in the community, either with family or elsewhere.[43]

THE DECLINE OF THE STATE hospitals happened over many decades
but became acute in the period around World War II. There were
more and more patients, which resulted in overcrowded facilities; at
the same time, many hospitals became even more drastically understaffed when doctors and attendants were drafted into the war. Meanwhile, state governments were dealing with the double demands of
the Depression and the war, and had no funds to help the hospitals.
Even before the war ended, a series of books and articles documented
overcrowded conditions, the lack of treatment, and the severe staff
shortages.

In 1932, for instance, Marle Woodson, a journalist who had himself
committed to an Oklahoma hospital to manage his severe alcoholism,
wrote that the doctor "is compelled to look on the patients in the mass;
he has no time to consider any of them individually."[44] Any notion of
treatment was largely abandoned, wrote journalist Albert Deutsch in
1943: "Our mental hospitals have returned to their 19th century status
as asylums for the custody, rather than the cure, of the mentally sick."[45]
Not only that, wrote reporter Mike Gorman in the *Daily Oklahoman*
newspaper in 1946, but "most [patients] do not receive even adequate
custodial care."[46]

That same year, a journalist named Albert Q. Maisel published a
scathing critique in *Life* magazine bluntly titled "Bedlam 1946: Most
US Mental Hospitals Are a Shame and a Disgrace."[47] The article
drew on Maisel's own reporting as well as information given him by

conscientious objectors who worked in the hospitals during the war instead of serving in the military. It was accompanied by an arresting spread of black-and-white photographs: emaciated men wandering naked through a unit in Pennsylvania; a woman hunched on a bench, arms wrapped tightly in a straitjacket; a man peering through the bars of a jail cell in Ohio, where he was awaiting transfer to an asylum. As Maisel wrote, "The vast majority of our state mental institutions are dreary, dilapidated excuses for hospitals...costly monuments to the states' betrayal of the duty they have assumed for their most helpless wards."[48]

Maisel reported that the hospitals were so overcrowded that people slept cheek by jowl in hallways: "We jam-pack men, women and sometimes even children into hundred-year-old firetraps in wards so crowded that the floor cannot be seen between the rickety cots, while thousands more sleep on ticks, on blankets or on the bare floors."[49] A 1948 national survey found that one state hospital had no nurses. In another area the doctor-patient ratio was 1 to 500, and the nurse-patient ratio in one was 1 to 1,320. Hospitals turned to retired general practitioners and, in some places, unlicensed physicians.[50]

Many hospitals, Maisel found, didn't bring criminal charges against employees who mistreated patients but either reprimanded or at most fired them, leaving them to seek similar employment elsewhere. Staff in many hospitals used both physical and chemical restraints to keep the patients under control so that they would be less trouble to the attendant. In *The Snake Pit* the narrator describes being drugged with paraldehyde, a soporific: "[She] went with the other Medication Ladies and drank her share of the hypnotic that made them smell like badly tended lions and then she went to her dormitory...you know it will be only a few minutes before you will sink into paraldehyde emptiness."[51]

Maisel described more quotidian abuses as well: "Through public neglect and legislative penny-pinching, state after state has allowed its institutions for the care and cure of the mentally sick to degenerate into little more than concentration camps on the Belsen pattern.... We feed thousands a starvation diet....We give them little and shoddy clothing at best. Hundreds...spend 24 hours a day in stark and filthy madness."[52]

Written barely a year after the end of World War II, this was no casual indictment. Yet the most alarming aspect of reading Maisel's and others' accounts nearly three-quarters of a century later is not how awful they are, but how closely we have replicated the appalling conditions of the asylums in our contemporary jails and prisons.

IN AN ARTICLE IN THE *New York Times Magazine* in 1947, George Stevenson, a psychiatrist and medical director of the National Committee for Mental Hygiene, a group "dedicated to raising the standards of psychiatric institutions and clinics," advocated for more community-based care. The state of the public hospital, he wrote, "is merely a symptom of an outdated system that is crying for a complete remodeling. What we need today is an entirely new *concept* of public psychiatry."[53] Stevenson's proposal was the beginning of what would become the twentieth century's biggest and best-known change in psychiatric care: deinstitutionalization. Moving people out of the dysfunctional state hospitals solved the immediate problem of overcrowding. It also changed some of the thinking around who should be held in hospitals and under what circumstances. It did little, though, to resolve the underlying predicament. Decades later, there is still not enough mental health care to provide to all who need it, it is still not clear how and where that care should be delivered, and we still can't agree on who should pay for it.

Three major changes led to the push for deinstitutionalization in the middle of the twentieth century: the development of new medications, new funding for outpatient treatment, and the creation of Medicaid.

The first big change came in 1954, when the FDA approved the use of the drug chlorpromazine—sold in the United States under the brand name Thorazine—to treat major mental illness. The compound had previously been used in a variety of ways—first in synthetic dyes, later as an insecticide, as an antinausea medication, and as an enhancement for anesthesia—before doctors began experimenting with it to control symptoms of psychosis.[54] Doctors had used medication to treat mental illness before, but none as widely or as successfully as Thorazine.

Mostly, the medication slowed the patient down. As doctors pointed out, it made patients seem to "lose interest in their surroundings, and their florid symptoms abated."[55] Some patients complained that it made them feel empty and impossibly drowsy. It also had serious side effects, including Parkinson's–like symptoms: a slow, shuffling walk, a blank stare, and tremors.[56] In some cases the tremors lasted even after the patients stopped taking it, which suggested that it caused permanent brain damage.

Still, Thorazine's ability to control the symptoms of psychosis, combined with a heavy marketing campaign targeting the state legislatures that funded state hospitals, made it one of the first blockbuster drugs.[57] As a government commission put it a few years after Thorazine was approved, the drug "revolutionized the management of psychotic patients." Indeed, barely a year after it was first brought to market, doctors had prescribed it to more than two million people.[58] That's an enormous number, especially considering that the overall population of the United States and the population of people diagnosed with mental illness, were much smaller than they are today. Today, Thorazine has mostly been replaced by newer medications that are more effective and have fewer side effects. What was truly revolutionary about the drug, though, was not the medication itself but rather the newfound conviction that we could prescribe our way out of our mental health problem. Doctors and the public suddenly believed that psychotropic medication could effectively eradicate mental illness, much the way vaccines had (mostly) eradicated measles and polio, and antibiotics had stopped people dying from infections. The thought was that by treating the symptoms of mental illness, pharmacological agents would allow people with severe mental illness to live meaningful, independent lives in the community. It's a belief that persists in some measure today, where the vast majority of psychiatric care focuses on pharmacological interventions.

Changes in mental health care spending even in the past three decades show how this has been borne out in practice. As recently as 1986, for example, more than 40 percent of mental health care spending was on inpatient care. By 2009, the figure was less than 20 percent. On the other hand, prescription medication represented only 8 percent of mental health care spending in 1986; in 2009 it was more than three times that. That growth is not evenly distributed across different types of medications, though: the number of prescriptions for antidepressants nearly tripled, from 55.9 million prescriptions in 1996 to 154.7 million in 2008.[59] Inpatient care represented 41 percent of spending in 1986, but only 17 percent in 2009; outpatient care accounted for 24 percent in 1986 and 32 percent in 2009. Residential care made up 22 percent of spending in 1986 and 15 percent in 2009.[60]

The second big shift was the move toward community-based care, which began soon after the end of World War II. In 1946 Congress passed two acts allotting money to build outpatient clinics in the community and to expand general hospitals to be able to serve psychiatric patients.[61] And on October 31, 1963, President John F. Kennedy signed the Mental Retardation Facilities and Community Health Centers Construction Act of 1963 (as it turned out, the last bill he would sign into law). "Under this legislation," he said in a speech at the signing, "custodial mental institutions will be replaced by therapeutic centers. It should be possible, within a decade or two, to reduce the number of patients in mental institutions by 50 per cent or more. The new law provides the tools with which we can accomplish this."[62]

The new act dealt with both mental illness and what we now call developmental disabilities; it distinguished between allocations for each, with most money going to the latter. It allotted money for states to build new community-based care centers, which would offer both inpatient and outpatient care and other services to people with mental illness. The idea was that patients could still see doctors and get cared for without having to live in an institution permanently. However, it was never specified, either in the act itself or in subsequent statutes, who would get the care, who would provide it, or what kind of care it would be.

Nonetheless, the passage of the act allowed state legislators to justify closing or drastically reducing the number of state hospitals, often over the objections of local politicians, medical staff, and broader communities, where the institutions often provided much-needed employment opportunities. (This last response is remarkably similar to what we have seen in recent years as states seek to downsize prisons.) Nevertheless, despite the opposition, numerous hospitals or parts of hospitals were closed; this downsizing of public inpatient care continues today in many parts of the country.

Many of the new community care centers either never materialized or ended up serving populations with less severe forms of mental illness or with other disabilities, rather than those with serious mental illness. (This complaint still surfaces today: a mental health program created by the first lady of New York has been widely criticized for not focusing on more serious forms of the disease.) Even where community care was made available, its success wasn't guaranteed because the approach assumed that patients had access to housing and family who could help care for them, while many in fact had access to neither.

The large-scale elimination of state hospital beds alongside the failure of the community clinic model has had consequences that continue to be felt today, with ever-greater numbers of people left scrambling to find care. The number of private psychiatric beds has increased since the 1950s but has declined from its peak.

A third big shift came in 1965 with the creation of Medicaid and Medicare, federally funded health care programs for the poor and the elderly, respectively. Medicaid has ended up having a significant effect on how mental health care is financed. But at the outset, the critical issue was a provision in the law designed to make sure that *states*, rather than the federal government, were responsible for funding for long-term inpatient psychiatric care. The Institutions for Mental Diseases (IMD) exclusion, found in section 1905(a) (B) of the Social Security Act, says Medicaid will not cover care for any patient under age sixty-five in an "institution of mental diseases," defined as a "hospital, nursing facility, or other institution of more than 16 beds, that is primarily engaged in providing diagnosis, treatment, or care of persons with mental diseases, including medical attention, nursing care, and related services."[63] In other words, the federal government would not cover inpatient treatment in psychiatric hospitals. This encouraged states to move people out of these kinds of institutions so they wouldn't have to pay for care and instead move patients to nursing homes or outpatient care in the community so that Medicaid would cover at least some of the cost. Today, Medicaid is the largest funder of mental health care services in the nation.[64]

In the decades that followed, other societal changes helped further the push toward deinstitutionalization, including significant changes to the laws around involuntary commitments, the growth of the disabilities rights movement, and a shift in public opinion. The number of people living in institutions dropped from a peak of more than half a million in the 1950s to barely over 100,000 by the mid-1980s. Since then, that number has continued to fall, with only negligible numbers of people living in psychiatric institutions.

So if deinstitutionalization is not responsible for the current crisis of mental illness in jails and prisons, then what is? Limited data are available, but best estimates suggest that in 1950, when jail and prison populations were far smaller than they are today, only about eighteen thousand people with serious mental illness were incarcerated.[65] The number of incarcerated people with serious mental illness is far higher today, namely because the total number of people in jails and prisons is higher. People with mental illness have simply been caught up—albeit sometimes in disproportionately higher numbers than the rest of the population—by the same forces that have driven the rise of mass incarceration, among them the War on Drugs, broken windows policing, and mandatory minimum sentencing.

The numbers are alarming, though, particularly when considered as proportions of total jail and prison populations. At the Cook County Jail, some 2,250 people have a mental illness, out of a total population of 9,000.[66] At the Los Angeles County Jail, it's almost 4,500 people out of a total population of 17,000. The California state prison system reports even higher numbers.[67] In New York City, it's roughly 4,500 of the 10,000 prisoners at Rikers Island. About 700 of those have what the city deems a *serious* mental illness, meaning diseases such as bipolar disorder and schizophrenia.[68] Furthermore, as overall jail and prison populations have begun to decline recently, the proportion of people with mental illness to those without has gone up. In New York City in 2010, for example, about 30 percent of people at Rikers had a mental illness; by 2014, the figure had gone up to 40 percent.[69] That's partly because people with mental illness continue to get arrested in large numbers and partly because, as discussed elsewhere, people with mental illness are less likely to get bailed out, less likely to get good plea bargains, and less likely to be given alternatives to incarceration, such as probation.

IT'S BEEN MORE THAN SEVENTY years since Lionel Penrose tried to draw a connection between the population of prisons and that of asylums. And while it's clear in hindsight, at least, that his explanation for the relationship is too simplistic, he was right in this respect: to understand how we got to the current crisis—and how to get out of it—we have to look as much at the history of the criminal justice system as that of mental health care.

Over the course of our history, punishment by incarceration has been our standard response to crime. But by the 1970s, as jails and prisons were beginning to grow dramatically, we had largely given up on the idea that incarceration should be rehabilitative. Lost with the notion of rehabilitation have been things like education programs, which made it possible. Instead, we have been left with an almost single-minded focus on punishment and retribution. According to sociologist David Garland, "Punishment...is once again a respectable, openly embraced, penal purpose....The language of condemnation and punishment has re-entered official discourse."[70] At the same time, the severe overcrowding and underfunding in many jails and prisons have meant that even if the political will were there, a program focused on rehabilitation would be difficult to sustain. As one state legislator recently said about overcrowding, "Basically, in Oklahoma, we're just warehousing people in prison, and we're not trying to rehabilitate anybody because of budget constraints."[71] We have come full circle from the old institutions.

On the mental health side, meanwhile, we have continued to cut funding, leaving even more people without access to care. According to an association of state mental health directors, in the years following the 2008 financial crisis, states cut $4.35 billion in mental health services from their budgets. In the same period, a million more people reportedly sought treatment at public mental health care facilities.[72]

In his 1948 book, *The Shame of the States*, journalist Albert Deutsch wrote about the relationship between mental health and criminal justice, complicated even then: "The finest, most up-to-date building I saw under construction at Milledgeville [a state hospital in Georgia], at a cost of $450,000, was intended to house the criminally insane!" Deutsch's guide told him that "there were really only 18 criminally insane persons eligible for this elegant housing, and that the rest would be given to choice civil patients. It appears that the building budget could not have been obtained without the plea that it was intended primarily for criminals, rather than for mentally sick people."[73]

This willingness to expend resources in the name of public safety but not public health still exists today as counties and states—while cutting budgets in the community—continue to earmark money for special mental health care units in jails and prisons. It's a strategy that has both upsides and downsides.

PART II

LOCKED UP:
WHAT HAPPENS INSIDE

4

Jail as Hospital

WHEN THE DAY BEGINS AT the Cook County Jail, the holding pens are almost always full. Most of the men in them were picked up the night before by cops in Chicago or the surrounding county. Their clothes are rumpled, hair messy, faces unshaven. Some have the dazed expression of somebody who stayed up all night. Others just look blank. They sit on the wooden benches that run around the perimeter of the high-ceilinged cinder-block rooms or lean against the chain-link fencing that forms the front of the pen. A few lie on the floor, too drunk or sick or high to stay upright. By noon, they will all be led out to eat lunch and then left in another set of holding pens to wait until bond court starts at one. But before that happens, each will stand in front of a tall wooden counter and get screened for mental illness.

Many jails, especially big ones, do mental health checks for new arrivals. What's different about Chicago is that it happens *before* you get arraigned. Diagnosing in jail can be difficult, especially in the first hours after arrest, when a person may still be intoxicated or high. The social worker who oversees these intake exams, a slight woman with long blond hair and glasses, plays detective, looking for clues about the newcomers, who often don't know or don't want to share their psychiatric histories. The secret "is to talk...about a medical problem, blood pressure, or diabetes. They're willing to talk about that," she says. Then you casually ask, "Where'd you get help? Where'd you get meds? They'll mention by accident a psych hospital. Ask what meds they were given, they'll name a medicine for hypertension and an older anti-psychotic." This early screening is important because it increases the chances that people with mental illness will be identified and treated. And it gives the jail a head start on getting them proper treatment and housing.

Besides comprehensive mental health screens, the jail boasts that a person with mental illness who comes there can now get individual therapy, group therapy, and special housing. Many of the corrections officers at the jail are trained in working with people with mental illness. There is a transition center to help them prepare for life on the outside, a program that includes both intensive therapy and job training. There are discharge planning services that help them enroll in Medicaid and figure out where they will get mental health care on release. And once people are released, there's a place for them to safely spend their first night in freedom and even a mental health hotline to call if they have a crisis. It's an enviable range of services, many of which one would be hard-pressed to find elsewhere in the community.

Between 20 percent and 30 percent of the Cook County Jail's nine thousand prisoners have a mental illness. Sheriff Tom Dart, who is responsible for the jail, is one of the loudest critics of a mental health care system that has helped turn jails and prisons into psychiatric facilities. But he is also a pragmatist and knows that this situation is not going to change anytime soon. This has made him a trailblazer in changing the way his jail deals with people with mental illness: "If they're going to make it so that I am going to be the largest mental health provider, we're going to be the best ones. We're going to treat 'em as a patient while they're here, it's like, we are going to think differently."[1] In a profession that tends to shy from publicity, he has taken the opposite approach, broadcasting his views in appealing sound bites and enthusiastically inviting members of the media to tour his jail.

Not everybody has embraced the new paradigm as enthusiastically as Dart. But most have at least come to acknowledge what Dart wrote in an open letter to sheriffs and jail directors in 2016: "Absolutely none of us signed up to run the largest mental health institutions in our respective communities. Yet that is where we find ourselves."[2] The letter serves as the introduction to a template he wrote for colleagues across the country about how best to respond to this crisis. Some jails—and prisons—have responded with to this new reality with a sort of "if-you-can't-beat-'em-join-'em" philosophy by building special mental health units—or in some cases separate facilities, adding new ways to screen people for disease and new ways to treat them. Others acknowledge the need but have done little to accommodate it, citing limited budgets and other constraints. But even when the money is there, is building hospitals behind bars really the solution? What happens when you try to turn an institution designed to punish into one that is meant to cure? Is there a danger that it will simply reinforce an already troubling reality, creating an incentive to send even more people with mental illness into the criminal justice system? On the other hand, what are the consequences when jails and prisons choose *not* to take on this new responsibility or when they do it half-heartedly? As with so much in the criminal justice system, the answer is complicated.

One place where you can see the rapid expansion of mental health care side by side with facilities that have largely ignored it is Rikers Island. In early 2016, New York City announced that it would spend $8.7 million in the coming year—with additional funding each year for a total of more than $24 million by 2020—to improve mental health care at the jail.[3] Around 70,000 people pass through the jail in a given year, and according to recent data, more than 40 percent of them have some form of mental illness. This is up from 30 percent less than a decade ago, a trend that has been apparent at many other jails across the country.[4] Among other aims, the additional funds for Rikers were meant to increase the number of special mental health units known as the Program to Accelerate Clinical Effectiveness (PACE).

Around seven hundred people at Rikers are too sick to live in general population and are housed in mental observation units, basic units similar to those in Los Angeles County and elsewhere. For those who need more care, the PACE units, introduced in 2015, are designed to provide an alternative that is more therapeutic. They are intended to replicate the kind of treatment found in the outside world, whether that of specialized behavioral health facilities or of psychiatric units in general hospitals. "My conceptualization of Rikers is as a hospital," Elizabeth Ford, the psychiatrist in charge of mental health care at the jail, told me shortly after taking the job in 2014. "You've heard that the criminal justice system is the new mental health system. We need to accept that fact and then, obviously, try to change it."

PACE units are small, with no more than twenty-five beds each, and like many units in hospitals on the outside, they are tailored to specific populations. Among the first four that were built, one was designed for people returning from an inpatient stay at the state psychiatric hospital, another for people returning from a stay at the forensic unit at Bellevue Hospital, one for patients at risk for needing inpatient hospitalization, and one for patients needing further psychiatric evaluation. In addition, the jail also runs two other units—one for men and one for women—called Clinical Alternative to Punitive Segregation (CAPS). These are, effectively, PACE units for people who repeatedly violate rules in the jail, replacing a series of punitive solitary confinement cells that were previously used to house prisoners with mental illness who repeatedly broke the rules.

The standard mental observation units, where most people with mental illness at Rikers are held, have typically had a shortage of clinicians and little in the way of programming. On PACE units, however, there are more staff and more services, such as group therapy and art activities. The medical staff and corrections officers who work on the PACE units train and work as a team, which helps reduce much of the tension between the jail's growing health care mandate and its primary function as a jail that has to guarantee everybody's safety. Staffing on the PACE units is also meant to be consistent so that the patient-prisoners see the same clinicians and have some degree of continuity of treatment. Patients have the opportunity to get to know the staff and become comfortable with them, which is important for successful treatment; likewise, both clinicians and security staff are also more likely to recognize problems or changes in patients they have observed over time. Hardly revolutionary in medical practice, this kind of consistency is nevertheless a departure from standard practice for many jails and prisons, in which prisoners may seldom see the same clinician twice.

Also different is the approach to discipline. On standard mental health units—including most of those at Rikers and at many other jails—medical staff often complain they are working at cross-purposes with the security personnel. On the PACE units, however, the security officers themselves are given special training in working with people with mental illness. Rather than relying on the usual combination of threats and punishments, PACE units use a reward system, where prisoners can earn socks, T-shirts, and even pizza parties for cooperation and good behavior. The units are also self-contained, which means that they are mostly protected from the chaos of the rest of the jail. In most parts of the jail, prisoners need corrections officers to be brought to appointments with the psychiatrist or therapist. That means missed appointments when there aren't enough officers or the jail is on lockdown. On the PACE units, clinicians come to the patients, so it's less likely they'll miss appointments. Even when the rest of the jail is on lockdown, people here can continue with their daily routines. So far, it seems, all of this is working well: according to Ford and the city, the first three years have seen half as many use-of-force incidents in PACE units as there are in other mental health units, half as many incidents of self-harm, and a 40 percent increase in patients taking their medication properly.[5] One activist attorney—long one of Rikers's harshest critics—called it a tremendous step in the right direction.

I visited one of the CAPS units. And while it's hardly luxurious—among other issues, the physical plant at Rikers is in terrible condition—the atmosphere is noticeably different from typical ones. Prisoners are encouraged to spend much of the day in the common room, which has table tennis and a television. Unlike larger jail units, it's relatively quiet. The therapy office—a converted corner cell—feels more human, thanks to prisoners' artwork on the walls. These are some of the toughest, most violent people at Rikers, but in most cases, treating them as patients rather than prisoners brings positive results.

Other states are taking steps as well. California recently spent $900 million to open the largest prison hospital in the country, the California Health Care Facility in Stockton. It has space for nearly two thousand patients with the "most severe and long term needs," including mental health care. And in April 2017, the state announced it is building a fifty-bed inpatient mental health facility at the California Institution for Men, a minimum-security prison for two thousand prisoners. The acute-care facility will provide crisis treatment for people from that prison and others.[6] The Special Offender Unit at the Monroe Correctional Complex in Washington State has some four hundred beds for people with mental illness.[7] In early 2017 the sheriff in New Orleans signed off on plans for a new building that will include eighty-nine beds for prisoners who have "acute and subacute mental health needs."[8] In southeastern Washington State, Benton County plans to build a $5 million, twenty-four-bed mental health unit in the county jail. "We are committed to not only develop, but create the best mental health system we can in the incarceration system," county commissioner Shon Small told the local newspaper.[9]

The need for in-house psychiatric care in jails and prisons has been acknowledged for a very long time. At its 1930 annual meeting the American Medical Association (AMA) adopted a resolution to support principles around "psychiatric service in criminal courts," a concept that had been put forth by the American Bar Association the year before. Among the principles was the idea "that there be a psychiatric service available to every penal and correctional institution" and that "there be a psychiatric report on every prisoner convicted of a felony before he is released."[10]

For more than four decades, little was done to put such an idea into practice. An AMA survey in the early 1970s found that only 14 percent of jails around the country had facilities for prisoners with mental illness.[11] To be sure, it wasn't just *mental* health care that was lacking in correctional institutions; the same survey found that in two-thirds of the institutions, the only medical care available inside the jail was first aid, and just over 15 percent didn't even have that. A US Department of Justice study around the same time reported that among larger jails, only one in eight had a specialized medical facility of any kind; the study made no specific mention of *mental* health.[12]

However, just a few years after those findings appeared, the situation changed dramatically. Today, prisoners have more of a right to health care than anybody else. As with so many criminal justice reforms, these changes were driven by a lawsuit—in this case, one involving prison labor. (Although many people know about prisoners making license plates, the reality is that prisoners have long been required to work on prison farms or in factories. Some private companies contract with prisons to provide labor, and in some states, such as California, prisoners are used to fight forest fires.)

In 1973 J. W. Gamble, a prisoner at the state prison in Huntsville, Texas, was unloading a truck at his prison job at a textile mill when a six-hundred-pound bale of cotton fell on him. Gamble kept working, but several hours later he went to the prison hospital complaining of back pain. After examining him briefly, the nurse gave him some painkillers and sent him back to his cell.

Gamble's back still hurt the following day, so he went back to the hospital. This time a doctor prescribed more painkillers and ordered him to stop working for a while—in effect, to take medical leave. Yet several weeks later, when the doctor declared Gamble healed and cleared him to return to his prison job, Gamble said his back still hurt as much as it had that first day and refused to start working again. The prison sent him to solitary confinement.

The cycle continued for several months. Gamble would refuse to work, citing back pain, and the prison would punish him with more time in solitary. Finally, Gamble filed a lawsuit *pro se*—that is, acting as his own attorney—saying that by denying him proper medical care the prison had violated the Eighth Amendment: "Excessive bail shall not be required, nor excessive fines imposed, *nor cruel and unusual punishments inflicted*" (emphasis added).

The case, *Estelle v. Gamble*, eventually made it to the US Supreme Court, and in 1976 the Court ruled in Gamble's favor. Writing for the majority, Justice Thurgood Marshall observed that because prisoners depend on the prison (or jail) to meet all of their needs, "deliberate indifference to serious medical needs of prisoners constitutes the 'unnecessary and wanton infliction of pain.'"[13] In effect, this historic decision established that people in jails and prisons have a constitutional right to medical care. They are the only population in the country that does.

The ruling laid the groundwork for the creation of a parallel health system within jails and prisons. The Supreme Court case clarified the fact that jails and prisons were obliged to provide medical care. It left it up to district courts and others to decide what, precisely, that was to mean in practice.

At the same time that courts began considering what mental health care in jails and prisons was to look like, state legislatures in places such as Indiana and California were ordering the closing of state hospitals. This could be seen as further evidence of "transinstitutionalization": as people with mental illness left the state hospitals and ended up in the criminal justice system, jails and prisons saw an increased need for correctional health care services. But a closer examination suggests a different explanation: that these were simply two opposite responses to the same need for mental health care. The state legislatures got rid of state hospitals on the grounds that they were unnecessary and beyond repair, while the *Gamble* decision to require medical care put the United States on a long path toward the normalization of jails and prisons as major health care providers.

What the Supreme Court did not do was clarify how and in what form health care should be provided in the criminal justice system. So in the following years, lower courts started to do so themselves. In 1980 *Ruiz v. Estelle,* a Texas class-action suit heard in federal court, laid out minimum requirements for mental health care in jails and prisons. Among these, the Court established that there must be a systematic way to screen people for mental illness, that treatment must be provided by trained mental health professionals and must go beyond simply putting patients in seclusion, that accurate health care records for prisoners must be maintained, that psychotropic medications must be prescribed safely and appropriately, and that every correctional facility must have some kind of suicide-prevention program.[14] Alarmingly basic, the requirements set down in *Ruiz* may seem so obvious that it would be surprising if they were not already being observed. Yet, as we will see in coming chapters, states still regularly fail to follow many of them. In *Madrid v. Gomez*, another class-action suit, this one in California in 1995, a federal court judge expanded on the minimum standards laid out in *Ruiz*. Prisoners must also have a way to let medical staff know what they need, and enough clinical staff must be available to provide prisoners with individualized treatment. Furthermore, the court ruled, prisoners need timely access to care, there has to be a quality assurance system, medical personnel have to be competent and well-trained, and systems must be in place for suicide prevention and for responding to health emergencies.[15]

Over the years, other organizations, such as the American Psychiatric Association (APA), have also laid out straightforward though nonbinding guidelines for the provision of mental health care in jails and prisons. According to the APA, inpatient care should be available either in the correctional facility itself or in an outside hospital; health care coverage should be available seven days per week, with twenty-four-hour nursing coverage for those with acute issues; patients should receive written treatment plans; and they should have access to a full pharmacopeia of psych meds, access to individual and/or group therapy, and access to programs "that provide productive, out-of-cell activity and teach necessary psychosocial and living skills."[16]

More generally, the APA suggests that treatment should be a mix of medication and therapy: "[P]atients with bipolar disorder are likely to benefit from a concomitant psychosocial intervention—including psychotherapy—that addresses illness management...and interpersonal difficulties. Group psychotherapy may also help patients address such issues as adherence to a treatment plan, adaptation to a chronic illness, regulation of self-esteem, and management of marital and other psychosocial issues."[17] Guidelines for treating schizophrenia, once the patient is stable, are similar.

For jails and prisons, the question of *how* to treat people with mental illness is relatively clear. As with diabetes and other chronic diseases, the medications and other therapies are well-known; they are the same inside a correctional facility as they are outside. The conditions needed for optimum care are also well-known. The larger challenge is how to reconcile these needs with the physical and disciplinary environment of correctional institutions.

To people such as Elizabeth Ford, the psychiatrist at Rikers, and Tom Dart, the sheriff in Chicago, it is a challenge that requires a great deal of pragmatism. People with mental illness in the criminal justice system need treatment, the same way people who are not in it do, and that treatment might as well be as effective as possible. "We're guardians of these people for the time they're with us," Ford said. It's a logical, laudable approach to this problem. Here is a literally captive audience, one that might not get health care otherwise. Of course it makes sense to provide the best care possible.

Some prison systems have taken a similar approach. Washington State has made it a priority to try to identify prisoners' psychiatric needs when they come into the system and to send them to prisons that can best accommodate those needs. There is also a weekly meeting, similar to what is done in hospitals, to discuss the most complicated cases. "What we've tried to focus on here is recognizing the continuum of care that is needed, and being able to provide it," Karie Rainer, who is in charge of mental health for the Washington State Department of Corrections, told me.

"The chief problem is that mental health care and criminal justice start with different philosophies," says Bandy X. Lee, a psychiatrist at Yale, "so the ethos itself of the criminal justice approach is incompatible with therapeutic means and methods." No matter how well meaning, in other words, efforts like the PACE units inevitably point to a far more intractable question: Can institutions designed with radically different priorities than maintaining psychic well-being under *any* circumstances be adapted to offer appropriate care? And should they?

Indeed, there are risks associated with programs like the PACE units at Rikers. For starters, they operate on the premise that there will always be a large and growing population of people with mental illness living in jails and prisons. Would it make more sense, one can legitimately ask, to invest in community-based care and other treatment options instead? At times, building new and improved facilities for prisoners with mental illness seems to be almost a knee-jerk response to a crisis. When two civil rights groups sued the Alabama Department of Corrections in 2014 for its treatment of people with mental illness, the department's initial response was to propose building four new prisons to replace the old ones. There is also the risk that if people can get better health treatment in jail than they can in the community, then it might encourage a new form of mercy booking—when a cop arrests somebody to make sure that the person gets "three hots and a cot"—that is, food and a place to sleep. This is a not-uncommon practice, even in places where correctional mental health care is less than stellar. Sometimes, judges or prosecutors will insist on keeping the person in jail, usually by refusing to set bail, either to keep him "safe"—i.e., off the streets—or as a way to get access to mental health care.

One argument against this kind of "mercy," of course, is that jails and prisons were never meant to be therapeutic environments. As Lee observes, the real problem with jail psychiatry, no matter how ambitious, is that it will always be "a correctional unit under correctional control." Such criticism is not new. In 1972, even before jails and prisons were legally required to provide medical care, criminal justice professor Marvin Zalman found that a "study of cases indicates that adequate medical care cannot be systematically provided in large prisons." In an analysis that predicted some of the root causes of poor medical care, he wrote that anything that was done to improve prison conditions overall—such as "reducing overcrowding, moving facilities closer to big cities and closer to a greater range of medical talent, and reducing prison populations and the number of people subject to prison medicine"—would also improve medical care.[18] Similarly, an editorial published by a group of public health experts in 1990 warned about the problems of leaving mental health care in the hands of jails and prisons: "The cost will be prohibitive and a change in prison philosophy supporting a more 'caring' environment will be impossible to develop. Medical and mental health services stand only to be overwhelmed by the escalation in the number of prisoners." The problem, they said, lies both with the correctional facilities themselves and with the public health system as a whole, and the only way to solve it is for prisoners to "come to be regarded as an important segment of society deserving proper attention."[19]

Still, John Wetzel, the corrections commissioner in Pennsylvania, sees few downsides to trying to find new ways of treating people with mental illness in jails and prisons: "I don't know who the hell would be afraid of trying something new, because the old stuff is not working at all. The outcomes are terrible historically. I don't know what the risk is in trying something different." He sought input both from his employees and from the prisoners themselves on how to improve. Like Washington, Pennsylvania has been working on its identification and classification of prisoners with mental illness and then find them appropriate housing. Some units now have psychiatrists on them forty hours per week. The state has been training its corrections officers on how to work with people with mental illness; it has also been exploring the use of peer specialists—people who have experienced mental illness and who are trained to help others—a practice that has become increasingly common in the community.

Successful mental health care in correctional facilities requires both money and leadership willing to make it a priority. But under the relentless pressure of cost control, overcrowding, understaffing, and, undoubtedly in some cases, a lack of will, in many places the reality is far from that. Setting aside the underlying question of whether there should be hospital-style mental health care facilities in jails and prisons, there are countless reasons why, in practice, mental health care too often falls short. At the California Health Care Facility, the new 1,700-bed hospital prison just outside of Stockton, the opening of entire wings was delayed by a shortage of psychiatrists. Worse, workers weren't doing the regular checks of patients on suicide watch because they didn't have time; the union representing those workers told the *Associated Press* in 2014 that supervisors had ordered them to falsify the records to make it look like they had indeed done the monitoring even though they hadn't.[20] In New Orleans a psychiatrist testified in a 2016 lawsuit that the mental health unit at the jail there was in name only, that the only thing differentiating it from any other unit was a sign on the wall identifying it as such.[21] And then there is Rikers itself: the introduction of the PACE units came only after years of scandals around an earlier mental health unit where several people with mental illness died hideous deaths.

And that's the issue: given a long history of abuse and mistreatment of people with mental illness in jails and prisons, whether under the guise of specialized "mental health care" or within a regular disciplinary structure, there is little guarantee that the latest reforms will in practice—and over the long term—be much better than what came before. The patients who end up in jails and prisons are some of the sickest in the country, yet the available resources will always be limited. And as we will see in coming chapters, when the system fails people, the results can be tragic.

5

Destined to Fail

EXACERBATING THE CURRENT MENTAL HEALTH crisis in many jails and prisons are several fundamental problems: a population of prisoners who are increasingly sick, often severely so; extreme overcrowding and shortage of qualified staff, both of which have particularly harmful consequences for people with mental illness; and chronic underfunding for incarceration facilities in general, which often means woefully inadequate resources for mental health care. Any one of these problems alone presents a tough challenge for corrections systems. Together they form an almost intractable puzzle, in which an attempt to address one of them is often offset by another getting worse: the addition of a special mental health unit for a small number of severely ill prisoners may quickly be canceled out by the increase in the number of prisoners with mental illness overall, leaving many of them back in the general prisoner population and subject to the same poor treatment that the health units are supposed to eradicate.

Add to this yet another challenge: the criminal justice system, with all its other problems, is not only receiving huge numbers of people with mental illness; it is also, in many cases, getting the sickest of the sick—those who most urgently need intensive treatment. More than a third of prisoners with mental illness show signs or have symptoms of their disease when they're arrested but haven't been diagnosed or treated within the past year.[1] Even in a regular clinical environment, these are the cases that would be among the most difficult, people whose psychiatric disorders have been minimally treated, treated only sporadically, or, sometimes, not treated at all. In this way, *mental* illness is like many other forms of illness. Patients do better when treatment is consistent and starts early. When an illness is left untreated, it almost always gets worse and harder to manage. With a physical illness, it's the physical problem that makes it hard to treat. In other words, Stage 4 breast cancer is harder to treat than Stage 1 because the tumors have spread to other organs; unchecked asthma might lead to permanent scarring of the lungs. And there is some evidence that this is also true in mental illness, that untreated psychosis may lead to neurological damage. But advanced mental illness may leave the person with less insight into his illness and thus less open to treatment. For jails and prisons, this means that they are left with the fewest resources to treat the hardest cases.

Further complicating matters, three-fourths of prisoners who have a mental illness also have a substance use problem; in some cases this is the result of self-medicating with alcohol or street drugs. For clinicians, this situation presents a variety of additional challenges. In the early days of incarceration in jail, substance use can mask the symptoms of mental illness. In other words, if a person is high when he is arrested, it can be very difficult to tell whether a symptom comes from the drug or a disease. It also means that a person may be dealing with withdrawal. (Withdrawal from alcohol, in particular, can be quite dangerous if not treated properly.) It also means that any effective mental health care treatment likely needs to include substance use treatment as well.

Many prisoners also have physical illnesses, which may, in turn, further complicate—or be complicated—by their mental illness: somebody who is psychotic will have trouble managing his diabetes or other chronic disease.[2] Meanwhile, extensive data show that incarcerating a sick person often makes the disease itself worse. The most obvious example of this is the use of solitary confinement, but there are other, subtler ways that prisons and jails can aggravate or even precipitate mental illness. For example, overcrowding makes basic living conditions extremely stressful—the noise or just the competition for bathrooms and other amenities. These stresses may be worse for people with mental illness. A good place to observe this phenomenon is among incarcerated women. Across the country, female prisoners have even higher rates of mental illness than their male counterparts, and research has shown that they are especially vulnerable to conditions in jail or prison.

Consider Oklahoma, which has the highest female incarceration rate in the country; between 2011 and 2016 the number of women going to prison rose an astonishing 30 percent—even as the number of men dropped slightly.[3] In Oklahoma, as in other states, women still make up a very small percentage of the overall jail and prison population even as they are the fastest-growing group of prisoners.

A large majority of Oklahoma's female prisoners are sick when they arrive; in 2016 about 70 percent were being treated for a mental illness. Far from anomalous, this figure is in line with, or slightly under, that of other states.[4] Nationally, an astounding 75 percent of women in state prisons have a mental illness, compared to about 55 percent for men. This is partly caused by the nature of mental illness: it is more common among women than among men. But it's also true that women in the criminal justice system are far more likely to have experienced trauma, physical abuse, and sexual abuse and/or to have substance use problems, all conditions that are closely connected to mental illness.

Susan Burton spent fifteen years in and out of prison in California after, consumed with grief over the death of her young son and with no access to mental health care, she became addicted to cocaine and crack. She now works with women who have recently been released from prison in California, helping them find housing, find jobs, and regain custody of their children. She says particularly for women of color, incarceration is yet another form of abuse for people who have, in many cases, spent a lifetime being abused. When women have problems with substance use or even when they defend themselves, "we end up criminalizing these women. Then the criminalizing [i.e., the incarceration] takes on another form of violence against them.... We are further traumatized and tortured through the prison experience."

The trouble is that many of these psychological issues are precisely those that may be worsened by a jail or prison environment, as I witnessed at Mabel Bassett Correctional Center, Oklahoma's largest women's prison. Mabel Bassett is officially in McLoud, some thirty miles east of Oklahoma City, but is far enough outside the small town to make the fencing and barbed wire that surround it seem superfluous. The buildings are low slung and painted gray, set around a large yard. Under a cloudless blue sky, one could almost forget that it was a prison yard but for the women in their dull uniforms.

About 1,300 women are at Mabel Bassett. Only 10 percent of them "have not endorsed any mental health issues or treatment," according to Deanna Gallavan, the psychologist in charge of mental health there. In other words, 90 percent are receiving some form of mental health treatment. She's an upbeat woman with shoulder-length blonde hair; originally from Oklahoma, she studied forensic psychology in New York before moving back to the state. Unlike many who end up in correctional medicine, she says she went into psychology specifically to work in corrections. At the prison, she oversees a staff of three master's-level clinicians and two other psychologists.

For many people, untreated mental illness is one of the reasons they have ended up in prison in the first place. "What I believe is that in the decades to come, mental illness will be the new Jim Crow," Burton said. "People's response to the ways they have been treated is actually a normal response, to build these defenses, but these normal responses [are] actually used against them." At Mabel Bassett, as in many places, substance use—a common form of self-medication for people with mental illness—is a major driver of incarceration: in Oklahoma prisons, almost a quarter of the women have been locked up for having or buying drugs. About a fifth were arrested for distribution of a controlled substance. The way Oklahoma's drug laws are written, it's very easy for a possession charge to get bumped up to distribution.

Paradoxically, for many of these women, getting locked up, even for a minor, nonviolent offense, often carries other consequences that make the symptoms of the mental illness itself often significantly worse. For example, it often means losing at least temporary custody of one's children; one reason that Oklahoma leads the nation in the proportion of children who are raised by their grandparents is that so many mothers are incarcerated. In many cases, children are placed with foster families, sometimes permanently. I met a woman in Tulsa whose parental rights for two of her children had been terminated after she was arrested on drug possession charges; she had a serious meth addiction and ADHD (attention-deficit/hyperactivity disorder), so her children were placed in foster care and then put up for adoption. The woman was enrolled in an alternative-to-incarceration program and was hoping to get well enough to regain custody of her remaining children.

Even if a mother doesn't lose her children while she's incarcerated, distance and cost often make regular visits tough to organize. In some places the institutional rules make the separation even worse. For example, the Tulsa jail forbids visits from children under age fourteen, so depending how long she's in pretrial detention, a woman could go months—or years—without being allowed to see her children. Anxieties about one's child, being separated from one's child, and losing custody of one's child are all traumatizing events that may trigger or worsen a mental illness. And the process for regaining custody after incarceration is arduous and, some say, nearly insurmountable. For a woman who has been the victim of physical or sexual abuse, even being ordered around by corrections officers may be traumatizing. These are among the many issues that Deanna Gallavan and her staff have to try to treat. The very high incidence of mental illness poses huge challenges at Mabel Bassett, as it does at other jails and prisons. Despite how pervasive the care needs are, there are only forty-seven beds in the mental health unit there—enough for less than 4 percent of the prison's population. The mental health unit, which has been around since at least 1990, is, in effect, a stabilization unit, a place for the sickest women in the state's prison system.

However, it's not meant as a long-term care facility. As Gallavan said, "The goal of the mental health unit is to get them off the mental health unit. We want to get them to the point where they can function in the free world." She wants to stabilize them quickly and move them back into general population. The building is two stories tall, with a double row of tiers around the perimeter. In the middle are a few tables and glassed-in staff offices. It's dim, almost dark, inside, or maybe it only seems that way after the astonishing brightness of the prison yard. There are women sitting at the tables and wandering around. A few peer out the scratched cell windows. There's also an outpatient clinic just off the prison yard, a few doors down from the dining hall. Gallavan tries to prepare those patients for the free world by trying to explain to them that if it's not an emergency, they can't just show up in the clinic without an appointment and demand to be seen on the spot.

Gallavan says she could use more therapists so that clinicians could give each patient more individual attention, come up with treatment plans, and give them therapy so that ultimately they wouldn't need to come back to the clinic. She would also like more safe cells for suicidal prisoners; she says she sees more suicide attempts among women than she did among men when she worked at other facilities. She says she could also use a step-down unit, a place for women who are no longer so acutely sick that they need the mental health unit but who are not yet well enough to return to general population.

EVEN FOR THOSE LUCKY ENOUGH to get into the special mental health unit, other aggravating factors may be making their disease worse. Part of the problem is that Oklahoma's prisons are so crowded. As of 2016, the prison population in state facilities (for both men and women) was at around 110 percent of maximum capacity. And this figure itself belies the actual stress on the system because the state also pays to contract beds at private prisons and local jails; without those overflow beds, the prisons would be closer to 150 percent of capacity.[5] (Other states sometimes manage overcrowding by sending prisoners out of state.) Overcrowding is exactly what it sounds like: an institution housing far more people than it was designed for. Although Oklahoma is an extreme example—its rate of incarceration is second only to Louisiana's—lack of capacity has been a serious problem across the United States for decades. The anticrime and antidrug laws introduced in that era not only brought more and more people into the criminal justice system, many with very long sentences; it also meant that far more people were going in than coming out. Many were not going out at all or were regularly being cycled back in. It was like a bathtub with the faucet on full-bore but with the drain only partially open; water comes into the tub faster than it drains out, so eventually it will reach the top and overflow. Numerous prisons were built or expanded to meet the demand, but not enough to keep up.

Technically, overcrowding is measured simply by comparing the number of prisoners that a given institution actually houses to the maximum number of prisoners it was built for. But corrections officials, psychiatrists, and criminal justice scholars point out that a shortage of beds is only one aspect of a problem that plagues institutions in many different ways. There is the question of basic services that a correctional facility is supposed to provide, whether mental health care or recreation time, both of which may be significantly compromised or curtailed as a result of overcrowding.[6] For prisoners with mental illness, the effects of overcrowding can be devastating, sometimes even deadly.

Coleman v. Brown—which in 2011 ended up in the US Supreme Court under the name *Brown v. Plata*—charged that severe overcrowding made it impossible for California to provide adequate mental health care to its prisoners as mandated by the Constitution. Over the years, the case has laid out in detail how, as the former head of the California Department of Corrections and Rehabilitation put it, "overpopulation makes everything we do more difficult."[7] It meant that two people were made to live in cells designed for a single person; as many as two hundred prisoners were housed in a single gymnasium, sometimes on triple-level bunk beds. The sanitary conditions were otherworldly: these prisoners were made to share just six showers, and more than fifty had to share a single toilet.[8] Some of the unsurprising results were less out-of-cell time for prisoners, more violence, and serious failures of the sewage and plumbing systems.

Given the inadequate number of mental health crisis cells, very sick people ended up housed in infirmaries or in "telephone-booth-sized interview stalls typically placed in corridors."[9] A psychiatrist testified that suicidal prisoners were known to have spent long weekends, from Thursday evening to Monday morning, being transferred between so-called dry cells—freestanding upright mesh cages with no toilets, used during the day—and wet cells—holding cells with toilets, at night.[10] Several committed suicide while they were waiting to be transferred to the appropriate mental health beds. In the 1990s, suicide rates in California's prisons were far higher than national averages. Mental health caseloads were so large that patients often had to wait months, or even as long as a year, to receive psychiatric care. And those delays created cascading effects on the whole system. "By denying prompt access to inpatient care, [California] is allowing patients to become more acutely ill than they would," a psychiatrist testified. "By the time those patients reach an inpatient bed, they will generally require more resources for a longer period of time to become well than they otherwise may have needed. This further backlogs the system, thereby exacerbating the shortage of beds and making it difficult to assess the demand for services."[11]

Overcrowding has also hastened the move away from rehabilitation as something that can happen in prison. It may not be as immediately apparent as dysfunctional plumbing or nonexistent medical care, but having too many people in an institution frequently makes it impossible to maintain anything beyond the most basic of services. Programs aimed at helping prisoners prepare to return to civilian life, whether through an anger-management program or a GED course, simply don't make the cut. This has multiple consequences: besides the more obvious purpose served by such programs, parole boards often look at attendance in such activities as evidence that somebody is serious about making a positive change. Sometimes, successful completion of courses is mandatory for a person even to be considered for early release.

In many ways, California's situation is extreme—it has one of the biggest prison systems in the country, and at its worst, some of its prisons have been at 300 percent of capacity. But it's also far from un-usual. At the end of 2015, prisons in eighteen states were operating at or above maximum capacity.[12] And while these states haven't necessar-ily reached the levels of California's worst prisons, their overcrowding has had similar consequences. In Nebraska, where a 2016 US Justice Department report found the suicide rate was 30 percent over the na-tional average, civil rights attorneys are suing over the treatment of prisoners with mental illness, who often end up in solitary confine-ment rather than getting treatment.[13]

THE MEASURES OF A JAIL'S or prison's capacity isn't just a question of having enough space for all the prisoners; it also has to have enough staff to take care of them. One issue that the technical definition of overcrowding fails to account for is how many people are on hand to oversee a given jail or prison population. A chronic lack of qualified staff was one of the problems in state psychiatric hospitals when leg-islatures began shrinking and closing them in the 1960s and 1970s. "There wasn't enough of anything at [the psychiatric hospital]," Mary Jane Ward wrote in *The Snake Pit*. "Not enough doctors, not enough nurses, not enough toilet paper, not enough food, not enough cov-ers for cold nights...there were not even enough beds. There wasn't enough of anything but patients."[14] Change "patients" to "prisoners," and this would be a fairly accurate description of many incarceration facilities today.

In state after state where the mental health crisis is most pronounced—states such as Oklahoma, California, Alabama, Illinois, and Florida—there is not just a large population of very sick people stuffed into facilities that were never designed to contain so many but also a chronic shortage of doctors and other personnel to care for them. In Arizona, between April and December 2015 the state prison sys-tem had only half as many psychologists and mental health nurse prac-titioners as it was supposed to have. There was a backlog of 377 mental health appointments; the waiting list for a psychiatric appointment was 1,385 patients long. By 2016, the state had a ratio of 1 psychiatric health care provider to 1,861 prisoners. Compare that to neighboring Colorado, where the ratio was 1 to 531.[15] This kind of extreme understaffing might mean that therapy sessions—when they happen—last only a few minutes. It might mean cell-side treatment, where clinician and patient have to shout through cell doors or through the tray slot. Or it could mean situations like the man with bipolar disorder who committed suicide in an Arizona prison after waiting two months for a psychiatric exam to be rescheduled.[16]

At the same time, many facilities often have far too few corrections officers. In parts of Florida, for example, more than 15 percent of prison jobs are vacant.[17] For prisoners with mental illness, this can have catastrophic effects on their well-being. When there aren't enough officers to maintain order, then more-stringent security and disciplinary measures become necessary to maintain control. More critical is the fact that corrections officers are essential to almost every aspect of health care provision.

Because everything that happens inside a prison or jail requires extensive security precautions, corrections officers are responsible for getting prisoners to medical appointments or escorting clinicians to cells if an appointment has to happen at the cell, either because the person is seen as too dangerous to come out or because there aren't enough officers for escort. (Because they are seen as particularly dangerous, prisoners in solitary confinement usually require at least two officers for escort.) Corrections officers also oversee pill call, group therapy, recreation time, showers, and any other activity in which prisoners are out of their cells.

Even making an appointment with a clinician often requires the help of a corrections officer. Although some prisons have switched to digital systems, in most places prisoners still file a sick call request—a slip of paper—with the corrections officer, who delivers it to the medical offices for scheduling. As I witnessed in LA County, psychiatrists and clinicians rely on the officers to be their eyes and ears, alerting them to people whose behavior has suddenly changed or appears to be abnormal. Doctors will sometimes even use corrections officers to corroborate symptoms that patients claim to have, complaints that they can't sleep, for example.

Once the person has an appointment, it is up to a corrections officer—or several—to deliver the patient to the clinic or the clinician to the patient. When there aren't enough corrections officers to escort patients, appointments have to be canceled. At Bullock Correctional Facility in Alabama, the shortage is so bad that as many as 70 percent of mental health appointments are reportedly canceled because clinicians can't access their patients. Even programs run by outside volunteers—religious services and AA meetings—are compromised by a lack of officers.

Why is it so difficult for prisons and jails to hire staff? Although the skill set, educational background, and job orientation are radically different in each case, the shortages of both medical and security staff are at least in part a result of the same problem. In both cases it begins with highly difficult working conditions, often in inconvenient or remote locations, usually in exchange for very low pay. And this has resulted not only in difficulties in hiring and retaining qualified people but also in the often poor quality of those who are employed.

Take doctors. There are many smart and well-qualified medical staff who choose to work in corrections. But according to correctional psychiatrists themselves, such people may increasingly be the exception. "No one who went to medical school said, 'I want to incur this much debt and spend my life working in prisons,'" Kathryn Burns, the psychiatrist in charge of mental health care for the Ohio prison system, told me. This seems to be true for other kinds of medical personnel as well. "I lost another [clinician] just this morning," Gallavan, the Oklahoma prison psychologist, said the day I visited Mabel Bassett. She said the problem is that the prison system pays as much as $20,000 less than similar community-based jobs.

Perversely, such conditions have sometimes meant that those least qualified for what is truly challenging work are the ones most likely to stay. A 2016 investigation in Oklahoma showed that more than a third of doctors working in its prisons had previously received some kind of sanction.[18] An investigation by the *Atlanta Journal-Constitution* found

that one in five doctors working in Georgia prisons had been cited for
misconduct.[19] And an investigation by New York City found that the
contractor who provided health care at the city jail for several years
didn't do proper background checks and ended up hiring eight mental
health workers with criminal records, including one who had been
convicted of second-degree murder. As one physician who works in a
large city jail put it, correctional facilities "tend to attract folks who are
looking for a place to hide out."

Sometimes, jails and prisons have even hired clinicians who are
unlicensed.[20] Or, as came to light in a recent case in Alabama, they
place people in positions requiring close supervision by a higher-level
employee, like a nurse practitioner or a physician. But because there
aren't enough supervisors, these inexperienced workers may have to
make important health care decisions—for example, whether a patient
needs to see a psychiatrist—evaluations for which they are not trained.

At least part of the problem has little to do with the criminal justice
system. There is a severe shortage of psychiatrists nationally, and particularly in rural areas, which is where many prisons are located.[21] For
a highly skilled doctor, these remote locations can make a correctional
job less appealing. But even in jails, which are usually in or near cities, the working conditions can be unpleasant. Employees are subject
to many of the same restrictions as prisoners: cell phones and chew-
ing gum, for example, are prohibited. Just getting in and out of the
building can be cumbersome, making nearly impossible the kinds of
out-of-office meetings or errands that many professional people take
for granted: going out to lunch or rushing out to pick up a sick child
from school.

One way that some prisons and jails have tried to make the job
more appealing is by allowing doctors to work at a comfortable distance from the institutions themselves. At Mabel Bassett a psychiatrist
"visits" the prison once per week via telemonitor, essentially treatment
via Skype. The office is a tiny windowless room in the outpatient mental health clinic that belongs to an employee who has been on military
leave for the past year. It doubles as a kind of a storeroom, so there are
paper towels and suicide blankets stacked up on one side. The monitor

where the psychiatrist appears is on a desk on one side of the room. A mental health clinician sits in the desk chair while the patient sits on the other side, closer to the paper towels and blankets. Even at a distance, the psychiatrist's time with patients is limited, so he or she relies heavily on other clinicians to find out what's going on with each patient.

In recent years, some states and counties have become so desperate they have started to offer bigger salaries to lure psychiatric staff, despite facing limited budgets. A former head of medical services for the Washington State prison system told me that pay was so uncompetitive for medical personnel that many of the résumés they got came from people "who had worse criminal records than the people they were going to be taking care of." Only by significantly raising the salary, he said, was he "able to get people I would go to as a physician." California began raising salaries for psychiatrists after the courts ordered them to hire more staff as a result of the Coleman case. Even so, in 2017 the system faced a vacancy rate of 30 percent among doctors.[22] But there is hope that the situation will improve after a new union contract, approved in 2017, promised pay hikes of 24 percent over the next four years.[23] The Cook County Jail proposed raising psychiatrists' salaries by more than 20 percent, from $190,000 to $230,000, after struggling to fill a third of its budgeted mental health care positions. And Illinois Senator Dick Durbin has talked about trying to add county and municipal correctional workers to a program that would allow them to get as much as $50,000 in student loan relief.[24]

But even with good doctors in place, facilities may face many of the same challenges when trying to maintain adequately trained corrections officers. As I have witnessed in facilities as disparate as giant urban jails like LA County and Cook County and smaller, isolated state prisons like Mabel Bassett in Oklahoma, corrections officers themselves have one of the most difficult, dangerous, and underappreciated jobs in the criminal justice system. Sometimes, it's just one officer responsible for a hundred or more prisoners. Corrections officers are subject to many of the same unpleasant conditions as the prisoners: many prisons, including those in particularly warm climates, such as

Texas, Florida, and Louisiana, are not air-conditioned. The hours are long, and the rates of both divorce and substance use are high.

And for all that, the pay is astonishingly bad. In Florida, for example, the starting salary for a state corrections officer was, until recently, $28,000. In 2017 the state agreed to give most officers a $2,500 raise; it was the first real raise they had received in almost a decade.[25] When I asked a recruiter for the Department of Corrections how she convinced people to take the job under those circumstances, she said the main selling point was the opportunity for advancement. With extraordinarily high turnover rates—22 percent in 2015–2016—it is, indeed, very easy to move up the ranks quickly; a new corrections officer could become a supervisor within months. Several veteran officers told me that it can be very dangerous to have so many new people working, for most don't have the experience to respond safely in an emergency.

Lisa Murray, a corrections officer in Florida, worked in state prisons for nearly twenty-five years. In 2013 she finally quit. Unlike many, she actually liked the job—liked the security and liked working with the prisoners—and was grateful for the opportunities it had provided her, a single mother who had never graduated from high school. (Her son, now grown, currently works as a corrections officer for the state.) She simply couldn't afford to keep the position. She had risen two ranks to lieutenant—was supervising other officers—but was making less than $40,000 per year. "I was close to losing my house," she told me. "There were times that I couldn't afford to put food in my refrigerator." She took a new job at the county jail, and although it involved a demotion—which meant she had to work nights again—the pay was so much higher that by the end of the second year, she had doubled her old salary. Over the last few years, so many officers made the same leap from state prisons to county jails that Florida's Department of Corrections sent the counties what amounted to a cease-and-desist letter, asking them to stop poaching state employees. (On this issue, Florida may be an anomaly. In many places, county corrections does not pay especially well, either.)

Murray described a cycle of people quitting regularly, which led to understaffed prisons. With severe understaffing, management required many hours of mandatory overtime. To hear Murray and other former officers tell it, it was especially frustrating because they often weren't told about the mandatory overtime until they were on their way home. "I've seen it so many times, where [officers] go to leave, and the control room won't open that gate," Murray said. Twice, she remembered, officers called 911 and told the police they were being held hostage: "The way the administration can treat people sometimes...they're so desperate because they don't have anybody to work." I couldn't corroborate the 911 story, although I did talk to several officers who described being on their way home when they were stopped at the gate and told they had to work another shift. The anger about the hours and the way they were enforced led to more people quitting, which made the shortages worse.

"It's hard, when you're trying to fill a roster, to figure out how you're going to fill all these positions when you don't have the bodies," Murray said. "OK, what am I going to leave unmanned? I can't leave a dorm, but where a dorm is supposed to have two, maybe three people, I got one. And what does that mean? That's dangerous, when you only have the one officer for a dorm. They can't even walk around in the dorm." It's dangerous because prisoners may take advantage of that absence to attack or otherwise threaten others; this is especially serious for those with mental illness, who are more likely to be exploited. It's also an issue medically: when clinicians depend on the corrections officers to keep them apprised of sick prisoners' day-to-day status, fewer officers means fewer eyes on them. Rampant dissatisfaction and poor working conditions may also encourage abuse and neglect on the part of the officers. Many of the worst cases of officer-on-prisoner violence have come out of overstretched institutions in places such as Florida and Alabama.

As the salary woes of both medical and correctional staff make clear, money plays a crucial part in the quality and quantity of mental health care in the criminal justice system. Yet it can be fiendishly difficult to draw any systematic conclusions about costs and needs. Part of the problem is determining how you define mental health expenditures: Do they include the cost of prescription medications? Do they include only people with serious mental illness or also people with dementia or developmental disabilities—a group that may sweep in a much larger proportion of a given facility's population? (Although I have made a distinction between those here, jails and prisons often don't.) Do you count the cost of additional security staff needed on special mental health units? The list goes on.

In 2011 states together spent nearly $8 billion on prisoner health care, which amounted to roughly a fifth of total corrections spending.[26] The Pew Charitable Trusts calculated that *mental* health care makes up about 14 percent of total prison health care expenditures nationwide, which meant states spent about $1.1 billion that year just on that category. Yet the amounts spent vary enormously by state. For example, California's total corrections budget for 2017–2018 is $11.1 billion; just over 3.5 percent of that—$405 million, or $3,487 per prisoner— goes to fund mental health care. (There are other marginal costs to housing prisoners with mental illness, including the cost of additional officers. Also, it's more expensive if a prisoner needs to be housed in a crisis bed or an inpatient psychiatric bed.) By contrast, Alabama, a much smaller state, paid an outside contractor about $12 million to provide mental health care in fiscal year 2016. A larger problem is that these figures give very little indication of the actual needs of any state or county system. Jails and prisons care for many of the same people as public health care providers and welfare agencies on the outside, yet as one expert in correctional medicine put it, "[Jails and prisons] are not funded as either [health care provider or welfare agency].... Their resources are often insufficient to do that job adequately for everyone."[27]

Who actually provides health care in jails and prisons also varies from place to place. Nearly half—twenty-four—of the states fully contract out their prisoner health care to private contractors; another twelve contract out some of their care. Only fourteen operate their own prison health care systems.[28] That is, in these states doctors and other clinicians are state employees. Jails also have a mix of providers, with some—like New York City and Los Angeles County—providing their own health care through county agencies and many others using outside companies. Although there is much discussion—and criticism—of the use of private prisons, far less scrutinized and more pervasive is the prison-industrial complex of for-profit companies that provide goods and services such as food, telephone access, and medical care in jails and prisons. Hiring outside companies is a way to control costs because most of the contracts are designed so that the private providers effectively act as an HMO for the prisoners. The government, be it state or local, pays a fixed price per person for a given time period; in exchange, the contractor must provide the contracted service, regardless of the actual cost. So, for example, a contractor who has agreed to provide psychiatric care for prisoners at a cost of $8 per month must provide that care, whether the person ends up seeing a psychiatrist once per month or twenty times per month.[29]

Does that mean that companies end up cutting corners to save money? As a former CEO of health care provider Corizon put it in a recent interview, "Our job is to walk the line. Our job is to provide all the care that a patient needs and only the care that a patient needs. Our job is to use the funds that are provided in the most efficient way possible."[30] Private correctional health care providers like MHM and Corizon are regularly sued for providing inadequate treatment. But Marc Stern, former health services director for the Washington State Department of Corrections, said the real issue is the lack of money for correctional health: "If you focus on privatization as being the problem, you're focusing on the wrong problem."

It's hard to believe that jails and prisons spend so little on prisoners' mental health care, especially given how much is spent on incarceration generally. A look at a recent deal between Alabama and a health care contractor can help us understand how companies and corrections systems negotiate this race to the bottom. In 2013 Alabama put out a request for proposal (RFP) for a company to provide mental health care to around three thousand prisoners. The state evaluated bids using ten criteria. Each factor, like the company's experience, the qualifications of its personnel, and the cost of its services, were scored for a possible total score of two hundred points. But the criteria were not weighted equally, and a look at how they were weighted shows very clearly where the state's priorities lay: "Qualifications/Experience/References" was worth a possible fifteen points; "Price—Total for first three (3) years" was worth eighty points.[31] In other words, Alabama valued low cost more than five times as much as it did experience.

Only two companies ended up submitting proposals. Alabama chose MHM, which had the lowest bid. It's a privately held northern Virginia–based company that, according to its website, provides correctional mental health care and related services to more than three hundred thousand people in sixteen states.[32] MHM responded with a letter that began "We are excited about our continued partnership with ADOC and the opportunity to negotiate a price more aligned with the State of Alabama's budget expectations," before laying out significant staffing cuts for the proposal: the company proposed cutting the number of psychiatrist hours by 12 percent and the number of psychologist hours by 25 percent. Companies involved in these kinds of negotiations will often come back with counteroffers. But at least in retrospect, it seems that this one went too far. Numerous prisoners later complained about not getting the medical attention they needed, and a federal judge later found that the health care provided as a result of this contract was unacceptable. In settlement negotiations with the state, attorneys recently argued that Alabama needs to double or triple the level of mental health staffing in its prison system to reach constitutional levels.

THERE ARE COUNTLESS STORIES OF the shoddy mental health care treatment that people get in jails and prisons. In a 2017 class-action lawsuit, prisoners at the federal penitentiary in Lewisburg, Pennsylvania, claimed that the Bureau of Prisons provides little one-on-one counseling and that the "supposed 'counseling'" mostly consists of conversations through the cell doors, conversations that can easily be overheard by others. More appalling was this: "The less-than-constitutionally-adequate care provided for people with mental illness at USP Lewisburg consists of prison staff passing out coloring books and puzzles and calling it 'treatment.'"[33]

Often the lack of resources simply means resorting to the least-labor-intensive treatment available: medication. The use of medication is controversial in some circles, a discussion that is beyond the scope of this book. The problem here is that, as in the asylums of old, medication becomes the only form of treatment, and it is, in most cases, far from adequate. As psychiatrist Kathryn Burns testified in a lawsuit against Alabama's prison system, "There is an over-reliance on psychotropic medication as being the only treatment intervention that is consistently available."[34] The American Psychiatric Association warns that treatment "needs to be broader, including verbal therapy and other skill-building activities."[35] Worse, problems of overcrowding and understaffing can mean that even medication management isn't handled properly. Patients may get their medications (and side effects) checked far less frequently than they should, or not at all.

The US Bureau of Justice Statistics reported that in 2000 some 10 percent of all state prisoners were on psychotropic medications; in five states (Maine, Montana, Nebraska, Hawaii, and Oregon), as many as 20 percent were.[36] A later survey by the bureau showed that the number of state prisoners on psychotropic medicines was rising: by 2004, an average of 15 percent of state prisoners were on psychotropic medication.[37] It's hard to know if too many people in those states are being prescribed psychotropic medications, but there are many cases where specific systems have been called out for it. In 2011 the US Department of Justice criticized the Miami-Dade County Jail for its overuse of medications.[38] In 2013 California was criticized for relying too heavily on antipsychotic medications in prison: "Anybody that comes in on mental health (referrals), we put on a psychotropic," the federal receiver in the long-running mental health care case in California said. "[A] lot of it, I think we overprescribe."[39] Between 2009 and 2011, more than 25 percent of California's budget for prescriptions for state prisoners went to psychotropic medication. By comparison, New York spent about 17 percent of its pharmaceutical budget on psychotropic medications.[40] Although the study did not explain what drove the increase, doctors themselves have acknowledged that, much as they did in the old state asylums, medications have become a quick, relatively cheap way to treat and control large numbers of patients. One physician who regularly visits jails and prisons around the country told me he'd seen people medicated over objection for months or even years as a means of controlling them.

Ironically, this eagerness to medicate does not extend to the time after incarceration. When people are released from jail or prison, they are given, at most, a few weeks' supply of medication to take with them. They are then somehow expected to find a clinic, make an appointment, get to the appointment, and get a prescription filled and hopefully paid for, all before that small supply runs out. It is yet another recipe for failure for people with mental illness.

ONE UNFORTUNATE ASPECT OF OVERMEDICATING prison populations is that it implicitly dismisses the problem of mental illness as fundamentally untreatable. Instead of promoting avenues to long-term treatment and psychological well-being, the widespread use of medications seems to promote a worldview in which it is assumed that particularly unruly prisoners have to be drugged simply to keep them under control. Focusing on medication "reveals a common prejudice about inmates with mental illness, that they are noncompliant, difficult to manage, violent, and otherwise undeserving of clinical attention or services," the Council on State Governments writes.[41]

We have made progress, if one can call it that, by recognizing that a large population of people with mental illness is in our jails and prisons. But to ignore the most basic needs of a very sick population by cramming too many into too small a space and then denying them access to appropriate care is almost as bad as pretending they don't exist. Worse, it may set the stage for terrible abuses.

6

Sanctioned Torture

"THEY'RE NOT THERE YET," THE man called out as I tried the door to the courtroom. It was early, and the door was still locked. He was sitting on the wooden bench across from the door; his T-shirt and baseball cap looked out of place in the imposing marble-lined hall. I walked over, and he introduced himself as Ray Echevarria. He had been there every day since the trial began, he told me.

It was December 2014, and I was at the federal courthouse in Manhattan to cover the trial of Terrence Pendergrass, a Rikers Island corrections officer who had been charged with violating the human rights of the man's son, Jason Echevarria, a prisoner on the special unit for people with mental illness that Pendergrass was supervising. Echevarria was twenty-five and had spent nearly at year at Rikers when he died from untreated medical complications after he poisoned himself. "I'm here for my son," the senior Echevarria told me later. "I'm here to support his spirits.... I'm pretty sure he knows I'm here."

With a long history of behavioral problems and a diagnosis of bipolar disorder, Jason Echevarria had been prescribed medication for much of his life. When he was growing up, his father had arranged his own schedule as a city bus driver so he could take his son to doctor and therapist appointments. But nothing seemed to help very much. "To hold a conversation with him?" his father said to me during the

Pendergrass trial. "No. Fantasies all the time, that he was a gang member, that he was a Latin King. All fantasy."

At Rikers, where he'd been sent on a robbery charge, Echevarria gained a reputation for being something of a troublemaker and was moved around repeatedly from jail to jail. (The complex is made up of ten different jails.) Some of his behavior seemed more annoying than violent or even actively disruptive: a corrections officer testified that once, after bringing Echevarria to his cell and removing his handcuffs, Echevarria refused to take his arm out of the tray slot; this meant the officer couldn't shut the slot. Another time, Echevarria stuffed his mattress into the slot, with the same result. Often, it seemed to stem directly from his mental illness. He tried to kill himself several times, including once by swallowing a battery. According to the criminal complaint against Pendergrass, it was the suicide attempts that had landed Echevarria on the special mental health unit—the unit where he ultimately succeeded in killing himself.

Astonishingly, this special unit was not designed to provide treatment for prisoners with mental illness. It was designed to *punish* them. Established in 1998, the "mental health assessment unit for infracted inmates"—known by the acronym MHAUII, pronounced like the Hawaiian island—consisted entirely of solitary confinement cells designed specifically for sick patients who broke rules ("infracted" in the jail euphemism). People were locked in their cells for at least twenty-three hours a day; when they did come out, they had to be handcuffed. The cells were bare: a fiberglass platform bed, a metal toilet, and a metal sink. Food and medication were handed to them through a slot in the door. Human contact was kept to a minimum.

"MHAUII was designed as a more treatment-oriented form of segregation"—i.e., solitary confinement—wrote Elizabeth Ford, the psychiatrist responsible for mental health care at Rikers, "with the opportunity to earn extra hours out of one's cell for good behavior. The idea was solid—positive reinforcement—but the practice was not. Within several years of opening, MHAUII was indistinguishable from regular solitary confinement."[1] With conditions like this, it didn't take much for individual officers to take the abuse even further. As one civil rights attorney put it, once you start to dehumanize people this way, there are no limits, and there is no sense of obligation toward them. Conditions on MHAUII got so bad, and led to so much abuse and neglect, that it was shut down shortly before the Pendergrass trial started.

The day before Echevarria died in 2012, there was a sewage backup on the unit. This happened often. Raw sewage flooded several cells, including number four, where Echevarria was being held. A corrections officer gave Echevarria a packet of concentrated detergent— known as a soap ball—to clean his cell. The detergent is caustic and extremely toxic, and even prisoners without a history of suicide attempts are supposed to get it only after it's been diluted in quantities of water. At around 4:30 that afternoon, Echevarria began banging on the door of his cell. When a corrections officer went to see what was wrong, he said, Echevarria told him he had eaten the soap ball and that he needed medical care. "He was yelling off the top of his voice," the officer testified, "panting as if he couldn't breathe, . . . saying he needs a doctor. Get me a doctor. I can't breathe." The officer went to Terrence Pendergrass, the supervising captain on duty. "Don't call me if you have live, breathing bodies," the officer testified Pendergrass told him. "Only call me if you need a cell extraction [a forcible removal from a cell] or if you have a dead body."[2]

Shortly after that, the officer reported, he walked past Echevarria's cell again and this time saw vomit on his window and on the floor of the cell. Again he reported it to Pendergrass, who said Echevarria should "hold it."[3] About an hour after Echevarria first reported swallowing the detergent, a pharmacy technician came around to deliver medications, escorted by another corrections officer. Noting the vomit and Echevarria's coloring, the technician told the officers that he could die without medical treatment and asked the officer escorting her to inform Pendergrass. The officer informed Pendergrass, who asked him to document what had happened. But before the officer could finish his report, Pendergrass led him away. Echevarria never got any medical care. At 8:30 the next morning, a physician's assistant found him dead on the floor of his cell, blood and white foam coming out of his mouth.

Even as jail and prison administrators become more aware of the needs of people with mental illness, there have been an alarming number of reports of abuse or neglect of sick prisoners. Jason Echevarria is far from the only one to die at Rikers in recent years. In 2014, Jerome Murdough, a homeless former Marine diagnosed with schizoaffective disorder, was arrested in the stairwell of a housing project in Harlem where, he told police, he had gone to escape the cold. Barely a week after he got to Rikers, he died in a mental health observation unit when a malfunction in the heating system drove temperatures above 100 degrees and corrections officers failed to check on him at appropriate intervals.[4] Psychotropic drugs, which Murdough was taking at the time of his death, make patients particularly susceptible to heat because it makes it harder for the person to recognize that he's hot, and they also make the body less able to cope with the heat.

These cases go well beyond the largest and most troubled institutions such as Rikers. In April 2015, for example, Jamycheal Mitchell, a twenty-five-year-old man with schizophrenia and bipolar disorder, was arrested for stealing five dollars' worth of junk food from a 7-11 in Portsmouth, Virginia. After his arrest, a psychiatric examiner found that "Mr. Mitchell's thought processes were so confused that only snippets of his sentences could be understood; the rest were mumbled statements that made no sense" and recommended that he be sent to the state hospital for competency restoration.[5] The state mental health employee who was supposed to have arranged Mitchell's transfer to the hospital instead stuffed the paperwork into a drawer along with the paperwork of others awaiting transfer. Mitchell spent more than four months in the Hampton Roads Regional Jail awaiting a transfer that never came. He eventually died of starvation.

Mitchell's family filed a lawsuit alleging that Mitchell had rarely been allowed out of his cell. Officers had turned off his water, the lawsuit says, a common response to prisoners who misbehave. His cell was covered in urine and feces. Mitchell had no clothes, mattress, sheet, or blankets. He was allegedly rarely fed; he lost between forty and fifty pounds. The lawsuit said he was rarely given his psychotropic medication; in the last month before he died, he did not get any at all. Perhaps worse than the neglect, though, fellow prisoners reported to attorneys for Mitchell's family that corrections officers taunted Mitchell, treating him "like a circus animal." Officers kicked and punched him, they said, even while he was handcuffed. Another officer allegedly twisted Mitchell's arm when he stuck it outside the tray slot.[6] An internal investigation at the jail cleared its employees of all wrongdoing. I visited the jail shortly before the family's lawsuit was filed; the warden told me that his employees took excellent care of the prisoners, including the ones with mental illness.

Other cases are even more grotesque. In 2012 Darren Rainey was serving a sentence for cocaine possession in a Florida prison. Because he had been diagnosed with schizophrenia, he was being housed on a unit for prisoners with mental illness. When officers found that he had smeared his cell with feces, they dragged him to a "special" shower to clean up. The water in the shower, which could be turned on and off only from the outside, was 160 degrees—the legal limit is 120 degrees.[7] According to other prisoners who witnessed the event, Rainey screamed repeatedly to be let out. Officers left him in the scalding water for two hours; by the time they took him out, he was dead, his skin so red it looked as if he'd been "boiled" and peeling "like fruit roll-ups."[8]

It's hard to imagine how anybody could justify this kind of cruelty, let alone perpetrate it; corrections officials are quick to suggest that such cases are rare. Talk to prisoners, though, or people who were formerly incarcerated, and abuse is the norm, though events that reach the level of what happened to Jamycheal Mitchell or Darren Rainey are rare. That they happen at all, however—that they are even possible in multiple prison and jail settings across the country—is a horrific indication of the flaws of the current system. Worse, this kind of abuse is often merely an extension of the discipline that facilities regularly use—including solitary confinement and restraints—to punish people who act out. For prisoners with mental illness, such tactics, even when not lethal, can have terrible effects on their illness; in some cases, they may result in permanent trauma.

All of this raises far-reaching questions about the provision of mental health care in the criminal justice system. How can institutions that are built around discipline and punishment, that rely on officially sanctioned forms of psychological pressure and duress, provide, under any circumstances, the kind of setting necessary for effective treatment? And even if they can, what does it mean for doctors and other medical staff who work within them and must adhere to the strictures of life inside them?

ADMINISTRATIVE SEGREGATION. DISCIPLINARY SEGREGATION. Punitive segregation. Protective custody. Room confinement. Special Management. Special Housing Units. Lockdown. Isolation. The Bing. The Hole. The Box. There are many names for it, some official, some not, but they all refer to the same thing: solitary confinement—the brutal and perfectly legal practice of keeping people alone, with no human contact, in cells the size of a small bathroom for twenty-three or more hours a day for weeks, months, years, even decades at a time. At last count, there were at least eighty thousand people in solitary in the United States, a number that does not include juvenile facilities, immigration detention facilities, and local jails.[9] Somewhere between a third and a half of those people are believed to have some form of mental illness.

The practice of solitary confinement rests on shaky foundations. It doesn't have any place in formal criminal sentencing; it is unrelated to the crimes for which a person has been incarcerated. Instead, it is mostly used at the discretion of corrections officials themselves either because somebody decided, more or less arbitrarily, that the prisoner was a danger to the prison or, as is most often the case, as a form of additional punishment for prisoners who have violated certain rules or are otherwise deemed to have misbehaved. As a result, solitary confinement disproportionately draws in people with mental illness, even as it makes many ordinary prisoners sick. Solitary is also expensive, costing states as much as two to three times more per prisoner than ordinary incarceration. Each year, Texas spends $46 million above its regular correctional budget to pay for solitary confinement.[10]

Yet placing prisoners in isolation cells has been a feature of the modern US penal system since its inception in the early nineteenth century. The original idea, developed at Philadelphia's Eastern State Penitentiary, was to cut the prisoner off from all human relationships so that he might focus his attention inward and rehabilitate himself. In recent years the practice has been justified as an important tool for managing jails and prisons. Even opponents of the practice acknowledge that it can be useful when used for short, determinate periods. Specific prisoners may need to be separated from one another, either for their own protection or the protection of others. Sometimes, an entire unit may need to be brought under control. Putting people into isolation cells can be a relatively safe and easy way to do that. More often, though, it's easier to put an "unruly" prisoner—whether it is someone who has refused to return a food tray properly or who has threatened a corrections officer—away, out of sight, than it is to try to deal with the underlying problems that might be causing the behavior. One important question is what constitutes a reasonable period to hold somebody in solitary. In England, for example, a prison has to jump through numerous hoops, including getting dispensation from the Ministry of Justice and ordering special psychiatric examinations for the prisoner, to hold a person in solitary confinement for more then seventy-two hours. By contrast, jails and prisons in the United States have no such limitations. There is a sad irony to the fact that a doctor wishing to keep a patient hospitalized against his will for longer than seventy-two hours must seek permission from a judge.

Whatever the motivation, observers of the practice have from the outset found it morally dubious. "He never hears of wife or children; home or friends; the life or death of any single creature," wrote Charles Dickens of one such prisoner, after visiting Eastern State in 1842, then considered the most modern prison in America. "He sees the prison-officers, but with that exception he never looks upon a human countenance, or hears a human voice. He is a man buried alive; to be dug out in the slow round of years; and in the meantime dead to everything but torturing anxieties and horrible despair."[11]

Solitary confinement today involves complete isolation in cells not much bigger than a closet: an average-sized man who stands in the middle and extends his arms will be able to touch both walls. Many don't have windows. The bed is stainless steel or concrete, with a thin mattress. The "bathroom," also stainless steel, is a combination toilet and sink stuck in a corner of the same tiny room. Officers hand meals through the tray slot. Prison food is hardly known for being delicious or plentiful, but prisoners and their families regularly report that portions in solitary units are even smaller. In a number of institutions, prisoners in solitary are fed the "loaf," a barely edible and hard-to-digest mix of various foods ground together, instead of an ordinary meal.

The only physical contact they have with other human beings is with the corrections officers who search and handcuff them before letting them into or out of their cells. The process is cumbersome. According to legal scholar Keramet Reiter, "[The prisoner] backs up to the cell door and reaches his hands out through the cuff port. An officer handcuffs him before opening the cell door completely. Once the cell door opens, the officer will cuff the prisoner's ankles together and tether his cuffed hands to a chain around his waist. The officer will grab the waist chain...and the two will shuffle slowly down the windowless corridors of the [solitary unit]. Usually, one or two additional guards will follow to ensure the prisoner remains under control."[12] In testimony before Congress in 2012, Craig Haney, a psychology professor at UC Santa Cruz and an expert on solitary confinement, explained that the recreation yard in solitary units "often consists of a metal cage, sitting atop a slab of concrete or asphalt or, in the case of California's Pelican Bay, a concrete-enclosed pen, one surrounded by high solid walls that prevent any view of the outside world."[13]

Observing the effects of solitary confinement at Eastern State Penitentiary nearly two hundred years ago, Dickens concluded that "this slow and daily tampering with the mysteries of the brain [is] immeasurably worse than any torture of the body and because its ghastly signs and tokens are not so palpable to the eye and sense of touch as scars upon the flesh; because its wounds are not upon the surface, and it extorts few cries that human ears can hear; therefore I the more denounce it, as a secret punishment which slumbering humanity is not roused up to stay."[14]

In the twenty-first century, these devastating consequences have been documented with clinical precision. For example, extreme isolation may exacerbate or cause symptoms of psychosis such as hallucinations, paranoia, sleeplessness, and self-harm. More than half of all prison suicides occur in solitary confinement.[15] A study of self-harm incidents at Rikers Island showed that people who had spent time in solitary were almost seven times more likely to try to hurt themselves than prisoners who had not.[16] At the same time, in many solitary units mental health treatment is almost nonexistent. In some places, prisoners stay in their cells or in cages for group therapy, with the therapist sitting in the hallway between or among the cells. Individual therapy, when it exists, may be conducted cell-side. That means either shouting through the steel door while the rest of the tier listens in or bending down to talk through the tray slot, which is typically about waist-high. I have spoken to prisoners through those doors; it's hard to hear them, and it's hard to be heard. Even a casual conversation is difficult, let alone something as personal and nuanced as a therapy session.

One of the terrible ironies about solitary is that because of the disciplinary structure of most prisons and jails, people who already have a severe mental illness are often those most likely to be put there. For sick prisoners, this means a two-part trap in which they are punished for their "abnormal" behavior with disciplinary measures that, in turn, make their condition worse. The system works something like this: when a prisoner breaks a rule, a corrections officer gives him a "ticket"—in other words, writes him up for the infraction. The "crimes" that can get somebody sent to solitary range from the ridiculous—having too many pencils in one's cell or not standing in the right place to receive a food tray—to the serious—assaulting another prisoner or throwing something at an officer. Not infrequently, tickets are given for behavior that is symptomatic of mental illness.

There is a hearing to determine the "sentence," but the judge is usually a high-ranking corrections officer or other prison system employee; to defend oneself in such a hearing, even when possessed of one's full faculties, is extremely difficult.

In a 2013 lawsuit in Pennsylvania, attorneys cited the case of one prisoner who was repeatedly sent to solitary for "behaviors directly attributable to his serious mental illness, including banging his head against his cell wall, smearing feces on his body and his cell, attempting suicide by making nooses from bedding material in his cell, making himself bleed, and harming himself in other ways."[17] The man eventually accumulated 2,000 days—nearly five and a half years—in solitary, a period significantly longer than his original court-imposed sentence. Worse, prisoners in solitary can also accumulate new criminal charges and, with them, new sentences, which can turn a relatively brief prison stay into a life sentence.

Time in solitary often triggers more extreme behavior. One prisoner in solitary at a federal supermax prison (the highest security facility), psychologist Craig Haney told Congress, "has amputated one of his pinkie fingers and chewed off the other, removed one of his testicles and scrotum, sliced off his ear lobes, and severed his Achilles tendon with a sharp piece of metal.... Another prisoner, housed long-term in a solitary confinement unit in Massachusetts, has several times disassembled the television set in his cell and eaten the contents."[18]

One case I found particularly heartbreaking was the man in solitary in New Mexico whose family told me he got so paranoid he stopped eating because he was convinced the food was poisoned. The prison would send him to the state hospital, where, removed from the inhumane pressures of an isolation cell, he would quickly regain his faculties, only to be deemed fit enough to be sent back to solitary again. This happened repeatedly over the course of several years.

Such cases, and there are a great many of them, show just how poorly suited current incarceration practices are to dealing with a large population of people with mental illness: not only are we, in a great many of our penal institutions, failing to give these prisoner-patients anything like appropriate treatment; we are also putting them in environments we know will make their symptoms much worse. Indeed, it would be hard to come up with a system more perfectly designed to inflict maximum damage to the psyche than solitary. Worse, we are actually making our sick population grow. One of the most tragic effects of solitary is the extent to which it renders ostensibly sane people mentally ill—sometimes profoundly so.

BRIAN NELSON SPENT TWENTY-THREE YEARS in solitary confinement, most of it at the now-closed supermax Tamms Correctional Center in Illinois, after being convicted of accessory to murder. Before coming to Tamms, he had been in a minimum-security prison in New Mexico. (States sometimes manage overcrowding in their own prisons by sending prisoners elsewhere.) The first time I met him, at a screening of a documentary about solitary confinement, he asked me to bring him a six-pack of beer. He needed the liquid courage, he said, before he could bear to talk about his experiences in segregation.

Now in his fifties, Nelson is a stocky white man with a shaved head and a kind of pulsing anxiety that he attributes to his time in "the Bing." After the screening, he barely managed to introduce himself before he asked if I'd brought the beer. I handed him a bag with six bottles of Corona and a bottle opener I'd bought at a drugstore on my way over. He took them to the men's room and downed them in what must have been rapid succession, but he was still too distressed to talk. We ended up meeting the following day in his Times Square hotel. He hadn't been able to sleep the night before—a lasting effect of his time in solitary, he said—and had spent the night just wandering the streets of Manhattan. We sat in his tiny hotel room, a box of a space not much larger than his old solitary cell, but, as he said, with more amenities. His attorney and boss stood just out of sight near the door, in case Nelson needed emotional support.

Nelson had never been diagnosed with mental illness before he was incarcerated when he was seventeen, he said, but within a year of going into solitary confinement, he was on the mental health caseload. Over the course of his incarceration, he was examined several times by an outside psychiatrist as part of a lawsuit over conditions in the prison. She found that he had major depression, a serious mental illness, but when he was prescribed antidepressants, the doses were far too low to be effective. She also determined that prison medical staff had medicated some of the symptoms—such as insomnia—while missing the underlying diagnosis; they had also described things such as agitation and endless pacing in his cell as intentional exercise.[19] Sitting in his hotel room, Nelson described being put on suicide-watch: the prison took away his clothes—ostensibly for his safety—and put him into a freezing cold suicide-watch cell. "The best therapist [in prison] was a child psychologist," he said. "She cared, and she would tell you honestly, 'I don't know [how to help] but I will try. I will listen to you and try.'" When he talked to her, he had to sit handcuffed and shackled on a cement block.

As preparation for getting out of prison, the administration promised to let him spend the last month of his sentence in general population so he could get used to being around people again. It's absurd to think that thirty days in a prison dorm—almost always a chaotic place—surrounded by other prisoners dealing with various degrees of social dislocation and quite possibly mental illness could make up for an adulthood spent in a tiny room by oneself. Still, it seems almost anything would have been better than what actually happened.

For security reasons that were not made clear to him, Nelson was never transferred into general population. Instead, when his mother and stepfather picked him up at prison, he came straight out of solitary. He had not touched another human being—let alone been in the same room with one or several—in more than two decades. He was given neither his medications nor a prescription for them. He ended up going cold turkey on five drugs, including Zoloft and Prozac. "It was terrifying," he said. Ten minutes after they got in the car, his mother suggested stopping for ice cream. Inside the shop, a man walked behind Nelson, and "I panicked. I literally panicked real bad," he said. "Get away from me! Everybody in the place is like 'What's going on?' For the rest of the ride home, I wouldn't get out of the car."

Like moles, which have evolved to have poor eyesight because they don't need their eyes, people in solitary become hypersensitive to any kind of stimulus. Nelson remembers that when he got out, his mother's cooking was too intense for him, and she had to cut back on spices for months until he got used to them again. He had spent so long alone in his cramped cell that he had difficulty being in larger rooms with other people; even now, more than five years after his release, he still spends much of his days alone. He couldn't find a mental health professional who could help him deal with all the trauma: "You go to talk to a shrink, and they look at you like what? They don't want to deal with it." He finally found a psychiatrist who is trying to help him—somebody who has experience working with victims of torture. It makes sense. "Considering the severe mental pain or suffering solitary confinement can cause, it can amount to torture," Juan Méndez, the UN special rapporteur on torture, told the United Nations.[20]

SOLITARY IS NOT THE ONLY kind of "sanctioned" abuse in jails and prisons. Prisoners, including those with mental illness, are regularly subjected to tactics—such as hog-tying or cutting off water to cells—that are effectively torture in the guise of control. I have heard from prisoners and their families who have long-lasting trauma, post-traumatic stress disorder (PTSD) even, from time spent restrained in cells.

Given the disastrous and increasingly well-known consequences of solitary confinement and other disciplinary practices for prisoners with mental illness, a number of states and counties are contemplating significant changes to their policies. And at the same time, court cases, like those concerning the Rikers deaths of Echevarria and Murdough, have brought harsh light on existing practices and sometimes imposed steep penalties.

In the Echevarria case the corrections officer in charge, Terrence Pendergrass, was convicted and sentenced to five years in prison for violating the prisoner's civil rights. The US Attorney's office brought civil rights charges because it couldn't build a criminal case against the officer: Pendergrass hadn't directly done anything to Echevarria that led to his death. Nonetheless, as the evidence and the outcome showed, Pendergrass was at the head of the chain of command that failed to get Echevarria the medical care that he, medical staff, and even corrections officers themselves had asked for and that could have saved the man's life. The charges were unusual: the first time in at least a decade that the US Attorney for the Southern District of New York had pursued such a case in connection with Rikers. Later that year, the Echevarria family also brought a civil case against the city, the jail, and Pendergrass, for which it won a $3.8 million settlement from the city.

Still, as with police officers, the penalties for the corrections officers involved have generally not been especially harsh. In the case of Murdough, the Rikers prisoner who died of heat exposure, the warden of the jail where he died was demoted and transferred to a unit that does not house people with mental illness. A corrections officer was suspended for thirty days in connection with Murdough's death, and the supervisor of mechanics, who had failed to fix the heat, was barred from working in housing units.[21] More notable is that the city ended up settling with Murdough's family for $2.25 million. And no charges of any kind were filed in the death of Darren Rainey in Florida.

Although this kind of abuse has never been condoned, growing awareness of the consequences of solitary confinement and other abusive practices has been pushing change. In September 2017, Colorado took it a step further by ending the use of long-term solitary confinement, the only state to do so. Fifteen days is the longest a prisoner will be in solitary, and then only for serious charges such as assault. "When did it become O.K. to lock up someone who is severely mentally ill and let the demons chase him around the cell?" wrote Rick Raemisch, head of Colorado's Department of Corrections, in an op-ed in the *New York Times*, describing his decision to end the practice. "What is wrong with us?"

Other states, including Pennsylvania, South Carolina, and New York, have changed laws in order to keep people with mental illness out of solitary confinement. That does not always mean that they are, though. In a recent report looking at the federal prison system, monitors from the Office of the Inspector General wrote the following: "Although the [Bureau of Prisons] states that it does not practice solitary confinement, or even recognize the term, we found inmates, including those with mental illness, who were housed in single-cell confinement for long periods of time, isolated from other inmates and with limited human contact."[22] In some places, prison officials and others have simply found ways around the rules, or flexible interpretations of them, to allow existing practices to go on in another form.

In 2008, the New York state legislature passed a law requiring prisons to take people with serious mental illness out of solitary. Between 2008 and 2011, the overall number of people in the system who were diagnosed with mental illness dropped dramatically, from nine thousand to fewer than eight thousand. In that time the overall prison population dropped by just over 6 percent; the population of prisoners with mental illness dropped by more than 12 percent. And among people who still had a diagnosed mental illness, the number with *serious* mental illnesses, such as schizophrenia, also dropped significantly, while the number of those diagnosed with *less serious* illnesses, such as anxiety disorders, increased even more. In other words, the prisons presumably changed patients' diagnoses in order to be allowed to punish them more harshly.[23]

New York has found other work-arounds. Take medication, for example. It's against the law to punish a prisoner who refuses to take medication. There are many reasons that people may refuse psychotropic medications, even when they are medically indicated: an inability to recognize that one is sick, paranoia that the medication is poison, or simply not being able to handle the often severe side effects. Nonetheless, New York's statute allows for this bizarre distinction: "Misbehavior reports will not be issued to inmates with serious mental illness for refusing treatment, *however an inmate may be subject to the disciplinary process for refusing to go to the location where treatment is provided or medication is dispensed*" (emphasis added).[24] So you're free not to accept treatment, but you can still get in trouble if you don't show up for it.

Likewise, prisoners in New York usually won't get sent to solitary confinement for attempting suicide, but the statute leaves room for interpretation: "[T]here will be a presumption against imposition and pursuit of disciplinary charges for self-harming behavior and threats of self-harming behavior, including related charges for the same behaviors, such as destruction of state property, *except in exceptional circumstances*" (emphasis added).[25]

Indeed, in New York and elsewhere, solitary is a common punishment for self-harm or suicide attempts. One attorney who specializes in prisoners' rights in New York told me about a man who tried to commit suicide by swallowing a razor blade. Although he wasn't punished for the suicide attempt itself, he was charged with possession of contraband after he passed the blade in his stool. Her office has seen numerous similar cases: a man charged with destruction of state property after tearing a sheet to use as a noose, another who set fire to his cell in an attempt to commit suicide. In the latter case, the man wasn't punished for the suicide attempt, but he *was* accused of damaging state property and was fined about $1,000 for damages. He was also put in solitary.

MANY PEOPLE WHO WORK IN the criminal justice system have described to me the conflict between the security imperative of correctional facilities and the ever-increasing therapeutic function these institutions have as health care providers. According to psychologist Craig Haney, "Modern prisons are largely about control…the control of prisoners, their behavior, the degrees of freedom with which they can act, their level of contact with the outside world, and so on." Prisoners with mental illness who refuse—or are unable to abide by the rules—threaten the prison's order. And, continued Haney, "When prisons are at risk of losing this control, those in charge feel compelled to intervene."[26] By contrast, mental health care, at its best, must be shaped around empathy, trust, and positive human connection.

This leaves anyone working in a correctional environment full of sick people with a frequent dilemma. Take the officers at the LA County Jail: their professional remit is expressly aimed at maintaining order and security and enacting disciplinary measures, yet, as with their colleagues in many other jails and prisons, they are constantly called upon to act as de facto mental health care staff, whether it is identifying a prisoner's mental illness or "cutting down"—literally cutting the noose—of somebody who has tried to hang himself.

These clashing responsibilities are felt even more acutely by medical staff, whose professional work—and Hippocratic duty as physicians— is supposed to be *strictly* therapeutic. First of all, there are the legitimate security concerns. Jails and prisons can be dangerous places, and medical staff depend on corrections officers for protection. "We are guests in their house" is a common refrain among correctional medical staff, meaning they are at the mercy of security staff for everything, namely access and safety, so they had better comply with what corrections officers and other officials demand of them lest they find access to their patients limited or their own safety compromised. "In jails, you really see how bad [it] is," Homer Venters, a physician who was medical director at Rikers for several years, told me. "Clinicians can't make decisions that security staff don't like. If you're a psychologist in jail, you have to walk in and out every day. You will not be able to continue to do that job if you continue to annoy the security staff."

This dual loyalty—the tension between medical staff and the correctional work environment—affects all aspects of the job but is little discussed.[27] Venters compares the situation to infection control in hospitals. In that case, everybody knows the hospital is full of germs, acknowledges it's full of germs, and spends time and resources to train every person who works in that hospital how to minimize their spread. By contrast, dual loyalty "is linked to massive loss of life. [But we] don't ever talk about it. Of five thousand jails and prisons, you'd be hard-pressed to find five where anybody talks about it. We bury our heads in the sand, don't give it a name, don't call it anything. All of these bad outcomes, we chalk up to other things, we look to prosecute an *individual,* but we go through all these flips and twists so we don't have to say we have this problem."

There are many ways that this tension can manifest itself.[28] Health care workers may be asked to search patients for contraband; they may witness, or even participate in, force against prisoners. A doctor or therapist may be asked to decide whether somebody with symptoms of mental illness can "safely" be put into solitary confinement, making the clinician complicit in a practice that is especially damaging to people with mental illness. In that case the clinician not only decides who will get punished, but by saying that some people should *not* be put in segregation, the implicit message is that other people may be safely put there.[29]

Situations in which a clinician is involved in a disciplinary action may also compromise the clinician-patient relationship—particularly necessary in psychiatry. For many mental disorders, effective treatment depends on the patient developing a strong rapport and high degree of trust with the care provider, and a patient is likely to be deeply reluctant to trust a care provider he believes has compromised him in some way.

A psychiatrist who spent four years working in the Michigan prison system—he was employed by a company that was contracted to provide mental health care—told me that by the end of his tenure there, the whole mission began to feel futile: "There's the rehabilitation initiative that has been largely lost, or there's still this unwillingness to see that what's being provided is not rehabilitation. I think there's still that old mentality that punishment is rehabilitation. That if you make someone feel pain, that's enough to rehabilitate [him]."

Clinicians may also be asked, explicitly or implicitly, to restrict or otherwise change care as a way to control costs.[30] (Some argue that this is no different from what insurance companies do in the outside world, but ordinary patients usually have options, whether it's negotiating with the insurance company or getting a second opinion from another doctor.) All of this is complicated by the fact that in many jails and prison facilities, the medical staff are employed—whether directly or indirectly—by the county or state corrections department.

So refusing to do something the prison or the correctional workers ask may be difficult or impossible.

It's easy to see how a system that allows the kind of "official" abuse such as solitary confinement or restraints could also end up leading to the kind of unofficial abuses that Echevarria, Mitchell, and others were subjected to. Problems like overcrowding and understaffing only make the conditions more ripe for such abuses, as angry and over-worked corrections officials are made to deal with angry and frustrated prisoners. Add in the kind of "difficult" behavior that is often seen in people with mental illness, and the results can be disastrous. In Alabama the combination turned into something close to a complete collapse of the system.

7

Better Off Dead

It would be easy to portray Jamie Wallace as a monster. He was a boy who, at sixteen, murdered his own mother in cold blood as his eight-year-old brother looked on. A boy who, when his step-grandfather tried to intervene, tried to kill him as well. A boy who, leaving his mother bleeding on the front porch where he'd shot her, stole a tractor trailer and tried to escape in it. A boy who was already heading for trouble before that, who as an eight-year-old stole Pokemon cards and who had, by the time he was twelve, moved on to stealing cars. Even absent the criminal history, his personal story can easily be spun to argue that he was a troublemaking ne'er-do-well: the kid who did badly in school, who was quick to anger, who desperately wanted to join a gang, and who frequently cut himself just to get attention.

There is another parallel though no less true narrative that portrays Wallace not as a monster but as a victim. A victim of the mental illness that he inherited from both sides of his family, of physical disabilities that required multiple surgeries and complicated his daily life, of developmental disabilities that made school difficult. A victim of a complicated family situation, a family that was struggling to survive on a trucker's salary. Most of all, however, it could be said that Wallace was a victim of the system: of the mental health system that failed to get his illness under control, of the court system that sent him to prison for a quarter century, and of the prison system that failed to provide the treatment that he needed and that it was constitutionally required to provide, until he died by suicide at age twenty-four.

We know more about Wallace's case than most because shortly before his death, two human rights groups in Alabama identified him in a lawsuit they filed against the Alabama Department of Corrections, or ADOC. Wallace was the first prisoner to testify; he died a week later. "The case of Jamie Wallace is powerful evidence of the real, concrete, and terribly permanent harms that woefully inadequate mental health care inflicts on mentally ill prisoners in Alabama," wrote Judge Myron Thompson in his opinion in the case. "Without systemic changes that address these pervasive and grave deficiencies, mentally ill prisoners in ADOC, whose symptoms are no less real than Wallace's will continue to suffer."[1] But neither Wallace nor Alabama is unique as either a person with severe mental illness suffering the consequences of incarceration or as a penal system struggling to meet the needs of a very large, very sick population.

Jamie Wallace was barely eighteen when, in 2011, he arrived at the Donaldson Correctional Facility, a maximum-security state prison southwest of Birmingham. He was a slight man—his younger brother said that Jamie took after their mother, who had been petite, rather than their father, who was over six feet tall and heavy—with a round face, close-cropped dirty-blond hair, and big blue eyes. The corrections officials at the prison were aware of his illness. He had been sent to Donaldson to complete his sentence after being processed and evaluated at another prison, the Kilby Correctional Facility, near Montgomery, the state capital.

At Donaldson he was placed in a residential treatment unit (RTU). These units are supposed to provide "a supportive therapeutic environment for treatment of inmates with serious mental illness who are unable to function in the general prison population." Among the "amenities" they promise are consistent and specially trained medical and security staffing, a multidisciplinary treatment team, treatment plans, and group therapy sessions on a range of subjects.[2] In short, Wallace was supposed to receive care that—on paper—sounds like the care available in any good inpatient psychiatric facility on the outside. Unfortunately, paper is about as far as it went: on December 15, 2016, after years of isolation and neglect, Wallace committed suicide.

The RTU where Wallace lived is made up of single cells, where he was effectively in solitary confinement. He had little contact with others and was rarely let out of his cell. The cell was eight feet by eight feet; he slept on a mat on the concrete floor. At least he had a cell, though. There weren't enough cells for prisoners who needed extra mental health care or were on suicide watch, so sometimes corrections officials housed them in administrative offices or library rooms with neither bed nor toilet.[3] There were so many rats running around the prison that people shoved towels into the space below the cell doors to keep them out. His cell was filthy, and, Wallace said, "[T]hey do not want you to clean it." It was hard to get access to cleaning supplies, he said, since a prisoner had broken a broom and mop and used the handle to attack somebody. Clean clothes and basic hygiene materials were also in short supply.

On this special unit, designated for some of the sickest people in the system, Jamie Wallace said the mental health staff "ain't come see me worth a damn," just "once in a blue moon," every two months or so. Look at the number of mental health care providers in the Alabama system and the number of prisoners who needed care, and it's easy to see why Wallace and his fellow prisoners would have trouble getting medical attention. There simply weren't enough people to provide it. One prison had 120 prisoners taking psychotropic medication and no regular coverage by a psychiatrist or even a psychologist. Another had sixty-four prisoners on psychotropic medications but no psychiatrist.[4] Ruth Naglich, who's responsible for overseeing medical and mental health care for the Alabama system, testified that there simply weren't enough people on staff.

When Wallace did get to see a counselor, the routine was like this: turn around, cuff up, and be led upstairs to the counselor's office, where, he reported, the sessions usually lasted between five and ten minutes before officers brought him back to his cell. Time with mental health professionals was so short that one outside psychiatrist

who visited the prisons said that it "simply cannot be called psychotherapy."[5] Often the only care Wallace got was a mental health check
in front of his cell front. A clinician would stop in front of his cell door,
ask how he was doing, and move on.

Among the services the Alabama Department of Corrections
promises on that level of care is group therapy on a range of topics.
At Donaldson, though, there was neither individual therapy nor even
out-of-cell group therapy. Where Wallace lived, there really wasn't
much of anything.

I HAVE SEEN MANY OF Wallace's court records and talked to his family,
his friends, and attorneys who knew Wallace. However, in some cases
because he was a juvenile at the time he committed his crime and in
some cases because of the way Alabama's open records laws work, not
all of his records can be accessed. We do know that for most of the
time before his conviction, roughly two and a half years, Wallace was
held at the Jefferson County Jail in Birmingham; after the first year,
he was briefly transferred to the state hospital to see whether he was
competent to stand trial. Once he was convicted, he was transferred to
Kilby Correctional Facility. It is what's known as a classification center, a hub where everybody is sent first so the prison system can decide
how dangerous they are, how sick they are, and what kinds of services
they need before they are dispersed to other prisons around the state.
With the capacity to house fourteen hundred people, Kilby receives
some thirty new prisoners every day, five days per week. Attorneys for
the prisoners say as many as nine of those have a mental illness, and
more likely go undiagnosed.

Wallace had been diagnosed with mental health problems as a
young child and had been in and out of treatment his whole life. Yet it's
unclear whether the prison officials at Kilby, or the Alabama Department of Corrections itself, were aware of his long-standing diagnoses
of bipolar disorder, schizophrenia, and attention-deficit/hyperactivity
disorder (ADHD). The gathering and sharing of prisoners' health

records are notoriously poor in most correctional facilities. Sharing of this information is often spotty even among prisons within the same system and even in cases in which mental health issues are manifest in the court proceedings. Prisoners sometimes go from one prison to another without their medication. So even though the doctor at Jefferson County Jail would have known that Wallace was on medication, it is entirely possible that neither that information nor the medication itself followed him to prison.

Based on what we know of prison protocols in place at the time, we can assume that, like everybody who arrives at Kilby, Wallace was screened twice. In the first exam, somebody from the Department of Corrections itself would have interviewed him and given him a couple of tests to evaluate his mental faculties, including his intelligence and education level. Then somebody from MHM, the private contractor that provides mental health care in the prison, would have done another exam, specifically to check his mental health. This exam is done by a licensed practical nurse (LPN), who can decide whether the prisoner needs to see a psychiatrist or not.

According to his subsequent testimony, Wallace told the LPN conducting the exam about the medications he was taking, including lithium and others. In his testimony Wallace said she never asked him about his history of mental illness. The class-action lawsuit accused the Alabama system of undercounting the number of prisoners with mental illness. Failing to ask questions, or failing to ask the right ones, may be part of the reason. Assessing a prisoner's medical case history is usually done by somebody with more training, an RN or other specialized mental health professional. Regardless, Wallace was at least referred to the psychiatrist for further examination. The psychiatrist recommended that he be placed in special housing for people with mental illness.

Sometime after that—days or perhaps weeks after his arrival at Kilby—Wallace would have been put onto a DOC bus for the two-and-a-half-hour bus ride northwest to Donaldson, a prison long known for being overcrowded, understaffed, and extremely violent. I tried to visit Donaldson, or any prison in Alabama for that matter, just to get an idea of what conditions were like. After a few back and forths with the spokesman, he said it wouldn't be possible, thanks to the litigation and an ongoing investigation by the US Department of Justice. "We suggest you investigate another state," he finally said. I drove out to Donaldson anyway, just to see what it looked like from the outside. It's less than thirty miles from downtown Birmingham, but it feels worlds away, off a winding wooded road. The square guard towers overlooking the dingy brown buildings give it the feeling of an old stockade building. A faded sign on the chain-link and barbed-wire fence that surrounds the prison reads "DO NOT STOP AND TALK TO INMATES."

At Donaldson, Jamie Wallace was never well enough to be put into general population. Does this put him in the category of what Ken Kesey called the Chronics? Possibly. It could also just be an indication of what a colossal failure the medicalization of the criminal justice system has been in many places. In other words, it's possible that Wallace was not so much irredeemable as that nobody made much of an effort to help him get better. It's also possible that he was irredeemable by the time he arrived there not because his illness was so severe but because he had spent three years in jail. "At [Donaldson], they don't check on you like they're supposed to," Wallace testified. "Mental health patients are not getting their help down there." The only way he could get seen by a counselor, he said, was if he kicked the door of his cell in or told somebody he was suicidal.

It shouldn't be surprising that conditions are so bad for prisoners with mental illness, considering the baseline: how bad conditions are for everybody there. The fifteen facilities that make up Alabama's prison system were built to accommodate just over thirteen thousand prisoners. At the end of 2016, though, twenty-three thousand prisoners were being housed there—175 percent capacity. The system is also understaffed, not just with clinical workers but also with corrections officers. One retired officer described a dorm with 220 prisoners guarded by one officer. A former warden described suicide watch checks that should have been performed every fifteen minutes getting done every three or four hours.

Alabama's prison system was—and at this writing still is—rife with violence. In 2016, there were hundreds of assaults. In 2017, at least eight people were killed. The physical structures are disintegrating. Prisoners have staged hunger strikes twenty-seven times in the last four years. In 2016 prisoners used an illegal cell phone to shoot a video of people rioting at one of the facilities. The video shows beds lined up very close to each other. Prisoners light a fire on one wall, but there are no corrections officers to be seen. The Alabama Department of Corrections has been the target of several major lawsuits in the last few years, alleging everything from lack of proper medical care to excessive violence. In late 2016, just months before Jamie Wallace killed himself, the US Department of Justice announced a statewide investigation to see whether prisoners are adequately protected from violence and sexual abuse by other prisoners and by officers, and "whether the prisons provide sanitary, secure safe living conditions."[6]

Wallace often complained to his attorneys that other prisoners were mean to him. He reported being taunted. He was punished for attacking a fellow prisoner, whom he said had a weapon and was getting ready to attack him. A couple of times, Wallace called home saying he needed money to pay off debts of some kind: "I gotta have [money] on my books by such and such, or I'm going to get hurt." There were also reports of abuse by corrections officers. A retired officer told me his colleagues regularly handed razor blades to suicidal prisoners, suggesting the most effective ways for them to slit their wrists.

If idle hands are the devil's workshop, then the RTU, the mental health unit where Wallace lived, is the devil's factory. On most days, Jamie Wallace never left his concrete cell. Asked what he did in his cell, he said, "Ain't nothing we can do but pace the floor." He had two books, the Bible and another book about Jesus that he said he'd read so much he'd gotten bored with it. (Wallace also had cognitive disabilities and read at around a first-grade level.) "I'll walk around my cell, and I'll rap or I may sing," he said. "If I had a radio, I would listen to a radio... but if you can't borrow no radio, you ain't got nothing to read or nothing in there."

Every other day, he was taken out of his cell for a shower. Regulations required two officers to accompany him from the cell to the shower and back. Keep in mind that Wallace was barely five feet tall and slight, and, apart from having shot his mother, his only significant history of violence was against himself. The officers would open the tray slot. Inside the cell, Wallace would put his back to the door so the officers could reach through the slot to cuff his hands behind his back. Then they would open the cell door and lead him to the shower. If there weren't enough officers to spare, there was no shower.

Once a week, or sometimes once every two weeks, officers would come to the door, and Wallace would again turn around to have his hands cuffed. The officers would walk him to the concrete yard for rec time. But there was nothing to do there—and even if there had been something to do, he had to stay handcuffed while doing it. So he would spend thirty minutes walking around "in handcuffs to our back." One begins to understand why prisoners refuse outdoor time.

In jail and prison, even basic functions like eating and sleeping can become means of low-level, unintentional torture. Read the logs of Wallace's (and others') incarcerations, and you see that breakfast was usually served at 3 or 4 A.M. Pill call, when nurses come around to administer medications, happened at all hours of the day and night. The timing is not just cruel, though; it's counterproductive. It should come as news to nobody that even for those without mental illness, sleeping and eating, regular exercise, and constructive activity are all part of basic mental health care.

These are the kinds of injustices that rarely make the news; legislatures don't hold hearings on the lack of activity—let alone meaningful activity—in state prisons. But such practices reinforce the idea that prisoners, particularly those with mental illness, are less than people: even dogs in shelters are given time to run around outdoors. Jamie Wallace was assigned to get some of the most intensive health care that was available in Alabama's prison system. What he got was essentially solitary confinement. He said he rarely saw officers unless they led him to the showers or delivered mail or meals: "They come in at nine o'clock. Do chow. Leave out. Pick up trays. They come back in about 2:30 that afternoon and do trays and leave back out."

SUICIDE IS THE LEADING CAUSE of death in jails and one of the leading causes in prisons. It is so common that companies supply any number of suicide-prevention products specifically designed for jails and prisons. The most common method of suicide in jails and prisons is hanging, usually with bedding or clothing, so besides the suicide-proof blankets and smocks that I saw at the LA County Jail and elsewhere, there are suicide mattresses, thin mats really, also said to be indestructible (though corrections officers in many places complained about a perpetual shortage because prisoners regularly destroy them), even suicide-proof sanitary napkin belts for women.[7] Grainger, the industrial supply company, sells a stainless-steel suicide-resistant toilet and sink combination, designed without handles that could be used to attach to a noose. There are suicide-resistant showerheads and faucet handles, suicide-resistant toilet paper holders.[8] Most of this equipment is similar to what might be found in a psychiatric hospital. What is disturbing is that there is enough of a market in correctional facilities that companies can market directly to them.

When a prisoner attempts suicide or tells staff that he is suicidal, he is put on suicide watch. What that means depends on the institution and how the health care workers view the person's condition. After a man in an Illinois prison attempted suicide, he was put into a cell with no clothes or property and, at times, not even a mattress. It took more than a month for him to see a psychiatrist despite, in addition to his suicide attempt, a long history of severe mental illness; over the course of three months in the so-called crisis cell, the only other mental health care he received were quick cell-side checks from a clinician. Even those brief checks showed that he was "increasingly incoherent, confused, and actively hallucinating." He regularly spread feces around the cell. Confronted with a disciplinary hearing for that behavior, he pled guilty, saying, "You use it for protection. Smearing feces keeps the voices down."[9]

In the jail in Oklahoma City, I saw a prisoner on suicide watch in a cell in a dim corner of the jail where the ammoniac odor of urine was so strong that it burned my nose. The man sat on the floor of the cell, arms sticking out of the food slot, yelling, while a guard stationed outside the door stared at him. At the jail in Tulsa, prisoners on suicide watch were housed in a pod of dark solitary cells; officers observed them via close-circuit television from outside the pod.

When a person attempts suicide, corrections officers are usually the first to respond. Sometimes that means rushing in to cut the person down or to perform CPR, but not always. In Florida, for example, several officers told me they won't enter a cell where a prisoner has cut himself until he passes out. "I'm not going to stop him because he has a blade in his hand," one longtime officer told me. "If he doesn't want to come to the door, I'm not going to go in and put myself or my staff in danger. If [he doesn't] want to stop, you can spray him [with pepper spray]. That'll get him to stop; especially if you spray it in the cut, maybe it'll sting enough that [he'll] stop." If somebody hangs himself—"hangs up," in jail parlance—she and others told me, it's not safe to enter the cell alone to cut him down, even if it may take several minutes for backup to arrive, because it could turn out to be an ambush. In the case of a person trying to kill himself, the officer is stuck deciding between how to keep himself or herself safe and how to save a life.

EVEN BEFORE HE GOT TO prison, Jamie Wallace had a history of hurting himself; he had been a cutter for years. It's a morbid thing to say, but there is something impressive about the sheer creativity of the ways that Jamie Wallace found to try to hurt himself in prison. Maybe it was just experience.[10] Or maybe it was desperation.

Every few months and sometimes more frequently, he found a violent way to harm himself. There was the time when he was sad about some family issues. "I opened the light," he said. "I opened the light fixture, busted the lightbulb that was in there, took the lightbulb out, and broke it on the ground." He used the glass to cut both sides of his neck. The following year, he used a chicken bone to cut his arm. "I sharpened it on the floor," he said. "See, the floor is made out of concrete in our cells. You can take a chicken bone, you can file it to a point and cut yourself or stab yourself."[11] Then there were the times when he filed the metal part of a pencil—the silver ring that holds the eraser in place—to cut his arm. The time he jumped off the sink and hit his head. The time he bit his arm so badly that he had to be taken to the hospital.

"He always showed me where he had hurt himself last," said one of the civil rights attorneys who worked with him extensively to prepare for the class-action lawsuit. "Some people would say he wanted attention. He wanted someone to care, so yes, he wanted attention. He was in a lot of pain, and he needed help." What he got instead was punishment. He was regularly put into disciplinary segregation—though, ironically, he said that he was never moved to another cell; he just lost privileges while remaining where he was. Twenty-one days, or thirty days, or forty-five days where he wasn't allowed to have visitors or use the phone or buy stuff from the canteen.

Wallace once took the metal top off a can of smokeless tobacco, somehow tore it in half, and used one side to cut himself. He hid the other half in his rectum to use another time. On this occasion, he said he cut himself because he was angry that he had lost visiting privileges: "I did that because I wasn't able to see my daddy that month because they put a disciplinary on me," he said. He got another disciplinary ticket for cutting himself.

There is extensive research showing that keeping prisoners connected to family and to community more generally is one of the best ways to ease reentry once they're released and to prevent recidivism. This is especially true for people with mental illness. Yet loss of visiting privileges is a common consequence of breaking rules, even for people with mental illness. In Michigan and Florida, among other places, refusing to take medication is considered a rule violation, no matter what the motive. In Michigan the regulation is surreal: not taking prescribed medication is a drug infraction, like being caught with marijuana or heroin. So is possessing prescription drugs past their expiration date or not being able to urinate when ordered to do a drug test. After a second substance use ticket, prisoners permanently lose their right to have visitors. Nor is it just punishment for drug infractions that often seem way out of proportion to the infraction itself. I met a man in Michigan who had tried to hang himself in his prison cell. In the course of being cut down, he kicked the officer. The officer refused medical treatment, but the prison called the state police, which asked that the cell be sealed as a crime scene so that the state could press criminal assault charges.

JAMIE WALLACE WAS SINGULARLY ILL-EQUIPPED to handle the stress of being in prison, particularly a prison environment as difficult as Donaldson. He was born in Alabama in 1992 to Mike and Michelle Wallace. Jamie was their oldest; Jamie's brother, Chris, was eight years younger. Jamie was born with multiple physical disabilities—"I've had a lot of surgeries at being born," he said. These included several serious defects of his digestive system that meant he had use a colostomy bag for years and left him partially incontinent as an adult. He also had intellectual disabilities: "[T]he way I function on a level is a kindergarten level. I mean, I can barely even read." He was acutely aware of his deficiencies: "It makes me feel sad I don't know how to read." Jamie was put in special education classes at school, but he dropped out after tenth grade.

Then there was the mental illness, for which he started getting treated when he was just six. That's early; most serious mental illness isn't diagnosed until the late teens or early twenties. I couldn't track down his medical records, but it's safe to assume that anyone who was getting treatment that early—especially in a state like Alabama, where mental healthcare has long been neglected and underfunded— was pretty sick. Certainly, later records indicate that his disease was serious and hard to control; he regularly saw a therapist growing up and was in and out of psychiatric hospitals right up until the time he want to jail, at age sixteen. He was eventually diagnosed with ADHD, bipolar disorder, and schizophrenia, although all three don't always show up in his prison health records. Some of the records mention post-traumatic stress disorder (PTSD) as well, but none specify which trauma that may have caused it.

Alabama has extremely high rates of mental illness. It also ranks in the bottom half of states for spending on mental health care.[12] In an annual survey that compares rates of mental illness and access to treatment, the advocacy group Mental Health America found that Alabama ranked forty-six out of fifty for having one of the highest rates of illness and the least access to care.[13]

Bipolar disorder appeared to run in the family on both sides: his paternal grandmother was reportedly diagnosed with it late in life, as was his mother. Two weeks after Wallace's mother died, his grandmother killed herself. Wallace's uncle, David, told me the grandmother felt guilty about the killing because Jamie had used her gun. Several people, including Mike Wallace's widow (not Jamie's mother) and his half-brother, told me they long suspected that Mike also suffered from bipolar disorder but that he refused to seek a diagnosis, let alone treatment.

For much of Wallace's life, the family—his parents and his brother, Chris—lived in Graysville, a community of two thousand people in the hills outside Birmingham. Originally known as Gin Town because it had the only cotton gin in the area, Graysville experienced a second boom when coal mines and steel mills brought work in the 1950s and 1960s. Today, it's mostly a collection of houses tucked into hilly woods; about 20 percent of the population is below the poverty line.

Mike Wallace—known to friends as Mikey T.—was a large man, over six feet tall and five hundred pounds by the time he died. He had grown up in Graysville. At the time his wife died, he and his family were renting a small yellow clapboard house in sight of the house where his mother and stepfather lived. He drove a semitrailer for a company owned by his cousin, hauling coal from the only mine still in the area to power plants in other parts of Alabama and Mississippi. Even so, money was tight, and sometimes the family relied on food stamps for extra help. He was, by several counts, a violent and abusive man who had a hard time controlling his anger. His estranged half-brother told me that he regularly beat his wife and told his son he needn't respect her.

Jamie's mother, Michelle Wallace, stayed home to raise him and Chris. She was an animal lover, and she always had dogs and birds in the house. She loved the outdoors: fishing, camping, and swimming. She was abused, but some say that she was also an abuser, favoring her younger son and regularly calling the older one "retard" and other names. Jamie said that his parents fought "like cats and dogs" and that he and his brother were once removed from the home because his mother had beaten him with a belt. Jamie said that she hadn't intended any harm, that she was merely whipping him.[14] (Chris Wallace told me that his father hit him to discipline him but never beat him up.)

As best as I can piece together, Wallace's childhood was a combination of the mundane—video games, pool parties, trips to McDonald's—and abuse, marked by regular visits with a therapist and semi-regular inpatient hospital stays to deal with his physical and mental problems. Chris Wallace remembers a happy childhood, being outside, playing board games with his brother, and helping him with his homework, even though Jamie was the older one.

Jamie's uncle David Bazzell—Mike Wallace's estranged half-brother—lived near them when Jamie was growing up. I met Bazzell, now in his fifties, at a Huddle House restaurant near his apartment not far from the house where Jamie grew up; he wore a baseball cap with the Confederate flag and the word "rebel" across the front. Throughout Jamie's childhood, he said he regularly took Jamie to church or to McDonald's. They would talk about Jamie's life, and Bazzell would try to keep him on the straight and narrow: "He had his problems, but all in all he was a pretty good kid; he was just rambunctious at times." Jamie didn't play sports, but he liked video games and spent as much time as he could at his grandparents' house, which he could see through the trees.

Even now, all these years later, Bazzell is still angry at his half-brother and his sister-in-law, who, he said, regularly hosted wild drug- and alcohol-fueled parties with the kids around. Jamie once showed Bazzell how to roll a joint and told him his father had taught him. Another time, at a July 4 barbeque, Bazzell said, Jamie and some friends found some meth and took it. (For his part, Chris Wallace told me he hates his uncle.)

Michelle Wallace's friend Dianne Skinner—their husbands were childhood friends—remembered a different, less-complicated version of the Wallace family life: barbeques and summer afternoons spent in the above-ground pool in the Wallace yard. When Jamie was sixteen and Skinner's daughter Savannah was twelve, an innocent romance developed between them. The parents agreed that they couldn't be alone together—Skinner was worried about how much older Jamie was than Savannah—but the two would watch television together at one family's house or the other. If they asked permission, they could hold hands, although kissing was not allowed. "Jamie was extremely good to Savannah," Skinner said. "He would save up his allowance, and for Valentine's Day, he bought her a big balloon, a teddy bear, some chocolate, and brought it over to the house to surprise her."

More tragedies followed Michelle Wallace's death. Two weeks after she died, Mike Wallace's mother killed herself, reportedly by overdosing on the medications she took for her bipolar disorder. Mike Wallace died seven years later, in February 2016, after a brief illness; he was severely overweight and died of related complications. Less than six months later, Jamie's step-grandfather, the one who grabbed the gun from him the day he shot his mother, died as well. It was a lot for Jamie Wallace to take in. He was especially devastated by his father's death.

At his son's court hearing after he shot his mother, Mike Wallace told a newspaper reporter that he "didn't want people to think he was a monster." He visited Jamie regularly in jail and in prison, put money on his commissary account, and, his widow said, paid off Jamie's thousands of dollars in court fees. He was even looking into a lawyer for him to help with a bid for parole, his widow said. (Jamie would not have been eligible for a parole hearing until much, much later.)

"When his daddy died, you could hear Jamie screaming," Jamie's stepmother said. She had called the chaplain at the prison to let him know. "It tore him all up." After that, Wallace spent several weeks in the stabilization unit at another prison. Prisoners who spent more than a few weeks there were supposed to be transferred to the state hospital for more intensive treatment, but in reality, it almost never happened. Wallace was never sent there.

I visited Graysville a few months after Jamie died. Both of his parents were dead by then, but I met his stepmother, Belinda Wallace, whom his father had married after Jamie's mother died. Since Mike Wallace's death, she's worked nights at the Waffle House a few towns over from 5 P.M. to 6 A.M. and then a day shift at the nearby Dollar Tree. She tries to sleeps for a few hours in the afternoon between the end of her shift at the store and before her shift starts at the restaurant. I met her on a Sunday, her one day off, at the Waffle House where she works.

She told me that Mike Wallace would take Jamie's brother, Chris, to see him every three months, which was as often as prison regulations allowed. Chris Wallace remembers those visits: "I'd love it because I got to spend time with my brother, even though it was in a [prison]; I just missed being with my brother." Sometimes, Belinda Wallace told me, they would make the trip only to be turned away by the officers for a minor transgression: once, the senior Wallace didn't have a letter from his doctor attesting that he needed a cane for walking. (He needed the cane to walk, but the prison officials wouldn't let him bring it inside.) Another time, his pants didn't meet the dress code. Often, Jamie would lose visiting privileges, sometimes for months at a time. Sometimes when they visited, Mike reported, Jamie would be so out of it from the medication that he'd be drooling on himself. His father would call the warden, but it often changed nothing.

Belinda Wallace never met Jamie; she was waiting to get on the prison visitors list when he died. She says she wrote to him regularly, though, and he would call her, often feeling suicidal: "He would call me and tell me 'This is what I'm going to do [that is, how he was going to kill himself]. I want to do this. I'm weary; I'm so weary.' I talked him out of it." She says he didn't always seem to understand what had happened to him: "Jamie didn't even realize his momma wasn't going to come back. I would tell him, 'Jamie, I'm sitting here talking to you. Your momma isn't coming back.'" Other times, she says, he was more aware of reality and would tell her things like "My mom's gone because of me. Now you're acting as a mom."

Jamie Wallace needed help, and he knew it: "I need someone that I can sit down and just sit there and talk to about what's going on in my mind and my chest and stuff." At Donaldson, "[T]hey change up so many folks on us. Like this [psychologist who had seen Wallace for a period], he was my counselor. Then he all of a sudden just stopped working there. He don't work there no more.... [My new counselor] she barely comes back there unless I say I'm suicidal or I kick the door down or something. We have to actually raise hell back there just to get somebody back there."

SIX DAYS BEFORE JAMIE WALLACE killed himself in his prison cell, he told the prison psychiatrist that he had been hearing voices. "He hears 'Momma's voice...she yelled before she died,..."help...please don't kill me,"'" the psychiatrist noted on December 9, 2016. "He hears the devil say 'kill yourself...you're not worth it.'"[15] Below that, the psychiatrist noted that Wallace's appearance was disheveled and his cell was messy, but his speech was coherent and he conversed easily. His mood, the doctor wrote, was blunted. Next to the part of the form marked "suicidal," the psychiatrist had checked the box that said "no." However, Wallace had been suicidal the week before and had just spent three days on suicide watch. He was depressed, he had told a clinician, "because he has lost contact with his brother and does not have any way of making contact with him. [Inmate reports] it has been several months since he has spoken with his brother."[16] Chris Wallace told me he wrote his brother once or twice: "He would write back, say he missed us and he loved us. We know he felt sorry for what happened and everything."

In the months before he died, two different mental health professionals—his own psychiatrist and a psychologist—had recommended he be transferred to the hospital for stabilization. By the time he told the psychiatrist about the voices, he had instead been moved to a cell on what's called a "stabilization unit." This unit promises specially trained corrections officers, a mental health nurse on site twenty-four hours per day, and an "expectation of providing mental health treatment for inmates in crisis, having cells modified to provide 'safe' environments."[17] It is, in other words, for the sickest prisoner-patients in the state, meant to be hospital-level care in the prison.

On December 15, less than a week after he told the psychiatrist that he was not suicidal, Wallace managed to find a piece of cloth—probably a sheet—which he tied to the fire sprinkler head. Two corrections officers found him hanging at 10:33 P.M., and a nurse tried to revive him. He was already dead.

JAMIE WALLACE STILL HAD MORE than two decades left on his sentence when he was buried on New Year's Day of 2017. His brother, Chris; his half-uncle, David Bazzell; his father's best friend, who later became Chris's guardian; a local television reporter who had taken an interest in the story; and three or four other family friends gathered on a piece of patchy lawn at the Crestview Memorial Gardens in Adamsville, not far from the yellow house where Wallace had lived before he went to prison.

The memorial park is an unassuming place of sloping lawns dotted with bronze memorial plaques and bouquets of artificial flowers, available for purchase in the funeral home office at the bottom of the hill. Jamie Wallace was in jail when his mother was buried there, a week after he shot her. He was in prison when his father died seven years later. Prisons sometimes authorize leave for prisoners to visit a critically ill family member or to attend a funeral, but Jamie was not granted either one. On the day of his funeral, the gravedigger dug a shallow grave between those of his parents.

The day was mild, in the low sixties; Bazzell says he didn't need to wear a jacket. The funeral director put the urn with Jamie's ashes into the hearse and drove it up the winding drive, past three large white crucifixes, to the plot. "In Loving Memory Mr. Jamie Lee Wallace" reads the funeral card that was handed out. Under the words is a picture from before his incarceration, showing a smiling Wallace in a blue shirt, hair cropped short. On the facing page is a poem about going to heaven. The wife of his father's best friend spoke briefly.

Jamie Wallace's grave doesn't have his name on it. The spot where he's buried is marked with a bronze plaque with his parents' names on it. "Together forever," it says.

"ONE OF THE THINGS THAT made me sad about working with Jamie is that it was hard for me to imagine where else he might have ended up," one of the civil rights attorneys who represented Jamie and other Alabama prisoners told me. Not in the sense of prison, necessarily. Rather that he'd been so abused—by his parents, by the mental health system, and, ultimately, by the criminal justice system—that it would have been hard for him to function independently.

At this point, it's hard to know whether the outcome of Jamie's story was really inevitable. Certainly his mental illness and cognitive deficiencies were severe enough that he might never have lived on his own. Getting proper mental health care in prison undoubtedly would have helped; it might have kept him from killing himself. It also seems possible that having better mental health care earlier in life could have kept him from killing his mother. He didn't have much of a criminal record to speak of when he killed her; as a twelve-year-old he had stolen a car and subsequently crashed it, but there was really little else in his history to suggest a life of crime.

What actually happened that day? The week before he killed his mother, Jamie Wallace had been released from a psychiatric hospital where his father had brought him to try to get his illness stabilized yet again. His father thought it was the medication that the doctor had just changed that caused him to kill his mother. Jamie's stepmother thinks maybe Jamie's mother found him trying to commit suicide. Jamie's uncle says he'd been planning it for a long time. The local newspapers reported, quoting a Jefferson County sheriff's deputy, that Jamie and his mother had gotten into a fight.

In any case it was a warm Sunday afternoon in March 2009 when Jamie's mother called his father, who was driving a load of coal out of state. She was scared, she said. Jamie, then sixteen, had stolen a .38 caliber pistol from his grandparents' house and was threatening her with it. Take Jamie's brother, Mike told her, and run. Go there and get help. The door to the house was right outside Jamie's room. Michelle tore it open, and pushing Chris, eight, ahead of her to protect him, she ran across the small front porch and down the six cement steps toward her in-laws' house. It would have been just dark, but not so dark she couldn't see as she ran across her lawn past the driveway, across the narrow street she lived on, and into the woods. It must have been harder when she ran up the wooded path alongside a small white church, then made a right turn onto the street where her in-laws' tiny one-story house sat.

It wasn't very far, less than a city block. It couldn't have taken more than a few minutes, even in the dusk, with a terrified eight-year-old. But it must have felt like forever, her younger son running in front of her, her older son chasing behind, gun in hand. Somewhere between the two houses, he shot. The bullet hit her in the hip. But she kept running, hurrying Chris along, until they got to the front porch of her in-laws' house. They might have heard her screaming as she ran, or maybe Mike Wallace had called to alert them. They certainly would have heard the shot, practically outside their window.

When she got to the porch, bleeding, almost certainly out of breath, her mother-in-law and stepfather-in-law were already there, behind the screen door. Jamie was right behind his mother, and as his grandparents and brother looked on, he shot her again, this time in the chest. By now she was lying on the porch. Jamie pointed the gun at her head and pulled the trigger again, but he was out of bullets. He didn't realize it, though, and turned the gun on his step-grandfather, Jerry Gilliam, who did realize it and wrestled the gun away. A sheriff's department investigator later testified that Jamie had said he would have shot Gilliam as well "if I wouldn't have been stupid and used up all of them [bullets]."

Weapon gone, Jamie bolted. The trucking company where his father worked was right across the street from his grandparents' house. He ran into the lot, found an eighteen-wheeler used to haul coal—imagine an extra-long dumptruck—with the keys in the ignition, and he jumped behind the wheel. He had no driver's license, but he had apparently learned enough from his trucker father and step-grandfather to pull out of the lot. By this time, his step-grandfather had called the police. The officers had to shoot Wallace with a Taser to get him to stop. The Jefferson County district attorney charged him with the murder of his mother, attempted murder of his step-grandfather, and resisting arrest.

Jamie Wallace spent most of the next three years in the Jefferson County Jail, waiting for his case to be resolved. His father and brother visited as often as they could, but as his brother remembers it, contact visits were not allowed, so they looked at each other through a thick glass window and talked on scratchy telephones. There were issues with his court-appointed attorneys, who twice had to be replaced, and the usual slowness of court proceedings, with endless hearings.

One of the biggest delays in his case, though, was the question of his sanity. He spent more than a year in the Jefferson County Jail before being transferred to the Taylor Hardin Secure Medical Facility, a 114-bed forensic hospital in Tuscaloosa, about an hour southwest of Birmingham. Even in a case where mental illness should have been raised early on as a factor, it took more than a year for him to get evaluated. After a brief stay there, he returned to Jefferson County, where he stayed for more than a year while his case worked through the system. When I called the jail's medical director, she knew who I was asking about before I mentioned Wallace's name: "He seemed like a typical guy that just really fell through the cracks of the system...."

He did a horrendous thing, and it was just too late to help him." She remembered him being on a medical unit the whole time he was there and remembered that he often sought attention. She suspects that he never really intended to kill himself and is adamant that the criminal justice system should not bear all the responsibility for what happened to him: "Far more injustices were done [to Jamie Wallace] prior to his criminal act than afterwards. He was just a young person in need of our help, and we did the best we could to take care of him."

In November 2011, nearly three years after he killed his mother, he appeared before the judge for the last time. He had been found competent to stand trial, but he was also barely eighteen years old, a high school dropout with developmental disabilities and severe mental illness. His confusion is apparent in the transcript of the proceedings. The prosecutor had previously offered him a plea bargain of twenty-five years in state prison; Wallace had to decide whether to accept the plea or to go to trial. His lawyer said he wanted to go to trial. But when the judge asked Wallace whether he understood what his choices were, Wallace's answer was polite but muddled: "I sure do, sir. I would like to speak for myself, because ain't nobody just let me speak. I don't need no hard feelings, but what are you wanting to offer? What are you willing to do, sir?"

When the judge explained that the prosecutor makes the offer, not the judge, Wallace asked to speak to his lawyer. The judge called for an adjournment so they could speak privately. When they came back, Wallace started to tell the judge what he wanted—"Judge, I have decided..."—when his lawyer cut him off. "Wait, wait, wait," the lawyer said. "Judge, just for the record, I want to let the Court know that we have...a disagreement as to...what...Mr. Wallace should do, which really makes me question his whole competency to stand trial, anyway....At this point, I don't know what he is going to say; whether he wants to say he wants to take the twenty-five years that's been offered, or whether he wants to withdraw the plea. But for the court record, I have communicated to my client that I recommend he withdraw the plea, and his father has given a note, which I have showed his son, that he recommends him withdraw the plea and go to trial."

The judge seemed unmoved. He reminded the attorney that Wallace, not Wallace's father, was the client and that it was up to the client to decide how to proceed. He did not acknowledge how young Wallace was or his cognitive limitations.

The lawyer tried again, telling the judge that he had spoken to his client numerous times about the possible consequences of either decision. Then Wallace asked to address the court. After another reminder from the judge that the decision was up to him, Wallace took the plea bargain: "I have been in jail for two years and seven months. My father has been on the outside for two years and seven months, coming and seeing me. I know that when you are locked up, it's hard for—not to cry and stuff. But, Judge, I'd like to get twenty-five, because simple fact is, is I have been waiting so long. I can't wait for no more sentencing or nothing. I'm sorry."

Wallace's brother, Christopher, now a teenager and living with his father's best friend and his wife, told me that afterward, he and his father got to go into a side room in the court and talk to his brother: "He said he was sorry; he just missed outside and everything. We actually got pictures of that day. You can see I was forcing a smile; there were tears rolling down my face."

In deciding to take the plea, Jamie Wallace is not so different from tens of thousands of people who take plea bargains. He just couldn't stand waiting anymore. And as for many others, it was a decision that had dire consequences. Before he imposed the sentence, the judge asked Wallace if he had anything else to say. "Yes, sir," Wallace answered, "I would like to say something to my father, if that's all right." The judge ignored the comment and asked again if Wallace had anything further to tell the *court*. "Yes, sir. I would like to say this here," Wallace said. "I feel very bad for what I done. I know as a man, a man is punished for what he has done by God. And if it wasn't for God being with me, he wouldn't let me do this today. That's it, Your Honor."

After the sentencing—which included more than five thousand dollars in fines—Wallace's attorney made another impassioned plea on his client's behalf. He reiterated the extent and severity of Wallace's medical issues, begging the judge repeatedly to make note of them in his sentencing letter.[18] Again the judge seemed unfazed: "I will certainly make them aware... at least of the physical conditions," the judge responded, "but ultimately [the officials of the Department of Corrections] decide how he is classified, where he is housed, and those issues."

Then Jamie Wallace asked to address the court again. "Can I say something to my daddy, please?" For the last time, the judge tried to redirect him to the court proceeding, and with that he concluded the hearing.

8

Guilty by Reason of Insanity

ON THE THIRD FLOOR OF the Fulton County Jail in Atlanta, Georgia, eight men are sitting around "spider tables," stainless-steel tables with stools attached. They are all wearing dark-blue scrubs with the words "Fulton County Jail Inmate" stenciled on the back in white letters. Some wear thermal undershirts or raggedy sweatshirts underneath. At the front of the room, a woman sits behind a desk, straight white hair pulled back with a single barrette. "Why are you here?" the woman asks.

"To be made *competent*," answers one man emphatically.

Another raises his hand. "How do I make myself competent?"

By studying hard, the woman answers.

"Can we learn to be a judge?" he continues. Without waiting for an answer, he launches into a long, rambling digression about judgment.

All have a pending criminal case (or cases), and all have been found incompetent to stand trial because of a mental illness, a developmental disability, or some combination of the two. They are not here to be made sane, or "better." As the man correctly responded, they are here to be made competent—that is, sane enough to appear before a judge and get a fair hearing.

A CRIMINAL CASE CANNOT PROCEED if the defendant is deemed incompetent. It's one of only two points in the criminal justice system where, legally speaking, the defendant's sanity matters. The other point in the criminal justice system when sanity is relevant is at the time the crime was (allegedly) committed. This is, of course, the basis for a plea of not guilty by reason of insanity (NGRI). But where questions about competency to stand trial are far more common— and indeed have widespread ramifications for the entire criminal justice system—NGRI has a reputation that far exceeds reality. It is one of the oldest and perhaps the most misunderstood concepts in the world of mental illness and criminal justice. Popular opinion holds that pleading NGRI is extremely common and that it is frequently used by sane but dishonest people as a way to avoid prison time. (Indeed, Randle McMurphy, the hero of *One Flew Over the Cuckoo's Nest*, had feigned insanity, thinking that the hospital would be preferable to prison time.) In reality, though, even without precise statistics, it's clear that both requests for a finding of NGRI and the success of those requests are quite rare.

Best estimates suggest that attorneys *ask* for the insanity defense in somewhere between 0.1 and 0.5 percent of felony cases. And most of the relevant studies were done using data from the 1970s to the mid-1980s, when the insanity plea was far more common than it is today. Of those 0.1 to 0.5 percent of felony cases, somewhere between 10 percent and 60 percent are thought to be successful; another study estimated that the plea succeeds in about a quarter of the cases in which it is raised.[1]

If he is found not guilty by reason of insanity, the defendant, like the fictional Randle McMurphy, will be committed to a psychiatric facility rather than to prison. In another indication of how rarely it succeeds, statistics from 1978—when, again, NGRI was far more common than it is today—show that NGRI accounted for only 8 percent of all admissions to mental hospitals that year. That translates to about thirty acquittals per state, annually.

Although psychiatric treatment might *sound* preferable to prison time, the truth is that it is often more involved. To be released from the hospital, even temporarily, the patient has to prove to a judge that he is not a danger to himself or others, either currently or "in the reasonable future."[2] Depending on the outcome of the hearings, a person who is found not guilty by reason of insanity could spend far longer in the hospital than he would have spent in prison, one reason that defense attorneys are hesitant to ask for the plea. Another reason to believe the plea is rarely used to pull a fast one on the jury is that few successful insanity acquittals are the result of a jury trial. Instead, they come from what amounts to a plea bargain, where the prosecutor agrees that the defendant is not sane enough to be tried and punished, and lets him plead NGRI instead.[3]

Whether somebody can be found not guilty by reason of insanity hinges on whether he was sane enough to understand what he was doing when he committed the crime. Although there are accounts of some form of insanity acquittal going back to at least the 1500s, our modern interpretations of it date to a case from the nineteenth century. In 1843 a man named Daniel M'Naghten went to London with plans to assassinate the prime minister, Robert Peel. Mistaking Peel's secretary, Edward Drummond, for the prime minister, M'Naghten shot and killed him instead. A medical witness in the murder case concluded that both what M'Naghten had done and his medical history "[l]eaves not the remotest doubt on my mind of the presence of insanity sufficient to deprive the prisoner of all self-control. I consider the act [of the assassination] to have been committed whilst under a delusion." The judge, for his part, told the jury that "If [M'Naghten] was not sensible at the time he committed that act, that it was a violation of the law of God or of man, undoubtedly he was not responsible for that act, or liable to any punishment whatever flowing from that act."[4]

M'Naghten was found not guilty by reason of insanity, a verdict that led to an intense outcry from both the general public and from Queen Victoria, who had herself been attacked by a man later found to be not guilty for the same reason. In response, the House of Lords asked the judges to clarify the circumstances under which somebody could be found not guilty by reason of insanity; their answer has become the basis for what are called the M'Naghten rules, on which modern definitions have been based: "[E]very man is to be presumed to be sane.... [T]o establish a defence on the ground of insanity, it must be clearly proved that, at the time of the committing of the act, the party accused was labouring under such a defect of reason, from disease of the mind, as not to know the nature and quality of the act he was doing; or if he did know it, that he did not know he was doing what was wrong."[5]

Richard Bonnie, a law professor at the University of Virginia who specializes in competency issues, says that for people in favor of the NGRI plea, "[I]t seems fundamentally wrong and inhumane to punish people and condemn them and, certainly, to execute them, if they were truly alienated from the moral reality of their conduct." At the same time, he acknowledges that in many cases, the magnitude of the crimes, set against the image of somebody who looks so outwardly "normal," makes the plea tough to justify: "These look like people who were capable of rational reflection on their behavior, yet do terrible things," he told me.

Although the insanity defense is rarely invoked, the debate about it exposes in many ways the central tension between the goals of our criminal justice system and the fraught question of sanity. We may agree, in the abstract, that it is unfair to convict somebody who didn't know what he was doing. On the other hand, we are deeply skeptical of people who attribute their behavior to madness (or have it attributed on their behalf), and we may even instinctively abhor violent or deviant behavior that is caused by psychosis.

As the M'Naghten case showed, a verdict in which a defendant is deemed insane and, thus, not guilty is almost always controversial. Bonnie says debates about NGRI force us to consider not just the question of punishing people with mental illness but also of punishment generally: "It puts before people the purposes of punishment, [asking] 'Why do we punish?' They talk about [NGRI] because by asking about the exception, we reaffirm the rule...by asking that, people then are really affirming the legitimacy of punishment."

In recent decades, however, the idea that a person who is insane should not be responsible for their crimes has been increasingly challenged, both by the US public and by state legislatures. This shift has been shaped in part by a number of sensational cases in which NGRI was requested by the defense: Jeffrey Dahmer, who was charged with killing fifteen people; Lorena Bobbitt, who cut off her husband's penis; and Andrea Yates, who drowned her children in the bathtub. (Dahmer was ultimately convicted, Bobbitt was acquitted, and Yates was convicted but later acquitted on retrial.)

However, the case that had perhaps the most effect on the laws around NGRI was the attempted assassination of Ronald Reagan by John W. Hinckley, Jr. It was March 30, 1981, when Hinckley, standing in a scrum of reporters and photographers on the sidewalk outside the Washington Hilton, shot President Reagan in the chest. He also shot the president's press secretary, James Brady; a Secret Service agent; and a police officer. Hinckley, then twenty-five, was the baby-faced drifter son of a wealthy Colorado oilman; he'd hoped the assassination would impress the actress Jodie Foster.

Just over a year after the shootings, a Washington jury found Hinckley not guilty by reason of insanity, and he was committed to St. Elizabeth's Hospital, the first federally run psychiatric hospital in the country. The response to the verdict was swift and angry: "There must be an end to the doctrine that allows so many persons to commit crimes of violence, to use confusing procedures to their own advantage, and then have the door opened for them to return to the society they victimized," Attorney General William French Smith said in a statement at the time. A Republican member of the House told the *New York Times*, "People are irate today. I think the country was stunned."[6]

In the years leading up to the assassination attempt, there had already been movement in a number of states to modify their NGRI statutes. In the years after, more than half passed laws doing so. Some states have added a question of *mens rea*—that is, the intent of wrongdoing—to their definitions. Many states also officially shifted the burden of proof onto the defendant, although Bonnie says that this has unofficially always been the case. (Four states—Kansas, Idaho, Montana, and Utah—have also abolished the insanity defense altogether.) More recently, a number of states have added a "guilty but mentally ill" (GBMI) verdict, which experts describe as being about as logical as declaring a defendant guilty but with high blood pressure—in other words, meaningless. According to law professor Christopher Slobogin, "The GBMI verdict, put simply, is a hoax.... [T]he GBMI verdict has nothing to do with assessing culpability, which should be in the central issue in a criminal prosecution involving a person with alleged mental problems."[7]

Conceived as a way to offer juries a third option besides guilty or not guilty, the GBMI verdict was also meant to guarantee defendants access to better mental health treatment while incarcerated. In practice, it has neither reduced the number of NGRI acquittals nor substantively increased access to care.[8]

Hinckley spent thirty-five years at St. Elizabeth's; he was released quite recently, at age sixty-one, to go live with his elderly mother in Williamsburg, Virginia. His release generated only mild concern, mostly among residents of that city.

In 2012, after shooting and killing twelve people and injuring seventy others in a movie theater in Colorado, James Holmes pled not guilty by reason of insanity. He was convicted. For the murders, he was given the otherworldly punishment of twelve life sentences without the possibility of parole. The sentence was calculated as one lifetime behind bars for each person he killed. In addition, he was sentenced to another 3,318 years for the seventy attempted murders and for filling his apartment with explosives.[9] Asked later whether she thought Holmes was mentally ill when he committed the massacre, the mother of one victim answered: "I don't care if he's mentally ill or not, that's irrelevant to me. He wanted to kill people, he managed to do it, and he should be held accountable."[10]

IN STARK CONTRAST TO NGRI, the question of whether a defendant is competent to stand trial has had a tremendous impact on both the mental health care system and the criminal justice system. A criminal case cannot proceed—either toward a trial or a plea bargain—if the defendant is found incompetent, and the epidemic of mental illness in the criminal justice system has presented a singular problem with respect to court proceedings. Across the country, thousands of people are stuck in jails simply because they are too sick for their cases to proceed.

Like NGRI, the discussion about competency to stand trial—and the notion that a person who is insane should neither be judged nor punished—has a long history. As far back as the mid-1600s, English courts differentiated between defendants who refused to answer questions out of stubbornness versus those who refused "by visitation of God." In his commentaries, which, when written a century later, became the basis of English and American common law, William Blackstone wrote that competency was critical. A defendant who was insane should not "be arraigned because he is not able to plead to [the charge] with that advice and caution that he ought." He shouldn't go to trial, either, because "how can he make his defense?"[11] In other words, it's not fair to charge an insane person with a crime because he can't make a rational decision about whether to plead guilty or not guilty. Nor is it fair for him to be tried because he can't defend himself. An English court reinforced that idea when, in the late 1700s, a man named John Frith—who believed that supernatural agents whispered in his ear and that when the moon was in the south, he could not sleep near heavy buildings—was brought to court in London for throwing a stone at the King's carriage.[12] The court told the jury that Frith should not be brought to trial in this condition: "[N]o man shall be called upon to make his defence, at a time when his mind is in that situation, as not to appear capable of so doing; for, however guilty he may be, the enquiring into his guilt, must be postponed to that season, when, by collecting together his intellects, and having them entire; he shall be able so to model his defence, as to ward off the punishment of the law."[13]

Throughout the nineteenth and early twentieth centuries, US states followed common law. Then in 1960 the US Supreme Court heard a case, *Dusky v. United States*, in which the plaintiff argued that he'd been too sick with schizophrenia at the time of his trial to fully understand what was going on. Therefore, he had been unfairly sentenced to forty-five years in prison for his part in kidnapping and raping a young girl. The Court agreed and laid out a new, two-part requirement for determining a defendant's competency. The judge must not only make sure "the defendant [is] oriented to time and place and [has] some recollections of events" but also consider "whether he has sufficient present ability to consult with his lawyer with a reasonable degree of rational understanding—and whether he has a rational as well as a factual understanding of the proceedings against him."[14]

The defendant has to understand why he's being charged—what crime is he being accused of committing?—and he needs to be able to understand the potential consequences of those charges—what kind of penalty could he face if he's found guilty? And he has to understand those concepts in a rational way. So, for example, he has to understand that he faces ten years in prison and that he faces those ten years because he stole a car and not because the CIA or God told the judge to send him to prison for ten years. The defendant must also have at least a rudimentary understanding of the workings of the justice system: Who is the judge? What is her job? What does a plea bargain mean?

The rest of the guidelines are often overlooked, although they are at least as important as the first. The defendant has to be sane enough to be able—and willing—to communicate with his attorney in such a way as to aid in his own defense. A law professor in New Orleans who specializes in competency issues told me about a client she had who met the first requirements easily: he understood the charges against him and the consequences. He had sufficient understanding of the criminal justice system. But his schizophrenia made him so paranoid that he was convinced the prosecutors could hear everything he told his defense attorneys. Sure, he was prepared to help his attorneys with his case, but he would talk to them only in a "code," a code that only he could understand. What's confusing about this is that narrow definitions of competency mean that a person could be very symptomatic and very sick yet still be found competent to stand trial. "There are a lot of people who would never get tried if we waited for them to get sane," one forensic psychiatrist told me. "The question to consider is not if he's sane, but if he can get a fair trial."

Since *Dusky*, subsequent cases have sought to come up with more-subtle interpretations that would accommodate the idea that different circumstances call for differing levels of competency. The idea is that a defendant facing the death penalty ought to be more competent than somebody who is facing only a low-level misdemeanor charge such as disturbing the peace or disorderly conduct. Note that we do this in other civil contexts as well: a person may be judged competent to make financial decisions but not medical ones.

It's also worth noting that the law does *not* differentiate between somebody who has a mental illness and somebody who is cognitively impaired for other reasons—because of a developmental disability or a traumatic brain injury, for example. This is important because, as we will see shortly, the reason for the impairment can affect whether or not it can be reversed. A person who is incompetent because he's psychotic from untreated schizophrenia may be "restored to competency" with medication and therapy. That is probably not the case for somebody who was born with developmental disabilities and who has never been able to function above the level of a five-year-old. Nonetheless, people with developmental disabilities are frequently referred for restoration.

ANY COURT OFFICIAL—A DEFENSE ATTORNEY, a judge, even a prosecutor—can refer a defendant for a hearing to determine whether he or she is competent to stand trial. In practice, though, it's almost always the defense attorney who does it. After the defendant is referred for an evaluation, one or more mental health professionals perform an exam to see how sane the defendant is. One common screening exam includes questions like "Where does the judge sit?" and "What is your attorney's name?" Others test for less tangible things such as the ability to assist one's attorney or rational understanding of charges. Tests often include components designed to ensure that the person isn't trying to fake the symptoms of mental illness.

Depending on the jurisdiction, the exam may take place at the jail, at the courthouse, or at a hospital. Sometimes, a person may be sent to a hospital for a longer period to give doctors a chance to evaluate him more closely over time. Wherever the exam happens, the psychiatrist or psychologist then comes up with a determination that is presented to the judge.

For defense attorneys there is sometimes a quandary about whether it is better to advise a client to simply accept a plea and be done with the case or to ask for the exam, even when the client would clearly benefit from treatment. That's especially true for clients who are facing low-level charges with minimal potential penalties. The evaluation and treatment often take so long that the person ends up spending more time in the hospital than he would spend in jail were he to simply accept a plea bargain. It's one more example of how the system hurts people with mental illness: the defendant will likely receive minimal treatment in the jail and little or no treatment once released.

However, the evaluation is not always simple. I've heard attorneys complain about the quality of the exams or that the examiner failed to consider the client's psychiatric history. Clients with means sometimes hire outside experts to do their own exams, but there is also no guarantee the court will agree with the outside expert. For example, a New York City man accused of the 2015 murder of his father, a hedge fund manager, hired an outside psychologist who found him incompetent, but based on the reports of the state's own examiners, the judge still found him competent to proceed. As of this writing, he has been at Rikers for two and a half years. His attorney still says his client has a mental illness; however, the defendant has refused to undergo another evaluation.

Nationwide, between fifty thousand and sixty thousand criminal defendants are evaluated each year for competency. Between 20 percent and 25 percent are found to be incompetent to stand trial. Like the men I saw in the Fulton County Jail, those people are referred for treatment designed to make them sane enough to stand trial, a process known as "restoration to competency."[15] Michael Perlin, a law professor emeritus at New York Law School who specializes in mental disability law, says the practice is relatively new. Until 1972, there were almost no attempts to restore defendants to competency. They were sent to a hospital but often ended up simply staying there indefinitely. The tongue-in-cheek story was that more defendants who were incompetent to stand trial left the Massachusetts state hospital in Bridgewater dead than by all other means put together.

There are usually two components to competency restoration today: the administration of psychotropic medication to control the defendant's symptoms and participation in what is often called legal education, classes that emphasize intensive repetition of basic facts about the court system—including what the difference is between a misdemeanor and a felony or what a jury does.

It is the kind of rote memorization that a reasonably intelligent four-year-old could be taught to parrot back, whether or not she actually understood the concepts behind it. It's not unlike the way one might cram for the written portion of the driver's license test, committing to memory just long enough to pass the exam such facts as how many feet away from a fire hydrant to park or how long to stop at a stop sign.

Perlin told me about a competency-restoration course he observed in Oklahoma some years ago. The class was held in an old schoolroom, where the prisoners—adult men—sat at elementary-school desks while the hospital instructor drilled them over and over on the role of various courtroom figures, including the judge, the prosecutor, and the defense attorney. The instructor held up a diagram of a courtroom and did what Perlin described as a call and response: "Who sits here? The judge. Who? The judge." Practice questions from a curriculum used in Virginia include things such as "tell me what the defense attorney's job is." Or "tell me how you should behave in court during your trial."[16] Many programs use movies such as *My Cousin Vinny* or television courtroom dramas such as *Law & Order* to help the patients understand how the justice system works.

One of the more absurd, and expensive, examples comes from Florida, which spends about $53,000 per defendant, some $50 million per year, to keep nonviolent felony defendants in state hospitals while they are restored to competency. As in other states, patients there participate in mock trials and watch *Law & Order* reruns.[17]

Less typically, Florida developed a mock game show that's supposed to introduce patients to different parts of the system. The production quality is 1980s-era open-access cable television: the set includes a large cardboard triangle outlined in small white Christmas lights, an amateurish approximation of the *Wheel of Fortune*, or the wall of screens on *Jeopardy*. There's even a cheesy game-show–style soundtrack. The "host" appears on the set dressed in a gray suit. "Welcome to Trial and Error, the game show that helps you achieve competency to proceed," he says, in a deadpan imitation of Alex Trebek or Bob Barker. "Today our categories are: courtroom personnel, plea options, witnesses, appropriate courtroom behavior, legal status and rights. Let's get right to it."[18] Another "episode" features a large *Wheel of Fortune*–style spinner. When the "contestant" correctly tells the host the penalty for a first-degree felony, he congratulates her heartily: "Congratulations, Miss Faust, you are now considered competent to return to court and face your charges." In reality, a mental health professional would have to administer a competency exam; this is not even remotely how a defendant would be found competent.

"The way we spend money now is ludicrous," said Steve Leifman, a judge from Miami-Dade County who has spent fifteen years working to reform the way mental illness is handled in the criminal justice system. "Our emphasis should be on recovery and community reintegration rather than memorizing facts about the justice system."[19] As Leifman points out, states spend enormous sums of money in what is effectively a charade to treat people's mental illnesses. Besides being disingenuous, it is a missed opportunity: here is a literally captive audience, potentially motivated to engage in treatment, and instead we have them watching *Law & Order* reruns so that they can correctly identify the judge in a diagram of a courtroom. (Certainly, many people, sane or not and facing charges or not, could use a refresher course on how the criminal justice system works. As mental health care, however, this seems like a questionable investment.)

Restoration typically takes place in state psychiatric hospitals, where a certain number of beds are reserved for forensic patients, a category that includes people in need of exams to evaluate their competency and those in need of restoration treatment. Because of this, the whole system of competency evaluation and restoration becomes part of the complex interplay between the public mental health care system and the criminal justice system. People who need to be evaluated for competency or restored to competency fill many of the available forensic beds. The average length of stay for competency-related issues is six months. Often it's longer. The 1972 US Supreme Court case *Jackson v. Indiana* ruled that defendants can be held for only a "reasonable period of time" but left it up to the individual states to define what was reasonable. Twenty states define *reasonable* as a year or less because research has shown that most people will be restored in six months to a year and that trying to treat beyond that is pointless. Others use criteria such as the maximum sentence for the alleged offense; some don't specify how long a person can be held. In some states, including New York, if a defendant in a misdemeanor case is found incompetent to stand trial, the case is automatically dismissed. On the one hand, this is a good thing because it gets the person out of the criminal justice system and saves both time and money, but it also means that the person misses out on any mental health care that might have been provided as part of a restoration-to-competency program.

Lengthy hospital stays for competency restoration mean that turnover in the state hospitals is very slow. With very few spots to begin with, it creates a shortage of hospital beds that in turn creates a backlog of people sitting in jail waiting for a hospital bed. For example, every month of 2015 saw nearly four hundred prisoners in California jails waiting for a place in a competency-restoration program. In Los Angeles County, the average wait time was more than two months.[20] (The county has recently begun experimenting with alternative models, including an in-house program in the LA County Jail.) For the people who are waiting, their cases are put on hold until they have been restored to competency or are found to be "unrestorable," and then the case could be dismissed, or they could be civilly committed to a hospital.

The ACLU filed a lawsuit in 2015 on behalf of eleven Pennsylvania prisoners who said they had been held in jail for months, and in some cases years, while they waited to be sent to a hospital for restoration. A quick look at Pennsylvania's mental health services makes clear why there is a capacity problem. Pennsylvania has two state hospitals with a total of just under 200 forensic beds. At any given time, there are an additional 220 people *waiting* for those beds.[21] A settlement reached in 2016 promised to create 120 additional treatment slots and to evaluate every person on the waiting list or involved in the forensic system to make sure that he or she is getting an appropriate level of care.[22]

Also in 2015, a federal judge ordered Washington State to follow state law, which requires that every prisoner sent for an exam to evaluate competency to stand trial receive one within seven days.[23] The state is fined $500 per day for any prisoner who waits longer than seven days for in-hospital services and $1,000 per day for delays longer than fourteen days. So far, according to the ACLU of Washington, which has been litigating the issue, the state has paid around $17 million in such fines and is still not in compliance. Meanwhile, counties are paying to house all of these people in jail who are awaiting hospital beds. Over a six-month period, a report by the state behavioral health agency showed, jails spent $1.7 million to house just those defendants who were waiting to be evaluated and another $1.4 million to house those waiting to be restored to competency.[24] There have also been lawsuits over wait times in other states, including Oregon and Arkansas, and cases are pending in California, Utah, and elsewhere.

Sometimes the delay is so long that it effectively cancels the case. In Oklahoma I heard about a defendant who had sat in jail for so long waiting to go to the hospital that he was finally released without ever getting either treated or tried: he ended up serving what would have been the maximum sentence for his crime without ever making it to the hospital, let alone to trial. When I tracked down his attorney to get more details on the story, he told me that he had so many clients who fit that description that he didn't know which one I meant.

For defendants whose cases don't time out in this way, though, court delays sometimes create a new set of problems. Once a person is found competent, he is sent back to jail to wait for his case to continue. But that can take awhile because court cases proceed slowly: there are often endless hearings and scheduling complications. Meanwhile, because jails are what is known as psychotogenic—that is, psychosis-inducing—environments and mental health care there, as we have seen, is often minimal, people sometimes decompensate (deteriorate psychologically) while waiting for the case to get resolved. If it gets so bad that the defendant becomes incompetent to stand trial again, he has to be sent back to the hospital for another round of evaluation and treatment, and the cycle begins again, sometimes dragging on for years.

AS A WAY TO MANAGE both the extraordinary wait times and the excessive costs, jurisdictions have begun experimenting with alternatives to the more traditional hospital setups: inpatient programs inside of jails and outpatient programs in communities. Started in 2011, the program I visited in the Fulton County Jail in Atlanta is an example of the former, though unlike many other jail-based programs, this one is not run by an outside contractor. Instead, it is a collaboration with the Psychiatry Department at Emory University's medical school, which means the program is overseen by a psychiatry professor there, and the clinicians, both the treating psychiatrists and the ones who do the competency testing, are part of the school's forensic psychiatry program.

In charge of the program is Victoria Roberts, a short woman with frosted blond hair who spent most of her career working at Georgia Regional, the state hospital in Atlanta. She was getting ready to retire when Emory's head of psychiatry invited her to take over this new project. It was a logical transition because of the overlap between the hospital population and the jail one. Often, she told me, she'll be walking through the intake area of the jail when she hears new arrivals calling out to her "Georgia Regional! Georgia Regional!" "It's the cycle," she said. "We're connected from in here, over there, forever. We recycle." That understanding is incentive for her to use the time she has with these men to do as much as possible, so her program offers more classes than many. In addition to things like legal education, the men in her program are offered classes in current events and literacy: "That's what we're really trying to do, interrupt this cycle. We try to do as much as we can while they're here, so when they do get out, [they won't come back]."

Some critics see treatment in jail for the purpose of restoration to competency as a contradiction in terms, just like treatment on a jail mental health unit. "It's virtually impossible to do meaningful psychotherapy in a jail context," said Michael Perlin, the mental disability law expert. But Roberts unabashedly uses the fact that it's a jail to her advantage: "We do a lot of things here that you can't do in a hospital. We have more control because it's a jail. We can do a little more coercion to come to groups. In the hospital, you can't cross a certain line because it's not ethical. In jail, they're supposed to do what we say. We try to do it in a way that supports independence. We actually will say 'If you don't go to groups, you're not going to get better [enough] for Ms. Roberts to work on your case to get to trial.'"

This is part of what worries critics of in-jail restoration programs. In Washington State the ACLU affiliate filed a lawsuit to block prisoners with mental illness in jails around the state from being sent to two alternative restoration programs, saying in part that mental health care should be provided in a hospital environment—where patients wear street clothes, can come in and out of their rooms at will, and have the full range of therapeutic programming.

Medically, the main difference between this and the restoration program in the state hospital is that the jail program does not medicate over objection. Except in certain emergency circumstances, forcing somebody to take medication when he doesn't want to requires a hearing before a judge, something with which few jails are willing to deal.

Instead, a patient who refuses medication will usually be transferred to the hospital, which is more equipped to handle such cases. (Some even have courtrooms inside the hospital to accommodate such hearings.) A 2003 Supreme Court ruling further complicated matters: it is now under extremely limited circumstances that a person may be forcibly medicated *only* to restore him to competency.

Days on the Fulton County Unit are heavily programmed. In addition to the various classes, there's substance use counseling, and each participant is assigned a counselor whom he sees once or twice a week; it's supposed to be more for legal issues than for psychiatric ones, "but of course things come out," Roberts said. They do mock trials once a month; a talent show, which she says promotes long-term thinking and planning skills; and celebrate holidays, from St. Patrick's Day to Christmas, designed in part to keep people oriented to the date and time of year. (Even for people without cognitive issues, jails are disorienting places: there's little access to daylight, lights may stay on all night, and the hours for things like meals and medication often have little to do with the chronological time.)

The walls of the unit are covered with laminated posters designed to reinforce what the participants are learning: "What does it take to be competent to stand trial?" (know that you are being charged with a crime, understand what your charges are, know how the court system works, etc.). Another lists the characters in a courtroom: the judge (the "Boss" of the courtroom), witnesses, the jury. Other walls have inspirational posters with messages like "Self-Control Is Knowing You Can but Deciding You Won't" and "If You Tell the Truth, You Don't Have to Remember What You Said."

Here, too, they use *Law & Order* and games: Roberts says it's useful to "immerse [the patients] in the language," for the same concepts play out in the show as in the real-life courtroom. After a break, another teacher, Ms. Brown, a woman in a blue knit beret and black leather jacket, organizes a game of bingo to review material from legal ed. It was a stark reminder of the difficulty, or maybe futility, of what they are trying to do. "What does it take to be competent?" Brown asks.

A man raises his hand. "I'm not," he volunteers.

Brown passes out laminated bingo cards and small squares of construction paper in lieu of chips and announces the beginning of the game. "Today we are reviewing some of the basic terms," she says. A white man with greasy hair and a patchy beard asks, "Is this game called limbo, not bingo?" Another man, the one who asked earlier about how to get competent, raises his hand and riffs off his classmate's question: "How do you arbitrate legal limbo?" Brown ignores them both and reads a clue: "A lawyer against you. He or she is paid to prosecute you."

"District attorney," a white man with a neat haircut and thick beard calls out.

"You admit what you were accused of doing."

"Guilty," somebody calls out.

Correct answers win the men candy, a choice of a Jolly Rancher or a Tootsie Roll, selected out of a plastic bag on Brown's desk. As I watched these men in class that day, the magnitude of the challenge really hit home for me. A few of them were able to engage fully and appropriately, answering questions and having relevant discussions. (Two of those had just been found competent.) Others were able to participate sporadically but had trouble sustaining interest and attention. And then there were those who were very much in their own worlds: one man sucked his thumb and rocked back and forth through most of the class. Another stared fiercely into space and periodically jumped up to punch or kick at invisible foes. Hopefully, all of them will eventually reach the level of the first group.

But here is the sad part: for many of these men, this may be the best mental health care they get. If Roberts succeeds and her patients are restored to competency, they will either be sent to prison, where treatment is likely to be as minimal as it is in other parts of the Fulton County Jail, or they will be released back to the streets, where the prospects are at least as bleak.

PART III

BREAKING FREE: TOWARD A BETTER WAY

9

Inside Out

THERE ARE TWO STATE HOSPITALS left in Oklahoma. One, Griffin Memorial Hospital, has 120 beds. It sits on what remains of the campus of the old Central State Hospital, whose elaborate neoclassical and Gothic red-brick buildings once dominated the town of Norman.[1] The other public hospital, officially called Oklahoma Forensic Center though widely known as Vinita, after its location in a town in the northeast corner of the state, has 200 beds. The patients at Griffin Memorial are civilians, referred there by psychiatrists and community health clinics, emergency-room doctors, and crisis centers because their mental illness requires longer-term inpatient treatment. On the other hand, the patients housed at Vinita all come from the same place, the criminal justice system, and have been sent to Vinita for one of several reasons: they need to be evaluated for competency to stand trial or to be restored to competency, or they have been found not guilty by reason of insanity.

Despite their different constituencies, Griffin and Vinita are very much health care facilities. "It's more secure than other psychiatric hospitals, and it has to be because of the population we serve," the spokesman for the state's mental health agency said of the forensic center. "But it's a hospital....The people who work here are mental health professionals."[2] And like Griffin, Vinita has a perpetual waiting list.

It might seem natural to divide the universe of mental illness—and mental health care—along the tidy line that seems to distinguish the populations of Griffin and Vinita: the good guys and the bad guys. The good guys are the ones in the outside world who may be seriously sick but do not present any obvious danger to their communities, where they live and get medical care. The bad guys are the ones who do pose a threat to society, who commit crimes and are locked up, and who access treatment through the criminal justice system.

Even setting aside the false—and oversimplified—assumption that everybody who ends up in the criminal justice system is "bad," it is highly misleading to draw a clear line between the two populations. It is true that many people with a mental illness never commit a crime, just as many people convicted of a crime don't have a mental illness. But it is crucial to understand that people with mental illness inside the criminal justice system and those outside it very often end up in the same treatment universe. Somebody who is a patient at Griffin Memorial this year might be a patient at Vinita next year, or vice versa. And in showing the many possible pathways into a civilian or a criminal justice mental health care facility, the two hospitals underscore a larger truth: just as there is no single cause for the crisis of people with mental illness in the criminal justice system—a crisis that must be properly understood as a public health crisis that goes well beyond jails and prisons—there is also no single fix.

To see why people like Bryan Sanderson or Jason Echevarria are so easily pushed into the criminal justice system, it's important to understand how community institutions that should be helping them—health care services, first responders, and courts—so often end up abetting this process. We also make it incredibly difficult for a person with mental illness, once out of a correctional facility, to stay out. In exploring these issues it's also possible to see some ways that our community institutions themselves might be reenvisioned and reoriented toward prevention and preemption: getting care to the most vulnerable before the criminal justice system takes them.

As NOTED EARLIER, DISCUSSIONS ABOUT the state of mental health care in the United States today often begin with a false narrative of causation, one that starts with the closing of state psychiatric hospitals and ends with the dramatic expansion of prison populations. What is true is that the landscape of mental health care has changed dramatically since the 1950s. We've gone from a situation with large numbers of people living long-term in institutions to one in which inpatient care has become increasingly rare.[3] The makeup of mental health care providers also changed significantly: today there is a far wider range of clinicians, including social workers, therapists, counselors, and psychologists, in addition to psychiatrists. Nonetheless, when you talk to people on the ground, it is clear that it is extremely difficult to access mental health care, either as an outpatient in the community or as an inpatient in a hospital.

All this has happened while, as has been shown, the population of incarcerated people with mental illness has continued to grow relentlessly. Yet there are many problems with the assumption that the one accounts for the other. Even if we had as many inpatient beds as we did before there might still be large numbers of people with mental illness in jails and prisons.

What is clear is that we do not need *all* of those beds we used to have. Improvements in medication and new understandings about where people with mental illness can and should live mean that for the vast majority long-term institutionalization is a largely outdated approach to effective treatment. In 2015, around 25 percent of all people with mental illness received treatment on an outpatient basis; just under 4 percent were treated as inpatients. But it is also clear that there is not enough mental health care available. As many as half received no treatment at all. Among people with serious mental illness, about 43 percent received treatment as outpatients, and 8 percent received treatments as inpatients; about 30 percent received no treatment at all. (Some people received both inpatient and outpatient treatment.)[4]

There is still a small population who could benefit from some form of long-term hospitalization. In a controversial article that appeared in the *Journal of the American Medical Association* in 2015, medical ethicist Ezekiel Emanuel, along with two colleagues, argued for the return of long-term care for people with mental illness. The article's provocative subtitle, "Bring Back the Asylum," obscured the authors' more critical point: that for some people with mental illness, we need to reconsider that kind of long-term care: "For persons with severe and treatment-resistant psychotic disorders, who are too unstable or unsafe for community-based treatment, the choice is between the prison-homelessness-acute hospitalization-prison cycle or long-term psychiatric institutionalization. The financially sensible and morally appropriate way forward includes a return to psychiatric asylums that are safe, modern, and humane."[5] I have spoken with a number of psychiatrists and others who agree that for a tiny population of people with extremely severe mental illness, some kind of humane and therapeutic long-term care would be the best outcome.

For most people with mental illness, however, the answer is both less dramatic and more complicated. For one thing, many communities have an acute shortage of outpatient mental health care, a shortfall that continues to get worse. In 2012 Texas had nearly ten thousand people on the waiting list for intensive outpatient treatment in public care centers, a 642 percent increase in demand over what it was less than a decade earlier.[6] As with the people in California's prisons who got sicker while they waited for treatment, when it isn't possible to get outpatient care, people may get sicker, to the point that they require inpatient care. It is here that the lack of beds can lead to crisis situations. Sometimes, the shortage is complicated by rules that hamper access to care or by simple dysfunction in its operation. It was a combination of those that caused a crisis in 2013, when Virginia State Senator Creigh Deeds's son, Gus, severely ill with bipolar disorder, became psychotic. The elder Deeds tried to have Gus involuntarily committed, but Virginia state law allows a patient to be held for only a certain number of hours while trying to find inpatient placement. When the agency responsible for finding the younger Deeds a bed failed to do so within the legally permitted time, Gus was released. He came home and stabbed his father nearly to death before killing himself. Creigh Deeds filed a lawsuit in 2016, alleging that the state had ignored warnings from its oversight board that its mental health care system was in disarray and that failure to fix it would have serious consequences for people with mental illness.[7]

Not all such stories end as tragically. Sometimes the person unable to find treatment or with treatment that is insufficient winds up instead in the criminal justice system after doing something that gets him arrested. A darker irony in this cycle is that all too often the shortage of inpatient hospital beds for civilians with mental illness is caused in part by the criminal justice system's own demands for beds in these same institutions: in many states, much of the remaining inventory of beds has been reserved for forensic (criminal) patients, at the expense of civilian ones.

Numerous states report that a large percentage of patients in state hospitals today comprises people who have been found incompetent to stand trial and have been sent to those institutions by the courts to be restored to sanity.[8] In Virginia, about *a third* of public inpatient psychiatric beds in 2011 were occupied by forensic patients.[9] *More than half* of Texas's 2,300 state beds are reserved for forensic patients, leaving only about 1,100 for patients who come through civil channels.[10] In Colorado the number of patients being evaluated for competency at one hospital increased an astonishing 500 percent between 2004 and 2014. In that time the average number of forensic patients went from 20 percent of the hospital's inpatient population to 60 percent, which meant far fewer beds available for civil patients.[11]

In other words, the criminal justice system is itself increasingly responsible for the shortage of community care that is sending more people with mental illness to jail and prison. As in other areas of health care spending, much of this comes down to money. The struggle over who pays for what, particularly in regard to people within the criminal justice system who need treatment, is long-standing. As a result of the US Supreme Court case *Estelle v. Gamble*, the payment for prisoner medical care must come, in the case of jails, out of the county corrections budget, and in the case of prisons, out of the state corrections budget.

In most places, though, if a prisoner is transferred to the state hospital, it is either Medicaid or the state mental health agency that picks up the tab. Sending an incarcerated person out for restoration or even just for intensive treatment means that the cost of his care now comes out of the state mental health budget instead of the state corrections budget. That adds up. In Louisiana, Maryland, Oregon, and Ohio, for example, at least *half* of state spending on mental health goes to forensic services. Although allowing correctional facilities to save money, this leaves states with ever less money to spend on treating people in the community.

But what about treatment before a person gets to the point of requiring inpatient care? What are states doing to keep people out of the hospital in the first place? Just over a fifth of state prisoners with a mental illness received no treatment in the year before their arrest, and less than a quarter of people in jail had, according to a 2006 study from the US Bureau of Justice Statistics.[12] Consider Oklahoma, a state with some of the highest rates of mental illness and some of the lowest per capita spending on mental health care. It also has one of the highest incarceration rates—*the* highest among women—in the country.

What I found was that Oklahoma is a dreadful place to seek treatment for mental illness. There are long waits for treatment: one man I spoke to described bringing his severely depressed son to the hospital for evaluation only to be told to come back two months later for an initial evaluation. Another woman told me about her stepdaughter who was turned away from the emergency room because she was not suicidal "enough" to be admitted. The lack of access to mental health care stands in stark contrast to the incredible access to the state's well-funded tobacco-cessation program. The ads for that are everywhere—on bus stop benches, highway billboards, and pamphlets in government offices: *No judgments. Just help.* Decide to stop smoking—or even just *contemplate* it—in Oklahoma, and there's a world of help out there for the asking, twenty-four hours per day, seven days per week: regular phone calls with a Quit Coach™ and nicotine patches, gum, or lozenges. Encouraging e-mails. Even text messages with "fun games to take your mind off cravings." And it's all free.

Generously funded by a settlement reached with the big tobacco companies years ago, the sheer range of what's available to smokers who are trying to quit is impressive. It's not just the size of Oklahoma's smoking program, although it's certainly more visible than what I have seen elsewhere. The program is also a tangible and striking reminder of what's possible when a public health issue is made a top priority. The trouble is that mental illness has rarely been seen as a top priority. In Oklahoma the government has consistently chosen to fund other things, including an enormous criminal justice system. Meanwhile, the state's per capita spending on mental health care is half the national average—$53 in Oklahoma versus $105 nationally.[13]

The funding issue has had a drastic effect on the ability of communities to provide treatment for sick people. "We really have to ration who gets what," Randy Tate, executive director of one of the nonprofit organizations that runs mental health care centers in the state, told me. The rationing occurs at every level of care, from the clinics his organization runs to the single remaining state hospital, from getting into group therapy to seeing a psychiatrist. He said that his clinics have twice as much demand as capacity; other organizations I spoke to report being similarly overburdened. In fact, public clinics across Oklahoma turn away so many people with mental illness each year that the state has stopped keeping track, calling it a bureaucratic burden. Chronic underfunding becomes a self-perpetuating problem, Mental Health Commissioner Terri White told the *Oklahoman* newspaper: "When we have a system that's underfunded and those people who are most ill are who receive services, the bulk of our money is tied up in community and inpatient care, which leaves very little money for prevention."[14]

As in other states, mental health care in Oklahoma comes from a hodgepodge of sources: public clinics, nonprofit care providers, outpatient clinics in general hospitals, and inpatient care in psychiatric units of general hospitals, public psychiatric hospitals, and short-term acute-crisis clinics. It's a confusing and far from systematic array of providers, one that can be especially hard for people with mental illness to navigate.[15] For those who get lost, the criminal justice system serves as a backstop.

And it's easy to get lost. Not only are the various treatment options challenging to access; in most places they are also so overstretched that only the most critically ill patients can obtain care. In its 2016 budget request, the state mental health department acknowledged that as money has been repeatedly squeezed from the state budget, "Services simply do not exist until [the patient's] disease progresses to a point that it becomes a crisis."[16]

Oklahoma's situation may be particularly dire, but it is far from alone. In 2017 the National Council for Behavioral Health, a group that represents mental health and addiction treatment providers, described similar conditions in many regions of the country. The report, which looks specifically at the shortage of psychiatrists, describes widespread rationing of services to only the sickest people in the system, which leaves people with mild to moderate illness little or no access to care. Instead, patients are left to rely on stopgap measures like appointments with nurses or case managers and extended prescriptions. When they do get to see a psychiatrist, patients often face shortened treatment sessions.[17] Besides causing more immediate problems, mental illness that is left untreated often gets worse and becomes harder to bring under control.

Each year, one in five Americans have a diagnosable mental illness; one in 25 have a serious impairment. Yet around half get no treatment at all; of those who get no treatment, roughly half say it's because they can't afford it.[18] For many people with mental illness, the Affordable Care Act, which mandated mental health coverage, has offered them access to behavioral health care for the first time. Before the ACA, little mental health care was covered by insurance anyway, so outside of the public system, people either paid out of pocket or did without. Thirty states and DC expanded Medicaid. This has been especially important for those in the criminal justice system because it expanded eligibility for single young people, a population that mostly was not covered before. (Oklahoma did not take the expansion.) Ironically, the Medicaid expansion and the new parity between mental and physical health care provided by the ACA and a 2010 federal law that increased access have in some ways made the shortage of community-based mental health care more acute.[19] With more people eligible for coverage, more have sought treatment, but the number of mental health care professionals has not increased.

Although they may have gotten worse in recent years, the severe shortcomings of community-based mental health care have long been known. Since at least the 1990s, numerous government commissions and other groups have done studies outlining the challenges faced by the mental health care system and proposing solutions to them. In 2002 a mental health care commission appointed by President George W. Bush issued a warning: "It is becoming clear that the mental health services system does not adequately serve millions of people who need care.... The system is fragmented and in disarray...from underlying structural, financing, and organizational problems.... The system's failings lead to unnecessary and costly disability, homelessness, school failure, and incarceration."[20]

A dozen years later, the situation had hardly changed. "We have replaced the hospital bed with the jail cell, the homeless shelter and the coffin," Pennsylvania Representative Tim Murphy told *USA Today* in 2014.[21]

What should a better mental health care system look like? People should have timely access to treatment at a range of sites, a 2009 report from advocacy group NAMI stated: "state hospitals, short-term acute inpatient and intermediate care facilities, crisis services, outpatient and community-based services and independent living options." Regardless of ability to pay, the report also said, any system must include access to medication, long-term care treatment, supportive housing, supported employment, and—crucially—jail diversion.[22]

Unlike other areas of the health care economy, most spending on mental health services comes from public sources: Medicaid and Medicare, state and local governments, and federal grants.[23] That's partly because people with mental illness are more likely to be disabled, unemployed, or employed in low-wage, low-skill jobs that do not provide health insurance. That leaves mental health care extremely vulnerable to changes in states' financial health, as became evident in the years after the 2008 financial crash. Between 2009 and 2011, states cut $1.8 billion from their mental health budgets. California alone cut more than $580 million, New York more than $130 million.[24] In practice, that has meant reductions in everything from prescriptions to clinics to inpatient hospitalization.

However, state budgets are only part of the story. Like jails and prisons, civilian clinics and hospitals face a critical shortage of psychiatrists; this is especially serious in rural areas.[25] Some of that is also about money: psychiatrists make considerably less than other specialties; a 2016 survey of physician salaries showed psychiatrists bringing in on average just over $200,000 a year, compared with more than $400,000 for specialties such as orthopedics and cardiology.[26] Even in regions that have enough psychiatrists, their services are out of reach to many. Few psychiatrists are willing to accept Medicaid because the reimbursements are so low.[27] In fact, 40 percent of psychiatrists don't accept any insurance; more than half of states have a critical shortage of psychiatrists who accept it. (The story behind those statistics may be slightly more nuanced; some psychiatrists don't accept insurance in their private practices but also spend some of their time working in community clinics, where insurance is accepted.)

In Oklahoma, services are so limited that a primary task of community mental health care centers is not to determine *what* treatment a person will require but *whether* a person will get treatment at all. Say a person is experiencing some symptoms of mental illness, such as withdrawing, having trouble sleeping, or even having auditory hallucinations. The person comes to the community mental health center, either on his or her own or brought by a family member. An intake specialist triages the person, rating the severity of the illness from one to four, with one being the most sick and four being the least. Because the demand for services is so high, the criteria are tough. To get rated a one or two—the level currently required to access treatment with a psychiatrist—a patient generally has to be either extremely psychotic or actively suicidal.

The shortage is so severe that people who are rated a three or four won't see a psychiatrist or, likely, even be seen at the clinic at all. Instead, the intake specialist generally refers those people out for case management, group therapy, or other less-intensive services. However, even those people frequently face a wait.[28] An Oklahoma statute requires health care providers to see any patient who rates a one or two. But even after weeding out all the threes and fours—broadly defined as people who are not an immediate threat to themselves or others—there are still enough ones and twos left that clinics regularly end up seeing far more patients than their state contracts cover. The two largest agencies that run such clinics—Randy Tate's and another—report that they regularly spend more than a million dollars over budget to provide care to the sickest people in the state.

A case manager may help with housing, employment, and other day-to-day issues, but if the person's condition deteriorates significantly, there's little left to do but for a family member to bring him or her to the emergency room or call the police to do the same. If the emergency room doctors decide the person is sick enough to need stabilizing in an inpatient setting, the answer is often a crisis center—a kind of in-between stopgap solution between treatment in the emergency room and inpatient hospitalization.

I visited one such crisis center in Norman. This one is housed in a cement building on the campus of the old Central State Hospital, a physical manifestation of the shift from long-term institutionalization to community-based care and of the problems that came with that shift. Many patients end up here, one psychiatrist told me, because they run out of medication and their symptoms get worse, "but they can't get into the outpatient clinic for two months [because of overcrowding].... People end up coming [to the crisis center] because they can't wait that long."

The quiet scene in the sunlit dayroom—a foursome playing cards at a heavy wooden table, a couple of men watching television in worn plush armchairs, a woman curled up under a blanket in an adjoining living space—belies the *crisis* aspect of the center. There are forty beds, which makes it, according to Medicaid's definition, a specialized psychiatric facility, and thus ineligible for Medicaid reimbursement. (The Institutions for Mental Diseases, or IMD, exclusion was designed to make states, rather than the federal government, responsible for the funding of long-term institutionalized care. In a time when most inpatient stays for psychiatric care last only a few days, it is a largely outdated, and unnecessarily complicating, rule.) Patients who receive Medicaid—about 30 percent of the agency's crisis patients—are sent to a psychiatric unit at the local hospital, which, with only fifteen beds, is small enough to avoid the Medicaid restriction.

Demand for any space is high. "However many we discharge today, we'll admit tomorrow," one of the center's two full-time psychiatrists told me. Patients may spend days waiting in hospital emergency departments for an available spot here. The state mental health department sends out a daily e-mail to let doctors and other clinicians know how many inpatient crisis beds are available and where. A psychiatrist at another center told me it's not unusual for the e-mail to read "no beds available anywhere in the state." When a bed does open up, there's also no guarantee it'll be anywhere near the patient's home, a point made more absurd in light of the short duration of most stays. I met one woman from a suburb of Oklahoma City whose daughter was sent to a psychiatric hospital more than a hundred miles away in Tulsa, only to be released a few days later.

Being released quickly is the norm. About 75 percent of the patients who come to the crisis center in Norman are subsequently released to outpatient treatment in the community. Coming from a crisis center bumps them to the front of the line for outpatient care, meaning they may be able to access treatment they likely wouldn't have been able to receive before. This kind of perverse incentive is not unique to Oklahoma. In some parts of Virginia, for example, people who have been getting mental health care in jail are also put at the front of the line for community care when they are released. The 25 percent of patients who come to the Norman crisis center and still need further care will be transferred to the "new" Griffin Memorial Hospital just across the way, once they can get in from the waiting list.

Despite the deficiencies, this makes for a relatively efficient process in the short-term. The trouble is, by its very design, it seems to exclude the kind of coherent, sustained treatment that is required to help keep people with mental illness out of jail.

10

The Cycle

WHENEVER EDGAR COLEMAN GOT ARRESTED, his lawyer remembers, he would pretend to be deaf. But it didn't really matter. He had been arrested so often that the entire police force knew who he was. "The officers had his full name and date of birth memorized because they ran into him so frequently," said Chuck Miner, a lieutenant with the University of Minnesota police, whose officers were often the ones doing the arresting. Coleman was *arrested* two hundred times between 1996 and 2012. And that number doesn't count the times when the cops—either university police or officers from the Minneapolis Police Department—just told him to move along or drove him to a homeless shelter downtown.

Coleman grew up in St. Louis and was a Minnesota Vikings draft pick in the 1970s, although he never actually played for the team. He studied psychology and later taught in both high school and college. He developed symptoms of mental illness; family members believed he had schizophrenia. His marriage broke up, he lost his job and his home, and he ended up living on the campus of the University of Minnesota.

UMN is a large, urban campus—more than fifty thousand students—making it an attractive spot for homeless people. "Edgar would find places in buildings to stay at night," Miner remembered. "[We'd regularly] get calls from custodians, faculty, students. We got a fair amount of calls." Coleman may have been trespassing, but he was also remarkably resourceful: "We'd get calls that he was stealing food from a buffet line. The university hosts lots of conferences; he would get in line between attendees and get a plate."

Sometimes, the cops would take him to jail; other times, they would take him to the homeless shelter. He would spend some time in jail or very occasionally in the hospital, but he would always be released quickly, and the cycle would begin again. Nancy Laskaris, the public defender who represented Coleman, said the police response was frustrating: "The university never did anything productive. They just had him arrested." Miner said the officers didn't really have other options: take him to the shelter or jail, or issue a citation. If he failed to respond to the citation, then a warrant was issued, and the next time they found him, they could arrest him.

Coleman is an example of what is known as a hot-spotter or super-utilizer—someone who cycles in and out of jail, often getting rearrested shortly after being released. Although we lack national statistics on the phenomenon, data from metropolitan areas show how widespread it is—and the extent to which it is tied to mental illness. Several cities have found that a large percentage of total arrests come from officers rearresting a small group of people over and over and that a disproportionate number of these super-utilizers have a mental illness, a substance use disorder, or both. In New York in 2013, for example, frequent arrestees were more than twice as likely as others to have serious mental illness, with nearly one in five having such a diagnosis. The frequent arrestees were also far more likely to be prescribed antipsychotic medication in jail, which means, among other things, that they are among the most expensive people to incarcerate. The vast majority of this group also showed significant substance use (97 percent versus 56 percent for regular arrestees).[1] This prevalence of substance use among people with mental illness who end up in jails and prisons is true more generally. Some studies have shown that co-occurring substance use and mental illness are a far higher predictor of rearrest than mental illness alone.[2] Likewise, substance use is one of the predictors for criminal behavior more generally.

Equally striking, most of the charges for which the super-utilizers were arrested were minor: petit larceny and criminal possession of controlled substances in the seventh degree—which means either residue or a small quantity of drug—together accounted for more than half of them. The rest were also low-level misdemeanors, such as criminal trespass in the second degree and turnstile jumping.[3] In New York, if a person charged with a misdemeanor is found incompetent to stand trial, then the case is automatically dismissed, so many of these people were likely released—only to be rearrested on a similar charge soon after.

Disturbingly, we continue to arrest such people for marginal offenses, despite clear evidence that incarceration is likely to make the illness worse. In fact, the practice of repeat arrests is often part of a broader reality faced by many people with mental illness: recurring stints in jails or prisons on the one hand and hospitals or crisis centers on the other. In both cases, intermittent stays in an institution can rupture one of the things that clinicians say is most important in treating mental illness: stability. Regardless of whether a stay is in a hospital, a jail, or a prison, it causes dislocation and instability—time away from the crucial social anchors of job, home, family, and, in the case of imprisonment, often from treatment.

For Edgar Coleman, the cycle of arrest and release ended only in 2012, when he was finally civilly committed to a nursing home elsewhere in the state. He died there in 2014 of a disease apparently unrelated to his mental illness. It's impossible to know if regular treatment and a place to live would have helped Coleman stay off the streets, although evidence increasingly shows that housing is an important stabilizing factor. What is clear is that arresting him over and over failed to keep him away from campus and cost both him and the criminal justice system a great deal of stress and money. Certainly, almost anything would have been better than getting arrested repeatedly while trying to survive on the streets of Minneapolis.

VISITING SOMEBODY AT RIKERS ISLAND Jail in New York City is a tortuous affair. There's the bus ride to the jail; the nervous excitement of the mostly young women, hair and nails carefully done; the babies and small children, scrubbed clean and neatly dressed; the older women carrying plastic bags of clothes and newspapers that will be scrutinized by officers before, hopefully, being handed off to people inside. During the ride, there's often a tense moment when a corrections officer, just starting his shift, gets on the bus at the stop by the parking lot just before the bridge to the island. When the bus reaches its destination, there's a mad rush for the visitors center, which is filled with grimy and battered lockers where people lock everything except their driver's license. (The ride back is usually quieter, with an almost palpable sense of deflation. Often, there are tears from exhausted children and anguished mothers alike.)

After the visitors center comes the interminable security line, which ends in a metal detector so sensitive it's set off by plain wedding bands and bra underwires. The waiting area is invariably full of squirmy toddlers, drug-sniffing German shepherds, and blaring televisions. A battered school bus painted white with grating on the windows takes visitors from the visitors center to the jail itself. The Anna M. Kross Center is the largest of the ten jails on the island and home to Rikers' mental health center. At AMKC, as it is called, visitors walk through another metal detector to yet another room full of battered lockers, where they lock up the key to their first locker—the one back at the visitors center—and anything else that may have made it through the first two rounds of security—say, a sweater or a diaper bag. The key to this second locker is among the very few items that visitors are allowed to bring into the visiting room.

A sign, hand-lettered on a dingy painted cinder-block wall, reminds visitors, among other things, that hands must stay outside of clothing during the visit and that they can be prosecuted for bringing money in. There is a tiny glass-walled room where corrections officers lock up people caught bringing in contraband until they can be properly arrested. I once saw an enormously pregnant woman handcuffed for hours to the hard bench inside; word was she had been caught trying to bring marijuana to her boyfriend.

Beyond the wall is a last search, a pat down this time, and still another waiting room, this one filled only with rows of uncomfortable plastic chairs, a desk for a corrections officer, and the inescapable blaring television that nobody watches. There are no windows, no clock, no watches, and no phones. From here, after a wait that could be five minutes or five hours, people are called into the visitors' room.

This is the excruciating ritual that families of some of Rikers's most seriously ill prisoners have to go through to have a brief face-to-face meeting with a parent, spouse, child, or sibling. AMKC currently houses more than twenty-three hundred prisoners in forty units. Among these are about seven hundred who are in "mental observation" units, a mix of single cells and dorms for those too sick to live in general population. Here, too, is where you'll find the new units that the jail's psychiatrist, Elizabeth Ford, described as part of her idea of Rikers as a hospital.

At AMKC the visiting room has low ceilings and is loud, with all the charm of a high school cafeteria. It was here that I first met Kyle Muhammad, a man with a long history of mental illness who was being held on an assault charge. I was accompanying Muhammad's mother on one of her regular visits to see him. Eula Muhammad and I sat in low plastic chairs, so close to the people next to us that we could have reached out and touched them. Eventually, Muhammad came out in the baggy gray jumpsuit, white socks, and plastic shower slippers that inmates are required to wear for visits. He sat in a chair opposite us, a low round table in between. Corrections officers watched over the noisy room, occasionally intervening to tell people to be quiet or to stop unauthorized physical contact.

Muhammad spoke hesitantly, often seeming to struggle to find the right word. His speech was peppered with the regular interjection of "What do you call it?" "My mother is my greatest support," he told me, over the din. She was, as far as I could tell, his only support; his daughters, his siblings, and his few friends had not visited him in the nearly two years he had been in jail. He likes to read but said that he hadn't been to the Rikers library in months. He saw a psychiatrist periodically, but he never saw the same doctor twice, and visits lasted only a few minutes. When the officers called that time was up, Muhammad thanked us both for the visit and walked away.

KYLE MUHAMMAD'S LIFE HAS BEEN marked almost equally by the criminal justice system and the mental health care system. Diagnosed years ago with schizophrenia, he has struggled for decades to build a stable life for himself. By my best count, he's been hospitalized more times than he's been arrested, although he's spent more *time* cumulatively in correctional facilities, a record that says much about our policy priorities for people with mental illness.

He's a soft-spoken man who always tries hard. His goals for himself are fairly conventional: a steady job, an apartment, a partner. Yet time and again, he is thwarted by some combination of his disease and his entanglements with the law. His periodic substance use, common among people with mental illness, complicates things further. Looking at his personal history, one gets the impression that every time he finds some stability in his life—a job, an apartment, a community-based treatment program that works—his illness is once again neglected or he has a run-in with the law, and he ends up in the hospital or jail—or both.

Eula Muhammad carries a photograph of Kyle in her wallet. It's one of his school pictures, maybe two inches by three inches, with a plain background. He was probably fifteen, thin, his white T-shirt hanging off his body, and he's smiling, the beginnings of a mustache on his upper lip. It was soon after that picture was taken that his behavior turned from what seemed like the merely rebellious—smoking marijuana, missing curfew, playing hooky—to the bizarre. There was the youth baseball game where he refused to bat. The time when he claimed to be a member of the Freemasons. The day he went around a McDonald's dumping other people's food on the floor. His mother was baffled. But kids are strange sometimes, she figured. And she was busy, working and going to school full time while raising four kids on her own. Then one day Muhammad told her he could use his mind to make people get off the subway. Now she was really concerned.

The part of the city where they lived was on the southern tip of Brooklyn; their station was the last stop for several different subway lines. Of course people would be getting off the train there—everyone had to. She took a ride with him, though, "just to see what was going on," and realized that her son was right, in a way. He couldn't sit still, and he was laughing bizarrely. Other passengers were, indeed, getting off the train. It just wasn't for the reason Kyle had imagined. She took him to the hospital, a public one near their apartment. The doctor said he had bipolar disorder and sent him home with some pills. He didn't get better, and within a few days he ended up back in the hospital. From that time on, he was on and off his medication and in and out of the hospital. His diagnosis was eventually changed, years later, to schizoaffective disorder, but even with the proper medication, the cycle continued, with varying degrees of frequency.

TODAY, KYLE MUHAMMAD IS IN his mid-fifties, although he could pass for a decade younger. He's African American, six feet tall, and two-hundred-something pounds. He's clean-shaven and always has a fresh haircut, one of those people who manages to look tidy even in a tracksuit or jeans. He's a fan of Burger King and diners, where he usually orders a cheeseburger and a Coca-Cola. He smokes—an old habit he picked up again after his most recent stint in jail; when he's short on money, he'll buy "loosies" (single cigarettes) or bum them from smokers in the street. He has two daughters, one a teenager and one in her twenties, from relationships with two different women. Since getting out of jail the last time, he has been working on building relationships with both of his children. The younger one, especially, he sees regularly, taking her to movies and helping her with homework.

In high school he got put into special education classes because of his mental illness, but by his own account he later managed to earn a bachelor's degree in psychology. (The school would not confirm it.) He speaks slowly, with a slightly flat affect that you might not notice in a single, casual encounter; sometimes he's more animated. Conversations with him can feel like a struggle; he often answers questions with short and sometimes brusque-sounding responses. Other times, though, he'll call or text—sometimes at odd hours—and just want to chat. Recently, he called me out of the blue to thank me for supporting his mother while he was locked up. (While I was doing research for this book, I accompanied her to his multiple court appearances and on her many visits to see him at Rikers as well.)

He does know that he's sick: "I will have to be on [medication] for the rest of my life," he told me once when I was visiting him in jail. "It's a fine line between sanity and insanity. It's a disease." He doesn't always recognize that, though. Over the years, he has periodically quit taking his medication, a decision that almost always ends badly. He's worked on and off as an EMT, a school-bus driver, and a janitor, among other things. But his repeated hospitalizations and incarcerations have made it hard for him to hold a job for very long. Each time he gets out, he has to start over again. And both mental illness and a criminal history carry stigmas that make it hard to explain gaps in employment or housing history when applying for a job or a new lease.

Because of his illness, Muhammad has relied on Social Security Disability Insurance (SSDI) for years. Still, his mother says he's rarely without a job for long, and he's always looking for the next gig or educational opportunity. Sometimes it's hard to tell with him what's wishful or possibly grandiose thinking and what's more realistic, although he's nothing if not ambitious. When he was in prison, he wrote a book of poems that he later self-published and that is available on Amazon.[4] Since getting out of jail most recently, he's been pursuing a certificate from a theological seminary. And, after some trouble finding a regular job, he took one as a caseworker for people with mental illness. He's told me he thinks he could make a living as an author, an inspirational speaker, and a professor.

His illness has cost him relationships and apartments. He doesn't talk about it much, but especially after two years in jail, he has few friends. His social circle consists mostly of his mother, his daughters, his brother, and his sisters. Shortly before he was jailed the last time, he gave up the apartment he was sharing with another man with mental illness. Muhammad has told me variously that the man was using drugs and that he needed to leave in order to stay sober, and that when he starts decompensating, he makes peculiar or sometimes poor choices, giving away all his belongings, for example, or giving up an apartment to move in with a girlfriend, only to change his mind a few days later. Other times, he's lost coveted spots in supportive housing because the amount of time he was made to stay in the hospital or jail exceeded the time he was allowed to be away and still keep the benefit.

BY MY BEST COUNT, THE police have picked up Muhammad at least eighteen times in the thirty-five years or so since he was first diagnosed. Mathematically, that's an average of about once every other year. In reality, the arrests ebb and flow with the state of his disease, so there are good years, when he isn't arrested at all, and there are not-so-good years, when he is picked up three times or more.

On at least two of these occasions, Muhammad was so obviously sick that when the police found him, they took him straight to the hospital. More often, however, he was arrested and booked for low-level misdemeanors: there were a couple of petit larceny charges and a couple of quality-of-life crimes, like jumping the turnstile and criminal trespass, a charge that can be leveled simply for lingering in the hallway of an apartment building or in front of a store when a cop thinks you shouldn't be. Once, Muhammad was picked up for selling cigarettes illegally.

There were also more serious crimes. He mugged somebody in New Jersey in the mid-1990s, for which he was given six months of probation and ordered to get a mental health evaluation and counseling.

Then there was the bank robbery. He was thirty-seven. It happened when he was working as a school-bus driver and living with a roommate. At the time, he had been managing his illness relatively well; he was on medication, and it had been five years since the last time he'd ended up in the hospital or been arrested. Then sometime around July 2000, he quit taking his medication. Six months later, he started decompensating. Then late one morning in early March 2001, he walked into a branch of the Fleet Bank in Queens. He handed the teller a note demanding money. He was unarmed but indicated that he had a gun. She gave him the money he had asked for, and as soon as he turned to leave, she called the police.

He was too out of it to notice, but he and the teller knew each other. Until two weeks earlier, Muhammad had driven the school bus that her child rode to school every day. Muhammad didn't get very far after the robbery. He was standing on the sidewalk out in front of the bank when the police showed up; a local newspaper reported that another officer had already noted the suspicious-looking man. According to the police report, Muhammad laughed when the money fell out of his shirt where he had hidden it. They arrested him, charging him with bank robbery, possession of stolen property, and possession of a controlled substance because the police also found cocaine on him.

After he was arrested, the judge ordered him to undergo a 730 exam—what competency exams are called in New York, after article 730 of New York's Criminal Procedure Law. (The number has been used in a number of rap songs to mean "insane.") Muhammad was given medication and found fit to stand trial. He took a plea bargain for two and a half to five years in prison and was sent upstate to Sing Sing. There he was housed in the Residential Crisis Treatment Program, a twenty-two-bed unit for prisoners who are believed to be a danger to themselves or others or who otherwise appear to need serious psychiatric help. For several months before he was released, he lived on another special unit for prisoners with mental illness, one designed to help with reentry into society. In all, he was locked up for about two years. Through all of it, he was ostensibly being treated for his disease.

Nonetheless, when he got out, doctors felt that he was sick enough to be discharged directly into a state-run psychiatric facility on Staten Island where he had been frequently before his arrest; it was the seventh time he had been admitted there in eight years. This time, Muhammad stayed at the facility for six months; when the hospital eventually discharged him, he was moved to a supportive housing program in Manhattan. He spent the next few years in and out of the emergency room and on and off his medication.

For the next few years, Muhammad was relatively stable. Then in 2012, he went to his psychiatrist and complained that the lithium he had been taking for several years made him feel like his chest was being crushed. He quit taking it. (I was unable to obtain the records from the clinic where he had been a patient at this time. According to both Muhammad and his mother, he told the doctor he was going off the drug, and the doctor agreed.) Six months later, he started getting paranoid—"It's like walking on eggshells," his mother said. "You have to watch what you say"—and very aggressive. He lost a great deal of weight and started giving away his belongings. He's described this behavior to me and says he's aware of it and is not sure why he does it. Even as he's doing it, he knows it's bizarre, but he can't help it.

It is agonizing to watch somebody decompensate and to know there's little to do about it. Because Muhammad is an adult, he can't be hospitalized against his will unless his mother can prove that he is a danger to himself or others, which is no easy task. And with Muhammad's history of arrests, it's not just a question of trying to get him into a treatment program; it's a race to see if she can make him get psychiatric help before he does something that gets him arrested again.

THERE HAVE LONG BEEN LAWS governing involuntary commitment. When Eastern State Hospital was built in Williamsburg, Virginia, a panel of three magistrates recommended patients for commitment; a second panel, the hospital's court of directors, made the final decision. However, despite such formal rules and processes governing who was to be admitted, there was little oversight of the actual practices at many of the newly built asylums. In the late eighteenth century, Massachusetts passed a law that any person "[l]unatic & so furiously mad as to render it dangerous to the peace or the safety of the good people, for such lunatic person to go at large," could be committed to jail.[5]

By the mid-nineteenth century, people sporadically began to raise concerns about involuntary commitment. One woman whose husband had her committed for refusing to be an obedient wife—she ended up spending three years in an Illinois hospital—spent two decades after her release pushing for civil liberties laws that would protect others from similar fates. Still, it wasn't until the 1970s, when the state asylums were coming under general scrutiny and a greater awareness of civil rights had emerged, that a broader push occurred for patient rights concerning confinement, treatment, and medication. Across the country, lawsuits questioned under what circumstances states could commit people involuntarily and, if they were allowed to do so, what kind of treatment those patients were entitled to.[6]

The result was dramatic legal changes that have since made it much harder to have a person with mental illness hospitalized against his will. Today a person needs to be considered either an immediate risk to self or others, or "gravely disabled," to be committed. Even if a patient meets these criteria, hospitals may hold him for only seventy-two hours without a hearing. Many family members I've talked to, including Muhammad's mother, believe the laws have gone too far in the direction of patients' rights. In her experience her son is often unable to recognize when he needs to get help, and the tough commitment laws make it too hard for her to intervene before he gets arrested. It's a concern echoed by many who cite the barriers to involuntary commitment as one of the reasons for the increased criminalization of mental illness. The connection between the two was suggested as early as the 1970s, shortly after the first new laws against involuntary commitment were passed. "[People with mental illness] are often charged with crimes such as public drunkenness, disorderly behavior, malicious mischief, or, interestingly, possession of marijuana or of dangerous drugs," wrote Marc F. Abramson, a court psychiatrist in California, in 1972. "Police seem to be aware of the more stringent criteria under which mental health professionals are now accepting responsibility for involuntary detention and treatment, and thus regard arrest and booking into jail as a more reliable way of securing involuntary detention of mentally disordered persons." He went on to say that "once the criminal justice machinery is invoked, it is frequently hard to stop." On this front, too, little has changed in the last four decades.[7]

In the 1990s, states began passing assisted outpatient treatment (AOT) laws, which allow for court-ordered outpatient treatment of people who are believed to be a danger to themselves and others. Most states now have some version of them—Kendra's law in New York, for example, named for Kendra Webdale, a woman who died after being pushed onto the subway tracks by a man with untreated schizophrenia.

It is still possible to get people involuntarily committed; it's just difficult. For those who are unfamiliar with the process, even *figuring out* how can be daunting. When I called New York City's public information line to ask to be connected to somebody who could tell me more about the process, the operator thought I was looking for animal control. Despite how cumbersome the process is, Eula Muhammad has had Kyle committed so many times she's lost count. And just because she can handle the bureaucracy doesn't mean she always succeeds in getting her son treatment. Her most recent attempt to have her son committed was just days before Kyle's last arrest. It was in late February 2013 when Eula Muhammad went to the courthouse in downtown Manhattan. The civil division of the New York Supreme Court is a beautiful, imposing Greek Revival building constructed in 1927. (In New York the Supreme Court is simply a trial court, not the state's highest one.) Unlike the criminal court building a half block away, this building's stately interior is orderly and quiet. Upstairs, beneath a grand cupola with a mural and through a heavy, padded door is a wood-paneled office where Eula filled out a form saying that her son was at risk of harming himself or others. At this point, a judge—one of a rotating panel of Supreme Court judges—needed to review her paperwork, review the evidence she presented, and decide whether to issue a mental health warrant allowing Kyle to be committed to the hospital against his will.

Even when successful, this procedure suggests how confused our system has become: It's one more way that the legal system makes what are effectively *medical* decisions, ones that judges aren't necessarily qualified to make. Judges have told me this kind of decision is not so different from what they always do, which is to use the information they have to make the best decisions they can under the law. Still, it's fair to say that a judge is unlikely to have the medical expertise to understand the complicated fluctuations in behavior resulting from a particular form of mental illness, the effects of medication or its disruption, and when the symptoms in question may require urgent intervention.

The law also gives the patients the right to fight their commitment. Had Muhammad ended up in the hospital this time, he would have been able to argue against his confinement there almost immediately. In some places, this is done by videoconferencing with a judge. In others, judges set up ersatz courtrooms within hospitals to hear cases. At Bellevue Hospital, the flagship of New York City's public hospital system, these hearings take place in a compact courtroom tucked away near the locked psychiatric ward. When I visited, the judge, a tall, thin man with a mane of wild white hair, sat on a blond wood dais with the flags of New York City, New York State, and the United States behind him. There were narrow tables in front of him for the patient and the attorneys to sit, and a roomful of low upholstered chairs for family and other observers.

I was allowed to sit for a day of hearings provided that I didn't disclose any patient's identity and that I agreed to leave if a patient asked me to. Only one did. The judge later told me that when asked whether he swore to tell the truth, the whole truth, and nothing but the truth—usually a perfunctory legal exercise—that patient said no. The judge said it was the first time he had encountered this response in twenty-five years on the bench; as a result, he concluded that the patient's testimony could not be included in the record.

Among the patients whose hearings I watched was a man visiting from Georgia who had hit a child on a playground in one of the outer boroughs. Concluding that the man was no longer a danger to himself or others, the judge released him to go free.

Another man was wiry and compact, with teardrop tattoos on his cheeks and a buzzing energy about him that made him seem literally wound up. He carried a flat-brimmed baseball cap with "Puerto Rico" printed on it and held a paperback book. He had a history of aggressive behavior. He had been brought to Bellevue on a seventy-two-hour hold a few days earlier. He had been smoking marijuana in Times Square when he got into a fight that ended with him throwing a chair. Before he walked into the courtroom, I saw his attorney quietly put the court officers on alert.

Patients are guaranteed the right to representation at these hearings; a special legal group provides free legal services. The man talked quickly when he answered questions from the judge and from both attorneys, his and the one representing the hospital. He drummed his hands on the table and laughed out loud while a psychiatrist testified about how badly he had behaved on the unit. The question before the judge was not whether the man was sick; about that, there was no dispute. He had been diagnosed years earlier with schizoaffective and bipolar disorders as well as with having an antisocial personality, and he'd been hospitalized multiple times in Florida and Puerto Rico. Rather, the judge had to figure out whether, in his current condition, the man was a danger to himself or others or was gravely disabled. "Are you aware that you have a mental illness?" one of the attorneys asked the man.

"I'm crazy and aware of it," the man said. "Everyone else here is crazy, but not aware of it." At the time the retort struck me as witty, although I assume he did not intend it to be. (It reminded me of a line from *The Snake Pit:* "You had always heard that crazy people think themselves sane," the narrator says. "Does it follow then that if you think you are crazy, you are sane?"[8]) But his response also hit on a profound idea, one with implications not just for the medical world but for the legal one as well. What does it mean to be mad? And who gets to decide whether you are mad or not?

We have set up all kinds of safeguards that are supposed to make sure that we accurately identify signs and symptoms of mental illness, whether for the purposes of confinement in a hospital or to stand trial in a criminal case. But it often seems like the people making the decisions—cops, judges, corrections officials—may know little about mental illness. Meanwhile, while it can be remarkably difficult to get a person admitted to the hospital for treatment of a mental illness, it is often shockingly easy to have the same person locked up in jail, even for the same behavior, driven presumably by the same illness.

Consider what ended up happening to Kyle Muhammad. After she filed the paperwork at the courthouse, his mother successfully obtained a mental health warrant from a judge to get him committed to a hospital. But to have this warrant executed—a warrant simply authorizing him to be sent to a medical institution for care—she had to call the police, tell them about the order, and let them know where to find her son so they could pick him up and bring him to the hospital. In other words, simply to get her son psychiatric help, Eula Muhammad had to involve law enforcement.

The police ended up finding him, but it was not because of the mental health warrant. When Muhammad gets psychotic, his mother says, he often wanders. Frequently she and his sister have driven around looking for him. On March 6, 2014, his mother tried to find him but couldn't. Then on March 8, Muhammad called her—from Rikers Island. He had been on the subway near his apartment in Harlem when he saw an elderly woman he thought he recognized. When the woman got off the train, he followed her. What happened next is a matter of some dispute. He says he went to kiss her on the cheek and accidentally knocked her over. The police say he pushed her.

"I don't know what happened that day," Eula Muhammad told me months later. "Something happened that day. Only Kyle, that lady, and God know what happened, but something happened that day." In any case the district attorney charged Muhammad with felony assault, a charge that his attorney says would have been a misdemeanor but for the age of the victim. She was over sixty-five and more than ten years older than he.

LINE UP KYLE MUHAMMAD'S HEALTH records with his criminal ones, and the connection seems clear enough. When his disease is not being treated, he sometimes makes choices or behaves in ways that get him arrested: jumping the turnstile in the subway, committing petty theft, or making a ridiculous attempt at robbing a bank. But can we definitively say that his mental illness causes him to break the law? What about the occasional substance use? Are there other motivations or factors that contribute to this behavior? As with many other people with mental illness who get arrested, there are no simple answers to these questions. It's part of why the relationship between mental illness and criminal behavior has been so difficult to square with our generally black-and-white understanding of lawbreaking and culpability. And it's one of the reasons it's difficult to know how best to reduce the number of people with mental illness who end up in the criminal justice system.

Certainly, there are cases in which complications of mental illness manifestly drive a person to commit a crime. The link is especially clear when the person in question has severe paranoia or is having delusions. The Texas man who stabbed his wife and two young children, each with a separate knife to avoid contamination, then put their hearts (and a piece of his wife's lung, which he mistook for her heart) into his pocket before walking out of the house would almost certainly fit this category. But few cases are so extreme.

The real challenge concerns the many people with mental illness who commit more ordinary, low-level crimes. One study found that less than 20 percent of crimes committed by people with mental illness were directly related to psychiatric symptoms. Furthermore, of that 20 percent, most of the people had, on other occasions, engaged in criminal behavior that had no apparent connection to the symptoms of their mental illness.[9] Part of the difficulty in drawing a direct link between mental illness and criminal behavior lies in the elusive nature of many forms of mental illness. Is somebody who is exceptionally impulsive exhibiting symptoms of bipolar disorder? Or does he just have trouble with impulse control? Even if a particular behavior is shown to be a symptom of illness, it can often be equally difficult to define the relationship between the disease and its symptoms on the one hand and the decision to do something illegal on the other. Another study looked at records of almost fourteen thousand people who had received treatment for mental illness. More than a quarter of them, the researchers found, had been arrested at least once. What was more interesting, though, was that a tiny subset of that group—just over 1 percent—accounted for nearly 20 percent of the arrests. Those high-frequency lawbreakers shared many characteristics with people in the general population who end up in the criminal justice system.[10] However, in addition to being poor and having substance use disorders, they also happened to have a serious mental illness.

Jeff Draine, a researcher at Temple University, thinks the answer lies in substance use: a sick person who engages in substance use is far more likely to engage in criminality than a sick person who does not. "If we look at people...with just uncomplicated mental illness going through the justice system, the things that explain whether or not they get rearrested are the same things that explain rearrest in the general population," he said. "[If you] then throw substance use in there, it's the substance use that so increases the likelihood of people with mental illness getting involved in the justice system." About 80 percent of people with mental illness in the criminal justice system have a substance use disorder in addition to the mental illness. Some studies have broken down the links more clearly. One showed that among people with mental illness, men with bipolar disorder and a substance use disorder are most likely to end up in trouble with the law.[11] Another showed that among people with schizophrenia who get arrested, substance use is the single most prominent factor they share.[12]

Jennifer Skeem, a professor at Berkeley who studies the intersection of behavior and criminal justice, says if you exclude crimes directly attributable to symptoms of a person's disease, you "still have lots and lots of criminal incidents that are left unexplained by mental illness." Criminologists know there are some factors that increase people's risk for breaking the law: people with antisocial behavior, people with family issues, or people who tend to hang out with the wrong crowd are all more likely to commit crimes. (Substance use is another one of these so-called criminogenic risk factors.) Skeem and others believe that those risk factors are much bigger predictors of criminal behavior than mental illness is.

Indeed, some studies have shown that people with serious mental illness commit the same kinds of "survival" crimes committed by other people who find themselves under economic stress: namely, they steal cars and other property. In other words, living conditions may be as important as or more important than the disease in shaping the behavior. As one social worker said to me, "[Mental] illness causes [people who have it] to be poor," because they can't hold a job or they can't find a well-paying one. (Approximately 80 percent of people who qualify for disability payments because of a mental illness are unemployed.[13]) And as it does for other people, the criminal justice system complicates the cycle: "'I have to go court, so I can't go to work, or I have to go to treatment Mondays,'" she continued, "'so I can't go to work Monday.'" Unemployment may make the person more likely to commit the crime, but mental illness may explain in part why the person is unemployed. This could be seen as further proof of our inadequate community support for people with mental illness, a failing that on some level is helping to push people with mental illness into the criminal justice system.

So what are we to make of all of this? The growing body of data shows how complicated the relationship is between mental illness and criminality. It is clear that keeping people like Kyle Muhammad out of the criminal justice system will require a much more nuanced understanding of that relationship. But if we truly want to solve the problem, we must also address the social and economic risk factors—including substance use and poverty, but also the stigma that so often come with it.

11

Shooting the Victim

IT STARTED OUT LIKE AN ordinary Sunday in early January. "We had coffee. Keith had hot chocolate," his mother, Mary Wilsey, recalled. Keith Vidal, who had turned eighteen just a month earlier, stayed home while she and her husband, his stepfather, went to the grocery store. Keith was handsome, with thick, dark hair and a sweet face. He was small—110 pounds, five-feet-six-inches tall. He also had schizophrenia and had been depressed. He lived with his parents and two siblings in a house that his stepfather, a contractor, had built on a wooded lot. He was a sweet kid who didn't get into trouble, his mother said, even if he sometimes acted like a typical teenager. "He didn't mow the lawn when you told him to," she said. He was athletic and was especially into soccer. But his real passion was music. He played the xylophone, then acoustic and electric guitar until he discovered drums. On YouTube and Facebook, there are still videos of him playing, legs bouncing, arms raging through the air, hair flopping wildly in his face. He and some friends started a band; his parents let them practice at their house. "We wanted to know where he was and what he was doing," Wilsey said. And with six children in their blended family, the house was always full of kids anyway.

It was the summer of 2012, when Keith was sixteen, that his mother started worrying that he might be depressed. He had recently broken up with a girlfriend, and at first his mother figured it was just teen angst. But it kept getting worse. He stopped hanging out with his friends; then he didn't want to leave the house. That fall, she got scared that he might try to hurt himself, so she had him hospitalized. Doctors diagnosed him with bipolar disorder and put him on medication.

It didn't seem to help. He became paranoid: he was sure that other kids were bothering him and chasing him. His parents pulled him out of school; instead, the school district sent teachers to the house a couple of times a week. He had been a boy who took care of himself, sometimes showering twice a day. He loved to wear T-shirts from his favorite bands. Now, his parents had to tell him repeatedly to shower, get dressed, change his clothes. He lost interest in food. He was hospitalized on multiple occasions; a couple of times, his parents called the police for help with him.

His parents took him to see other doctors, and about a year later a psychiatrist finally diagnosed him with schizophrenia. The psychiatrist started him on other medications, and for several months, it seemed like he was finally on track. But the Friday after Christmas, his parents had become worried again. He seemed depressed; they were afraid he might try to kill himself. His mother called his psychiatrist, who told her to bring Keith to the hospital. The plan was to admit him for two or three days, just long enough to adjust his medication, then send him home. But because Keith Vidal had turned eighteen a few weeks earlier, getting him hospitalized was suddenly much more complicated. Under the law, he was now an adult, and he could decide for himself whether he wanted to be hospitalized. If he didn't want to be hospitalized, then his mother would have to petition for an involuntary commitment unless the police or EMTs brought him in.

So on that Friday, she called the police. Boiling Spring Lakes, North Carolina, is a small coastal community near the border with South Carolina. Wilsey says the officer who responded knew Keith and his diagnosis. He was sympathetic. "Listen, Keith," he reportedly said. "I have a son your age. He has depression problems." The officer gave him a choice: agree to go to the hospital with his mom or get taken anyway, in a squad car or an ambulance. Keith agreed to go with his mother. At the hospital, a clinician asked Keith questions about how he was feeling. (His mother says she doesn't think he ever saw a psychiatrist that day and is unsure of the qualifications of the person who examined Keith.) She says nobody would listen when she tried to explain that Keith's own psychiatrist had sent him for a medication adjustment. When Keith said he was neither suicidal nor homicidal—not a danger to himself or to others—the hospital said he was free to go.

Things might have turned out very differently if he had been admitted that day and examined by a psychiatrist. Instead, his mother took him home, kept an eye on him over the weekend, and took him to see his psychiatrist the following Monday. The doctor increased Keith's medication. That week, he seemed unhappy but OK.

By the following Sunday, it was clear that he was not OK. When his parents got back from the grocery store that Sunday morning, "[Keith] thought I was somebody else," Wilsey told me. He asked if she wanted to fight. "I was never afraid of Keith. The only thing I was afraid of was that he would try to hurt himself because he didn't seem to be comprehending what I was talking about." She called the psychiatrist again, who told her to call the police in order to make sure that he really would be hospitalized this time. Wilsey stayed with her son while her husband called 911.

Two officers soon arrived, a Boiling Spring Lakes police officer and a Brunswick County sheriff's deputy. Because of a mutual aid agreement among neighboring law enforcement agencies, it was not uncommon for officers from different agencies to respond to the same call. An ambulance came, too, but Wilsey said the cops told the EMTs to wait in the hallway while the cops cased the scene. Keith had pulled out of a kitchen drawer what his mother described as a small screwdriver, which he often used to tighten screws on things around the house. One of the officers began talking to Keith, who was reluctant to put the tool down.

Although Keith was calm, the officer called for backup. Bryon Vassey, an officer from the neighboring Southport Police Department, showed up. Vassey is in his mid-forties; he has broad shoulders and a thick neck, with a ruddy face and close-cropped hair. He'd been on the Southport police force for eleven years. "I don't have time for this shit," Mary Wilsey heard him say as he came in. Two EMTs later testified that Vassey had announced, "I'm here to kick ass and take names."[1]

The first two officers were still talking to Keith when Vassey walked in. He had barely entered the house, Wilsey said, when he yelled for the other officers to Tase the boy. Hearing the order, Keith turned and ran into the bathroom. When he came out, one of the officers Tased him. He fell to the ground, stunned, and "at that point," Wilsey recalled, "we all rushed him." There were two officers across his chest; his stepfather was at his side, trying to get the screwdriver. Wilsey was behind her husband. Seconds later, Vassey pulled out his gun and shot the boy in the chest. The EMTs rushed him to the local hospital, where he was declared dead.

IN 2015 AND 2016 COMBINED, nearly five hundred people with mental illness were fatally shot by the police, according to calculations by the *Washington Post*.[2] This means that for each of those years, one in four police shootings was of a person with mental illness. Other reporting and analyses have arrived at similar numbers: in the first half of 2017, police in San Jose, California, shot six people, four fatally. All had a mental illness.[3] *The Portland Press Herald* found that nearly half the people shot by police in Maine between 2000 and 2011 had a mental illness.[4] A 2014 report from San Francisco public radio affiliate KQED showed that almost 60 percent of people killed by police in San Francisco between 2005 and 2013 had a mental illness that "was a contributing factor in the incident."[5] And an analysis of police shootings in Florida in 2013 and 2014 by the *Daytona Beach News-Journal* showed that more than a quarter of the people shot by police in that state had a mental illness or a substance use problem.[6]

Behind all of these statistics is a long list of individual tragedies. In October 2016 a New York City police officer shot and killed Deborah

Danner, a sixty-six-year-old woman with schizophrenia. Neighbors in her apartment building had called 911 because she was acting erratically. When a police officer went into the apartment, he found her in the bedroom, holding a pair of scissors. According to newspaper reports, he convinced Danner to drop them, but then she picked up a baseball bat. He shot her twice; she was declared dead at a hospital shortly afterward. In a poignant essay she had written four years earlier about living with schizophrenia, Danner observed: "We are all aware of headline news stories about persons with serious mental illness who commit horrendous acts of violence—a minority of the mentally ill. We are all aware of the all too frequent news stories about the mentally ill who come up against law enforcement instead of mental health professionals and end up dead. We *should* all be aware that these circumstances represent very, very serious problems that need addressing."[7]

It's easy to find numerous examples to support Danner's argument. In 2012 a SWAT team in suburban Atlanta responded to a call from Lisa and Nick Messina that their sixteen-year-old son, Andrew, was suicidal. Sheriff's deputies dressed in combat gear, including riot shields, surrounded the Messina house, where Andrew was inside, alone with a pistol. A sniper, wearing camouflage, set up his rifle in a neighbor's yard and shot Andrew through the window, killing him.[8]

In 2014 a man named Dontre Hamilton, whose family said had a mental illness, was asleep in a park in Milwaukee. A police officer, responding to complaints about him sleeping there, came up behind him and began patting him down. The two struggled, and the officer pulled out his baton, which Hamilton grabbed. The officer shot Hamilton fourteen times.

Also in 2014 Audrey Latham called the police in Norfolk, Virginia, hoping to get help for her son, David, who had schizophrenia and had stopped taking his medication. He was holding a knife when the police arrived; within seconds of telling Latham to put down the knife, one of the officers had shot him six times. Latham was one of two people with mental illness shot by Norfolk police *that week*.[9]

In 2017 a woman named Charleena Lyles called Seattle police to report an attempted burglary at her apartment. Two officers responded.

While they were in her apartment, Lyles, who had a history of mental illness, took out a knife. The officers shot her seven times in front of three of her children. (The autopsy showed she was also several weeks pregnant.[10]) Lyles was just one of more than 230 people with mental illness who were killed by police in 2017—as in recent years, one in four of all fatal police shootings during that period.[11]

PART OF THE PROBLEM IS that it generally falls to the police—rather than, say, EMTs—to respond to mental health crises. It's a burden on municipal law enforcement that has increased as the availability of community health care has declined. In 2015 the New York City Police Department estimated that it responded to more than four hundred mental health calls per *day*, more than twelve thousand per month.[12] The police department in Tucson, Arizona, said that it responded to more calls about mental illness than it did about burglaries or stolen cars.[13] In 2012 Chicago police got roughly twenty thousand calls specifically concerning a mental health issue, which the department believes is but a small fraction of the true number of mental health calls.[14]

These calls don't just come from bystanders who want to report someone's strange or dangerous behavior. Often, it's a person's family, like Mary Wilsey, who calls 911 for help: To keep somebody who is threatening suicide from killing himself. To ask for protection when a relative with mental illness is threatening. To calm a person down. Or to help the person get admitted to the hospital. Or just to get the person *to* the hospital.

Law enforcement is not health care, mental or otherwise. And to those who have not dealt with a family member who has a mental illness, having the police responding to a medical emergency sounds bizarre, especially if you replace *mental* illness with a physical one: who would even think of calling the police to help deal with diabetes or an asthma attack? Yet families, for the most part, know that when they call 911, police will respond rather than EMTs. Many realize there are risks in involved, but they also know it's the only option. Organizations like the National Alliance on Mental Illness (NAMI) publish guides on how to mitigate the danger when calling the police to help a loved one during a mental health crisis.

There are various explanations for why police have ended up as first responders for mental health crises. It's partly historical: in colonial Williamsburg, for example, it was up to sheriffs to deliver patients to the Eastern State Hospital. They were paid five pounds of tobacco for every mile they had to travel; if they needed additional guards to help with the transport, there was a further payment of three pounds.[15]

In some jurisdictions, these duties are also codified in the law. In Oklahoma, for instance, just as was the case in colonial Williamsburg, the police are responsible for transporting people with mental illness to the hospital for involuntary commitments, and the state mental health department budget includes money specifically to pay law enforcement for these transports. (For fiscal year 2016, it was $200,000 of a $10 million proposed budget.[16]) But the reliance on police has been reinforced in more subtle ways, too. As Keith Vidal's parents knew, it's much easier to have a person involuntarily committed when the police deliver him to the hospital. There's a practical element as well. From a medical perspective, mental health crises are less urgent than other health emergencies, such as a heart attack, where a speedy response can mean the difference between life and death. For a medical event like that, 911 may dispatch an ambulance or firefighters because they are usually closer.

However, more worrying is the perception that people with mental illness are potentially so dangerous that only police are equipped for the job of getting them under control. "We would never want to put [first responders] in a situation where their safety is jeopardized," a former longtime dispatcher told me. David Klinger, a police officer-turned-criminology professor at University of Missouri–St. Louis, put it a different way: "Shit rolls downhill, and cops are at the bottom of the hill," he said. "If somebody is in crisis, people call 911, and if there is a threat involved, then police get dispatched."

More often than not, people with mental illness are not dangerous, but using the tools of law enforcement to deal with them helps perpetuate the notion that they are.

FOR POLICE, THERE IS a disconnect between their training and the job they are asked to do. Most police training focuses on how to manage situations where people really are dangerous. For those like Keith Vidal who are not dangerous (and perhaps not even full-grown adults) but are facing a true mental health emergency, that classic law enforcement approach can quickly turn tragic.

Seth Stoughton, a former police officer who studies policing as a law professor at the University of South Carolina, says that the first rule of law enforcement is that you "do whatever you need to do to go home at the end of your shift." So training programs often emphasize the worst-case scenarios, the "ways the situation could go bad or...the ways the person could hurt you." It "teaches officers that the relationship that they have with the community is confrontational and adversarial. They are at risk, and they must take proactive steps to limit the risk." The idea is that if you treat everybody you encounter as a potential threat, then you will be better prepared to handle a real threat when you encounter one. "Officers are being trained in a school that really likes vinegar, because it's believed that vinegar will keep you safer," said Stoughton, referring to the adage about catching more flies with honey than with vinegar.

In practice, that means teaching officers to be intimidating, to gain control of a situation completely and quickly. Officers are taught to make themselves look commanding and threatening by standing with their legs spread wide, chest out, hands on weapons. Voices should be loud, commands shouted. If the suspect doesn't obey or doesn't obey quickly enough, the police are trained to move in closer and shout louder, effectively escalating the situation until the suspect responds. It's meant to be scary, but for a person with mental illness, particularly one who is psychotic or paranoid, it can be downright terrifying. And sometimes it produces the opposite of the intended response, driving the person to lash out rather than to obey. As with people in jail or prison who have trouble following orders from corrections officers, the problem may be compounded by the illness itself, which can make it hard to follow directions.

Officers also complain that superiors expect them to deal with emergency calls as quickly as possible in order to get back on the streets as quickly as possible. That encourages them to escalate the situation rapidly and discourages slower, more thoughtful responses. And for many cops, talking a person down from a crisis doesn't count as "real" police work.

Nonetheless, despite the amount of time officers spend dealing with people with mental illness, it's clear that few academies offer much guidance. A 2004 survey of police departments in Pennsylvania found almost half of respondents felt unqualified to manage people with mental illness.[17] A more recent survey of police academies reveals that some spend as little as four hours on mental health training.

This disconnect between training and practice has existed for decades.[18] "Not only do [police believe that they] lack training and competence in this area, but such dealings are stylistically incompatible with the officially propounded conception of the policeman's principal vocation," wrote sociologist Egon Bittner in 1967. "It involves none of the skills, acumen, and prowess that characterize the ideal image of a first-rate officer.... [I]t is a foregone conclusion that conveying a 'mental case' to the hospital will never take the place of catching [famous bank robber] Willie Sutton."[19]

At the same time, traditional policing strategies may make the situation more likely to spin out of control, especially when the person in question is paranoid or doesn't understand what is happening. That's exactly what happened with Dontre Hamilton, the man who was shot to death in the park in Milwaukee. Even when the outcome is not fatal, it may be traumatic for the person involved. Kyle Muhammad described one such encounter to me. He and I were at his mother's kitchen table one morning looking through old court records when he came across one that said that police had picked him up for marching in the street. "I remember this," he said. "The police used to mess with me because I would march in the street." Completely deadpan, he added that "I never saluted." I couldn't tell if he meant the remark to be funny, but what he said next made a lot of sense. "They would stop me, frisk me, handle me. I guess it was bizarre, because what am I marching for? [But] why would you approach me and say 'get against the wall' and then handcuff me? I wasn't sure what was happening. Of course I was angry."

The police didn't arrest him that time. Instead, they brought him to a hospital, albeit in four-point restraints. But it's easy to see how it could have escalated into something worse. Investigations by the Obama-era US Department of Justice (DOJ) found ample evidence of police mistreatment of people with mental illness. For example, the DOJ found reason to believe the Portland Police Department "is engaged in a pattern or practice of using excessive force against people with mental illness, or those perceived to have mental illness." It also found that those encounters too frequently ended up with police using force or a higher level of force than necessary: for example, cops often used Tasers when it was unnecessary (or more frequently than they needed to). The DOJ further found that when people with mental illness were arrested for low-level offenses, "there is a pattern or practice of using more force than necessary in those circumstances."[20] The department came to similar conclusions in Cleveland and elsewhere.

Escalation is something that Keith Vidal's mother, Mary Wilsey, thinks about a lot. I met her in a town about halfway down the southern shore of Long Island. She grew up nearby, and since her son died, she's been spending more and more time here. She's on the short side of average, with straight honey-blond hair; she wore a cable-knit sweater with a thick turtleneck. She told me she's been having trouble sleeping, that she struggles to get out of bed before late morning. Sometimes marriages can't sustain the loss of a child.

We sat in a booth where she ordered a salad and sandwich, which she mostly didn't eat, and iced tea, which she drank. She used a ballpoint pen to draw a diagram for me on one of the brown paper napkins. It shows the hallway of the family's house, the doorways, and the walls; it shows where the police officers were standing and the spot where her son was killed. "You know what was disgusting?" Wilsey said. "We did that walk [from the end of the driveway to the hallway of the house], and [Vassey] wasn't in there more than twenty seconds before Keith got shot. How do you assess a situation in twenty seconds? He came in and escalated the situation. You don't take out your gun if you're not going to use it." She calculates it took just over a minute from the time Vassey pulled up at the house until her son was dead.

I exchanged several e-mails with Bryon Vassey's defense attorney. He initially suggested that either he or Vassey might be willing to talk to me, but despite numerous follow-up calls and e-mails, I never heard back from either of them.

Vassey was charged with voluntary manslaughter. The case went to trial in 2016, two years after Keith died. Under a law that had recently been enacted in the state, Vassey opted for a bench trial, where the judge, not a jury, decides the case. In it, Vassey testified that he had not known that Keith had a mental illness when he arrived on the scene. He said he was filling in on patrol for a fellow officer and chose to wear detective attire—a business suit—so he was not carrying his Taser. And he testified that he felt he had a duty to protect his fellow officer. "I feel horrible, sir," he told the judge. "[I]t is the single hardest thing I've had to do in my life."[21] After the trial, which lasted nearly three weeks, the judge found Vassey not guilty. Wilsey thinks the trial was a charade, that the district attorney had no intention of letting him get convicted.

Whatever the merits of the case, his acquittal was certainly far from uncommon. As with other officer-involved shootings, police who shoot people with mental illness are rarely prosecuted and even more rarely convicted. The officer who shot Deborah Danner in New York City was charged with murder, manslaughter, and criminally negligent homicide; as of this writing, the case is still pending. In late 2017, the Seattle Police Department determined that the officers who shot Charleena Lyles had acted within protocol.[22] The district attorney in Milwaukee declined to prosecute the officer who shot Dontre Hamilton, saying the officer had acted in self-defense. (The police department did fire the officer, saying he had violated department policy by conducting a pat down on the man without reasonable suspicion for doing so and had failed to follow proper procedures for self-defense and arrest tactics.) A jury in Norfolk acquitted the police officer who shot David Latham. And a Georgia district attorney found no wrongdoing on the part of the police officer who shot sixteen-year-old Andrew Messina through the window of his parents' house.

These cases have proven hard to prosecute, but they have also proven to be expensive. In 2017 Wilsey won a million-dollar settlement in a civil case against Vassey, the police departments in both towns, and the county sheriff, claiming, among other things, that the Southport Police Department failed to properly train or supervise its employees. The family of Dontre Hamilton reportedly received a $2.3 million dollar settlement from the city of Milwaukee.[23] David Latham's family got $1.5 million, while the family of another man with mental illness killed by Norfolk police the same week settled for $90,000.[24] The money is cold comfort to the families. Mary Wilsey says her son was let down twice, first by the mental health care system and then by the criminal justice system. "They failed Keith in life," Wilsey said, "and they failed him in death."

The death of a child is unthinkable. Death at the hands of a police officer—one you called to get urgent help for that child—is even worse. "I wanted my son to get hospitalized and come home," Wilsey said. "If I had had any thought they were going to kill him that day.... There was no reason to kill this kid. He did nothing wrong except be mentally ill."

12

The Good-Cop Solution

WHEN MEMPHIS POLICE OFFICER JAMIE Lambert responds to a 911 call, he always stands to the side, just in case somebody decides to shoot through the door. "I stand with my right shoulder... toward the frame," he said. "I'm making myself smaller and... [putting myself] in line with [it]; that's the strongest part of the door.... One of the worst things is when you knock on the door and you hear the person yell. When you hear 'Who is it?' that's pretty normal. But when you know they're... talking to you, but it doesn't make sense. [When the person says] 'I'm gonna kill everybody,' [that's when you worry]." It's one of the challenges of being a police officer: you never know who's on the other side of the door or how he is going to react to your knocking on it.

"You don't know the individual you're going toe-to-toe with," former New York City Police Department officer Steve Osborne wrote in his memoir. "You don't know how crazy or desperate he is. You don't know if he's armed. You don't know if he is wanted for a homicide somewhere and is willing to do anything to stay out of jail. You just don't know!"[1] It means that in every encounter, officers can hope for good results but have to be prepared for the worst-case scenario every time. Lambert says you have to trust your gut because "fear is what keeps you safe." You also have to keep other people safe: your partner, the person on the other side of the door, bystanders. Your first instinct might be to go in, take control, and get out, all as quickly as possible. But sometimes your first instinct is wrong, especially when the person you're dealing with has a mental illness. What if training could change that?

I GOT TO SEE HOW a different approach might work on a blindingly hot summer day in Miami Beach. There was an impressive stream of obscenities coming from the backseat of the Ford Explorer. I was in the passenger seat up front, where some of the sound was muffled by the window separating the front and back seats. Sometimes the yelling was generic. Sometimes it was directed at the driver, Ysidro Llamoca, an officer with the Miami Beach Police Department. "Fuck you, Llamoca," the woman screamed. "Why did you rape me?" The shouting alternated between English and Spanish, and only let up for the occasional burst of jagged sobbing.

Dealing with people with mental illness is a regular part of the job for police in Miami. Like other temperate places, Miami is an appealing destination for people who are homeless because they can sleep outside here year-round without freezing. Access to mental health care in Florida is notoriously poor.

The woman in the back of the car, who wore shorts and flip-flops and had close-cropped blondish hair, was a regular. Llamoca had picked her up a few times before, often from the same doorway where he had found her that day. The cycle was mostly the same: she would camp out in the doorway, and the building's owner would get mad and call the police. An officer would come to collect her. Occasionally, he would take her to the hospital; most of the time, he would arrest her.

Llamoca is not an ordinary cop, however. He is a trained Crisis Intervention Team (CIT) officer, somebody who has received special training in how to handle people with mental illness. On that day in Miami Beach, the ride to the hospital took nearly half an hour; except for the occasional gentle shush, he ignored her screed. At the hospital, Llamoca pulled into a parking spot designated for police officers, where his partner was waiting. The police department's protocol dictates that Baker Acts—involuntary hospital commitments—are always done in pairs. Llamoca grabbed the woman's pink duffle bag out of the back and led the woman, still cursing and glaring, into the hospital.

The emergency room was crowded, and people stared as the two officers led the woman past people on stretchers and the nurses' station to the behavioral health area, two private rooms at the back of the emergency department. Llamoca coaxed her to put on a hospital gown and sat in the exam room with her until the hospital staff took over. In under fifteen minutes, the hospital staff had taken custody of the woman, and Llamoca and his partner were free to go. What happened that day shows how the CIT approach can work at its best: there was no confrontation between the woman and the officers. She didn't get arrested. The hospital system streamlined her admission, so the officers didn't have to spend hours in the waiting room with a psychotic and handcuffed patient. Llamoca could have arrested her for any number of things: criminal trespass or resisting arrest, for example. He could have lashed out at her—and some would say it would have been justified—for her rude language and false accusations. He didn't do any of those. But the incident also highlights the system's failings: while there's no doubt that having the woman Baker Acted was a far better outcome than arresting her (or worse), taking her to the hospital likely did nothing for her long-term stability.

Over the past several decades, dozens of police departments across the country have implemented CIT programs to respond to crisis calls involving mental illness. As with many aspects of policing, the true impact of these programs is hard to measure, and there are few data available to analyze. But the anecdotal evidence is encouraging. Several studies have shown that such programs can help reduce arrests, instead diverting clients to mental health care programs; others have shown that using CIT officers can help reduce use of force.[2] Cities, including Miami, have also found that fewer people with mental illness have been shot by police after a CIT program was implemented.

It was the shooting of a man with mental illness by police officers in Memphis, Tennessee, that provided the impetus for the development of the first CIT team. It took place some thirty years ago, in an incident depressingly similar to some of those we still see today. Early on a Thursday morning in September 1987, a woman called 911 and asked police to come to the LeMoyne Gardens public housing project in Memphis. A man—newspaper reports later identified him as the caller's brother—with paranoid schizophrenia and possibly high on cocaine had been cutting himself with a long knife. Several police officers—all white—arrived and shot Joseph Dewayne Robinson—who was African American—ten times. He died at the hospital several hours later. Officers said Robinson had lunged at them, a claim that witnesses disputed.

Residents of the housing complex were outraged. "If he was trying to commit suicide, they should have brought a psychiatrist with them when his sister called them," a friend of the family told the *Commercial Appeal* shortly after Robinson was killed. "His sister called and said he was trying to kill himself and they came and did it for him. I thought they were trained to disarm people like that."[3] Compounding residents' anger was the fact that Robinson's death came amid a long-running discussion about police accountability and the relationship between law enforcement, especially white law enforcement, and the African American community. Just days before the Robinson incident, officers had shot and killed another African American man in a nearby neighborhood. The deaths added an urgency to the conversation, and in the days and weeks afterward, there were numerous community meetings to talk about how to demand accountability from the police department and how to make sure something like this didn't happen again.

One of the community's demands was for the police to develop a team of officers specially trained to respond to mental health crises. "With the proper training and the proper type of unit, this man could have been subdued without a shot being fired," a longtime civil rights activist argued. He raised the idea of a "crisis intervention team" to a neighborhood commission that dealt with police-community relations, saying, "We feel the actual human relations training police officers get ought to be more beefed up. They spend more time learning how to shoot than how to relate to people."[4]

Sam Cochran, then a young lieutenant in the Memphis Police Department, was part of the discussion. At that time, he says, the Memphis police academy already offered eight hours of training in mental health issues, more than a lot of places. But he agreed to help develop a more robust program. Along with people in the mental health care community, Cochran and his colleagues came up with a new forty-hour training program that includes extensive role-play and meetings with people with mental illness and their families. Today, thousands of officers around the world still receive training based on this model. It has also sparked numerous copycat training models, all with the same goal of teaching officers to interact better with people with mental illness and other disabilities.

I went to the Memphis Police Department Training Academy, where Cochran, long retired from the Memphis police, still guest lectures during CIT training sessions. He's tall and slightly stooped, graying hair combed back from his forehead. That day, the academy's auditorium was filled with officers from around the area: some from the Memphis Police Department, others from around the state, and a few from Mississippi. Not all of them were cops: there were court officers, TSA agents (the officers responsible for security at airports), and a handful of 911 dispatchers as well. There's some disagreement in the world of CIT about who should get trained. The question is not about which agencies should be involved but rather whether every officer in a police department should get the training. Cochran and others believe that only certain officers have the disposition for it. Other people believe that interacting with people with mental illness has become so commonplace that all officers need to be trained.

Police training varies enormously among different departments and jurisdictions, so it's difficult to draw general conclusions about officer training. The United States has more than 12,000 city police departments, 3,000 county sheriff's departments, and state police and other law enforcement agencies as well.[5] There are 650 academies across the country, some run by individual law enforcement agencies, others by local community colleges. What those academies teach is dictated by state rules, although even within a given state, there is much room for interpretation. Still, there are some givens: most of the officers in the auditorium in Memphis had almost undoubtedly been taught certain things— weapon use, defensive tactics, criminal investigation. They likely also learned to do things quickly: walk in and take command of the situation.

CIT is different. CIT is slow policing, Cochran told the room. Like a football coach, he laid out a series of plays for officers to follow. "Verbal Crisis Plan: Things Your Mother Taught You," one of his first slides said. "Start: A Greeting or Introduction. Be respectful and polite. Keep the 'greeting or introduction' simple." Play number two is to introduce yourself and ask the other person's name. Other plays include asking how you can help and repeating back to the person what you perceive as the problem he is expressing. If these seem obvious, it's because they are. In many ways, the rules of play for CIT simply harken back to earlier days of community policing, when police served more as social workers and neighborhood fixtures than as armed crime fighters. (In the early part of the twentieth century, there was a shift toward professional policing—police as trained crime-fighting specialists, experts who shouldn't have to waste their time as social workers with guns. The latter half of the century saw a shift back toward the community policing model, but some argue that law enforcement is still driven by that vision of "professional crime fighters" rather than social services providers.) Mike Woody, a retired Ohio officer who is now advises police departments through the CIT community, said part of the idea of CIT is to undo that: "We are trying to change the warrior mentality back into the guardian mentality." It's an approach that Seth Stoughton, the police officer turned law professor, says is really just *good* policing: "It is a mistake to limit the concepts of the police side of CIT to individuals who are in crisis. The same basic considerations, tactics, verbal communication, de-escalation apply across the board to all individuals. Or they *should* apply to all individuals."

The goal of this training is to give the officers the skills they need to be able to defuse a situation—whether the person is contemplating suicide, threatening a family member, or just in need of hospitalization—without resorting to force. To do that, officers have to think like mental health workers or at least not think like cops. In practice, it might mean asking somebody calmly—"Hey, do me a favor. Would you mind putting down that knife?"—rather than shouting—"Put the knife down now! I *said now*! Put the knife down, or I'll shoot." It could mean being prepared to ignore insults from the suspect. Or it could mean letting somebody pace around his house while you're talking to him. (In standard situations, letting somebody wander around is seen as dangerous because he could be retrieving a weapon or otherwise putting the officer in harm's way.) Jamie Lambert, the officer from Memphis, has been a trained CIT officer since 2012, but he says taking the gentler approach can still feel dangerous sometimes: "You don't want to come across as mean, but in the back of your head you're [wondering if you are] sacrificing your safety to appease this person."

Skeptics of CIT training often deride it as a hug-a-thug approach. But Mike Woody says the goal is still to have officers going home alive at the end of their shifts: "There is a time to be a warrior, but there is also a time to be that guardian." He says this means teaching officers to do everything possible to defuse a crisis but also to be prepared to resort to more-traditional tactics—including force—if they need to: "What it means is that you have your tools, or your weapons, have them protected with elbows pretty close. Have hands out in front of you, [in what] looks like a welcoming manner but [in such a way that they] can protect you. [And] still keeping enough distance that you can react if, all of a sudden, this person would charge you."

Jamie Lambert told me about a situation recently where a woman called for help getting her teenaged son—who had not been taking his medication—to the hospital. Lambert said he had managed to calm the boy down and convinced him to go to the hospital, but when the boy suddenly punched a hole in the Sheetrock wall, Lambert and his partner had had to tackle him. (The boy calmed down in the back of the squad car.)

After a morning of learning CIT plays, it was time for officers to try out their new skills in elaborate role-play scenarios. One criticism of academy training is that new recruits spend many hours practicing how to shoot a gun or how to take down a suspect and very few—or zero—practicing how to help a person in crisis. Here, Memphis police officers played the parts of people in a mental health crisis. In one scene, officers tried to talk a depressed vet out of killing himself. The man kept putting his hand in his pocket—which makes cops nervous because he could have a weapon in there—and he kept wanting to stand up. The officers were encouraged to ask him about his military service; one connected by sharing that he, too, was a vet. In another, a woman was dancing in the street, risking her life and disrupting traffic; the officer who "responded" started by complimenting her dancing, then pointed out that standing in the street was dangerous and offered her a bottle of water. Another scene involved a man who wanted to get revenge on his girlfriend who'd left him. He told one officer he was planning to burn the house down, another that he was planning to call and threaten the woman. The 911 dispatchers took part, too, adding questions about diagnoses, medications, and plans for committing suicide to the usual ones about the location and nature of the emergency. Cities are increasingly coming to the realization that identifying calls as mental health calls is an important part of improving law enforcement responses: it means they can dispatch CIT-trained officers to the scene and that the officers who respond will have some idea of what they're walking into. I got to try the negotiations, too, talking to the man who wanted revenge on his girlfriend. It was harder—and more nerve-racking—than I'd anticipated.

OVER THE PAST SEVERAL DECADES, the CIT approach has become a cornerstone of police policies for dealing with people with mental illness in big cities like Miami and San Antonio as well as in smaller jurisdictions like the Chicago suburb of Orland Park. And the concept is moving beyond just police. Correctional facilities such as the Cook County Jail and the state prison system in Indiana have begun training their corrections officers in it so they can respond better to prisoners in crisis. There are far fewer correctional facilities with CIT-trained officers than police forces, but the number is growing rapidly. Correctional facilities have realized that, as with police in the community, corrections officers are often the first to respond to mental health crises in jails and prisons, and that abuse is more likely to occur when officers have not been trained properly. In some cases, as in Indiana, the training has been imposed on the state by a court order or as part of a settlement negotiation.

There are as many versions of CIT programs as there are cities, and even beyond the question of whether all officers should be trained in it, there is little consensus on how best to structure them. Does a CIT officer respond to every mental health crisis call or only ones where the regular officer calls for backup? Does a mental health professional accompany the officers? Who takes the "lead"—i.e., who is in charge on the scene—if a CIT officer arrives when a call is already in progress?

In Orland Park, the CIT program was developed after the police force started receiving large numbers of mental health calls when the local state hospital shut down. (The police chief in Orland Park has a stronger connection to mental illness and criminal justice than many; he was the Secret Service agent who got hit trying to protect Ronald Reagan when John Hinckley, Jr., shot him in 1981.) In Miami, CIT officers are part of a county-wide program to divert people with mental illness who commit low-level misdemeanors out of the criminal justice system and into treatment.

Sam Cochran, the retired Memphis lieutenant who helped start it all, believes CIT programs are only the first step: "The law enforcement officers are just a mere reflection of the community [they serve]. It's not about law enforcement; it's about the community." In other words, things won't really change until the rest of us start to see a person having a mental health crisis the way he teaches his officers to: as somebody who needs help, not as somebody who is a threat.

At the same time, changing the way communities see people with mental illness also means having the right institutions and networks in place to support them. It's great to have officers who know how to manage a mental health crisis, but training goes only so far if there's no place to take the person to get help. This was the problem Leon

Evans found in San Antonio, Texas, in 2000 when he took over community mental health care in Bexar County. The county jail was full of people with mental illness, many who had committed only minor offenses. His last job had been to oversee community mental health care across the state, and he felt partially responsible for the crisis. "[In that job] I really became painfully aware of all the people who had been criminalized because of failure of the mental health system which I was in charge of," he told me. Texas, like Florida, is perennially at the bottom of the mental health care spending list.

As a first step toward dealing with the crisis, the San Antonio Police Department began doing CIT training with its officers in 2003. The original plan was to train about 10 percent of the force; today, nearly the whole police department has received the training. But Evans saw the problem very quickly. He's a large man with white hair and beard, and he has spent his career working with children and with people who have mental illness. He tells a story about going to one of the early training sessions where none of the cops wanted to be there: "They were *forced* to be there by the chief or the sheriff. I heard [one say]: 'I'm a cop, I'm not a social worker. I don't believe in these hug-a-thug programs.'"

At the first break, Evans approached the cop who had been complaining the loudest. "How often do you encounter people with mental illness?" he asked the officer. "How about last night?" the officer responded. The night before, he had been working the graveyard shift when he got called to a McDonald's on the south side of town. There he found the restaurant empty except for a man in the corner who was screaming the Lord's Prayer over and over again. When the officer got the man to settle down enough to talk, he explained that he heard voices in his head, which were calmed when he shouted the prayer. "So what happened?" Evans asked.

"I took him to jail," the officer answered. In that moment, Evans realized that "if you don't have an alternative to jails or emergency rooms or putting somebody back on the street, [the police] are going to have to take them to jail or the emergency room or put them back on the street. This vicious revolving door."

For officers like the one Evans talked to, the emergency room was the last resort because, as anyone who's ever gone to an emergency room knows, it nearly always involves waiting for endless hours to be. seen. No police officer wants to sit in the waiting room of the ER with somebody who is psychotic or suicidal. And no police supervisor wants her officers doing that. In this, too, we have apparently learned little from the past. As sociologist Egon Bittner wrote in his 1967 article, officers complain that trying to get a person hospitalized "is a tedious, cumbersome, and uncertain procedure. They must often wait a long time in the admitting office.... They must also reckon with the possibility of being turned down by the psychiatrist in which case they are left with an aggravated problem on their hands."[6]

The San Antonio police chief at the time started tracking hours spent waiting in the ER and discovered that his officers were spending twelve to fourteen hours a week there, mostly with people who were in a mental health crisis, intoxicated, or both. In part because of that, the city was spending $600,000 a year on overtime for its police officers. Jail was decidedly the faster option, but it wasn't cheap, and it was rapidly getting crowded. Finding a solution to this became an obsession for Evans. With the help of a local judge, he created a partnership in San Antonio among the police, the courts, and the mental health care system. Much like CIT, the idea was at once both absurdly simple and dauntingly complicated: get people with mental illness out of the criminal justice system and into effective treatment programs instead.

The result is the Restoration Center, a kind of mental health care mall that is open twenty-four hours per day, seven days per week. It has a mental health crisis center for people who need short-term stabilization; a sobering center, where a person can sleep off a rough night of alcohol or drugs; detox and rehab programs; and a methadone clinic. Across the street, a homeless shelter offers a place to sleep for people who are ready to engage in mental health and/or substance use treatment, and a safe place, in the courtyard, for those who aren't ready for treatment but still need someplace to sleep.

On the face of it, the Restoration Center sounds similar to the crisis centers in places like Oklahoma, a place for people in a mental health crisis to get emergency care. What sets the Restoration Center apart is that it is a whole social services ecosystem. As Evans realized years ago, the police, the jail, the hospital, and the outpatient facilities were each dealing with different parts of the same problem. To resolve it, all the players would need to work together.

Today the center is housed in a single-story concrete building on the wrong side of downtown that used to house a diagnostic laboratory and, before that, the county medical examiner's office. The structure sprawls across a baking-hot parking lot, the monotony of its glaring off-white walls punctuated by a handful of dark red doors. Now, when a San Antonio police officer encounters a person in crisis, she doesn't have to take him to either jail or to the ER. Instead, she can bring him to a designated entrance at the back of the building that leads straight into the crisis center. Once inside, the officer finds free coffee and a desk for writing reports. (In the hospital, filling out a report often means standing up at a borrowed corner of a busy nurses' station counter.) The drop-off process is streamlined, so officers are back on the streets very quickly.

The center's annual budget is just over $100 million per year, and the facility is bare bones. The mental health crisis center consists of a couple of exam rooms and two identical dorm rooms, set side by side. The only windows face onto the nurses' station. Through them, in the cramped rooms I can see a man asleep on one bed and a woman in blue shortie pajamas sitting on another. A third patient paces back and forth across one of the rooms while a nurse in blue scrubs watches from a desk in the corner. The center doesn't intend for people to stay here very long. Evans believes that if there were more longer-term beds—as so many communities say they need—doctors would find reasons to keep patients longer: "If the only tool you have is a hammer, everything looks like a nail, right? In reality, a lot of these people can be stabilized fairly quickly." Once they're stabilized, they're discharged into care in the community, which the center helps arrange.

The admissions process is just as easy at the Sobering Center down the hall, a big room with mattresses on the floor, plus a few lounge chairs, where people can sleep off a drinking or drug binge. It has water, a bathroom, and an EMT for emergencies; it's overseen by a substance use counselor named Manuel. Once people are sober, Manuel offers—but does not push—detox or rehab. I was chatting with Manuel and watching three men sleep—one has the blanket pulled over his face; another hasn't managed to take his shoes off—when the doorbell rang. In the glaring sunshine outside stood two officers in sunglasses and polo shirts, a young blond woman in large plastic-frame glasses and turquoise hospital scrubs between them. She stepped awkwardly inside, carrying a computer bag and a pocketbook. The officers quietly introduced her as a public intox.

"I am not a PI," she said too loudly, before asking for the bathroom. Walking with a strange stiff-legged stagger, she lurched her way across the room. When she came back, Manuel quickly inventoried her belongings; somebody else checked her vital signs. It was all much faster than any ER intake and less traumatic than being booked into jail. The officers were free to leave as soon as she was admitted.

Leon Evans will tell you not to copy his model—it's specific to the needs of San Antonio, he says—but the Restoration Center has indeed become a model for communities around the country. So many criminal justice and mental health people come to observe the center that when I asked for the interview, the program assistant e-mailed me a standardized form with a checklist of all the things I might want to see. Evans retired a few months after my visit, but the program is continuing to evolve. For example, the county recently started screening new arrestees at booking to see if more people could be diverted from the criminal justice system.

The San Antonio model doesn't solve the whole puzzle. There still isn't enough mental health care available in the community, and people accused of violent crimes still end up in jail. Nonetheless, the record so far is impressive: since its founding in 2008, more than 60,000 people have been diverted from the criminal justice system. The program estimates that it's saved Bexar County taxpayers more than $50 million per year. Evans says the program is responsible for an 80 percent drop in homelessness in San Antonio's downtown, a 50 percent drop in the number of ER visits, and a decision by the county not to expand the jail by a thousand beds. Evans says it's really that collaboration—among cops, courts, and mental health care—that makes the approach work. Mental illness is not, Evans says, "a homeless issue, this is not a jail issue, this is not an emergency room issue…it's an issue for all those things."

AT ALMOST THE SAME TIME Leon Evans was starting to divert people in San Antonio into treatment, Steve Leifman, a judge in Florida, began diverting people in the Miami-Dade area out of the court system. He and Evans like to say they attacked the mental health crisis from opposite angles and are now—some fifteen years later—meeting in the middle.

There are two stories Leifman likes to tell about how he came to see mental illness as the most serious problem facing the criminal justice system. The first happened when Leifman was a high school student interning in a Florida legislator's office. A call came from a constituent who said her son was being treated terribly in the state hospital where he lived. Leifman was sent to investigate and was horrified by what he saw. He remembers finding the man—who, he later learned, had autism, not a mental illness—tied to a bed and heavily medicated. On a tour of the facility the same day, Leifman saw a group of male patients getting literally hosed down by hospital workers, in lieu of a shower.

The second story takes place years later, in 2000. By this time, Leifman was a new judge. He was getting ready for court one morning when an older couple came to his chambers. Their son had a case on the misdemeanor docket that morning, and they begged Leifman to help him. He had schizophrenia, they said, and needed help. When his case was called, the defendant who appeared before the judge was a young man, smart and well-educated. Except for appearing rather disheveled, he seemed fine. Suddenly, however, in response to one of the judge's questions, the man began to scream. He begged Leifman to kick his parents out of the courtroom. His real parents had died in the Holocaust, he told the startled judge; the people who had come to his chambers that morning were imposters from the CIA who had come to kill him. Leifman ordered a competency exam, and the man, not surprisingly, was found incompetent to stand trial. But from there Leifman was stuck. He wanted desperately to get the man medical help and was dismayed when he realized there was nothing he could do.

Today, there is something he can do. Leifman runs one of the most successful—and widely copied—jail diversion programs in the country. The basic idea is this: when a person with mental illness is arrested on a misdemeanor—and some nonviolent felony charges—he is offered the possibility of being diverted into treatment instead of going through the criminal court system. Leifman says that 80 percent of the people who are offered the option choose to join the program. Once they are enrolled, the program—called the Criminal Mental Health Project—helps connect them to mental health care and housing in the community. Participants appear in court periodically to make sure they're complying with what they're supposed to do.

I watched one afternoon as people came before Leifman to report on their progress. The judge is a short man with startling blue eyes and dark hair combed back from a receding hairline. His mouth looks like it's been caught in a perpetual half-smile. Sitting on the bench, he seemed genuinely happy to be there. He bantered with an older Jewish man who had been accused of stealing from a synagogue. He congratulated a blond woman who, Leifman said, had come so far since her arrest. He dismissed the case of a man who had, for the last thirty years, had a severe drinking problem. The man told me later he never would have quit had it not been for the program.

About 600 people are referred to the program each year; there is an active caseload of about 125 at any given time. "It should be more," Leifman says. He estimates that over the last decade his program has managed to divert about 4,000 people out of the criminal justice system. Recidivism rates among participants are low. Where Evans managed to keep the jail in San Antonio from expanding, Leifman says he diverted so many people out of the Miami-Dade system that the jail closed down an entire wing, saving the county $12 million. In a segment about the program, the television comedian Samantha Bee joked on her show "Full Frontal with Samantha Bee" on June 13, 2016, that the city made an extra $3 million by turning the empty jail into a water park called the Slipper Slammer.

As in San Antonio, the police have a critical role in the program. More than 4,500 cops in the Miami area have been trained in CIT; by being identified as potential participants early, people can be referred to the system without getting arrested. One challenge for both cities is what to do with people facing violent charges. Many diversion programs are reluctant to accept such people—judges, district attorneys, and community programs are all concerned about the risk involved. For example, one district attorney who works in a mental health court told me he never allows arsonists into the program; they're too hard to place in treatment and too much of a liability. For now, the only option for people who can't be diverted is to go through the criminal court system.

In 2020 Leifman plans to follow San Antonio's lead with the construction of a comprehensive care center. He has begun converting an old psychiatric hospital into a center that includes crisis stabilization units, short- and longer-term housing, vocational training, and a courtroom. He wants to focus on the toughest cases, the ones nobody else wants. "The center is going to do the opposite of what's done now," Leifman told me. Usually, "people go to a crisis unit, and the easy cases get dealt with. [Instead, we're] going to really go after the real problem."

San Antonio and Miami offer tantalizing glimpses of what broader reform might look like. It's especially encouraging that these programs were developed in large cities and were developed relatively quickly. Police forces and courts around the country, including in big cities like New York and Los Angeles, are exploring alternative approaches for people with mental illness that incorporate many of these ideas. Still, old prejudices die hard. As one cop in Memphis (who had not received CIT training) told me, anybody who's well enough to commit a crime is well enough to be arrested for it. More concerning, though, is a more fundamental reality: the crisis of mental illness in the criminal justice system is so pervasive that even broad multiagency responses like those in San Antonio and Miami touch only a small part of it. Neither city's model addresses the stark inadequacy of day-to-day access to mental health care in the community for people who don't come through the criminal justice system. Nor do they address the large number of people who have already been shunted into the prison system. Until now, moreover, few reformers have been pushing for alternatives for people with mental illness who commit more-serious or violent crimes—even when it is clear that these people are likely to fare poorly in conventional court systems.

13

Disorder in the Court

IT WAS APRIL 2014, SOME six weeks after Kyle Muhammad had been arrested. Because he couldn't make bail, he had sat at Rikers while a grand jury decided whether to indict him. Years ago, Eula Muhammad told her children that she would not bail them out if they ever got arrested. She has stayed true to that promise, even as she visited her son in jail regularly, called there repeatedly to demand better medical care for him, and sat for hours in the courtroom every time he had a hearing. On that day, as she would on every other day he had a hearing for the next two years, his mother came in through the court's front entrance. The courthouse, an imposing granite and limestone building built in the late 1930s, is just down the block from the Manhattan civil court where his mother had arranged to have him taken to the hospital before his arrest. The grandeur of the lobby, with an enormous art deco clock at the center, is obscured by the barriers that contain the crowds waiting to go through security, walking through metal detectors and putting their bags through X-ray machines. Even past the security check, it's bustling and chaotic: the tiny snack bar in the corner, the line of people waiting to get court records, and attorneys and their clients consulting in far-from-confidential spots in the hallway outside courtrooms.

Muhammad, like the other defendants brought over each day from Rikers Island, didn't see any of that. After a 4 A.M. wakeup and quick breakfast, he was searched and then, along with dozens of others with court dates that day, loaded into a bus—a white school bus retrofitted with metal grates over the windows and "CORRECTION, New York City's Boldest" painted on the side—and driven across the bridge to lower Manhattan. At the courthouse, the bus drove into a bay north of the civilian entrances, where its riders were searched again and then brought to the "pens," a series of holding cells in the basement of the building where they stayed until it was time for them to appear in court.

The courtroom, like many in the building, is large but shabby. The benches are made of wood, like church pews, and are filled with a motley audience of participants and observers that thins out as the calendar progresses. The front rows are reserved for the lawyers, private ones in dark suits, public defenders in hipper variations of court clothes. Defendants out on bail and waiting for a hearing, some looking uncomfortable in pants and shirts, others looking out of place in sagging pants and baseball caps. Family—mothers and wives or girlfriends, usually—hoping to catch a glimpse of and blow a kiss to the defendants bused in from jail. Court officers patrol the room, warning people caught texting or talking to take it outside. The judge has a narrow face and long, curly brown hair. She presides, in alternation, with compassion and a strictness that sometimes borders on irritation.

Muhammad was the fifth person on the calendar that day. His attorney and the prosecutor had barely identified themselves for the record when Muhammad began to shout. "I need to hear what you're going to say. You can't touch me," he yelled, addressing his lawyer. "I'm a free man. I need my paperwork. I need to speak to the judge. I have rights, and my rights have been violated by the Constitution. And my constitutional rights have been violated. This man [his lawyer] has given me a force order not to contact him. I've been mistreated by the staff and the whole judicial system."

The judge stopped him: "If you cannot follow these rules, you're not going to be brought back here," she told him. "So if you want to make sure your rights are protected—" Muhammad interrupted again, and the judge asked the court officers to escort him out. The judge put it in the record that Muhammad had had a meltdown and that she was arranging to get him the care he needed. What the record doesn't detail is what his lawyer and mother described later: Muhammad screaming at the judge, kicking at the court officers, and holding onto his chair like an oversized toddler as they dragged him out of the courtroom. Every time Muhammad came to court after that—at least a dozen times—she put her bailiffs on alert. The day of the meltdown, the judge ordered Muhammad sent to get a 730 exam to see if he was competent to stand trial.

The next time Muhammad came back to court, he still hadn't been evaluated. It had now been four months since he had been locked up, and he was getting effectively no treatment in jail for his schizophrenia. These kinds of delays are common; it's part of why places like Fulton County, Georgia, have been experimenting with competency restoration in jail.

Meanwhile, Muhammad's mother continued to visit him at Rikers, where she saw evidence of his continued psychosis. She always brought him a freshly laundered shirt before court appearances so he'd have something to wear besides the rumpled jail scrubs that can make the neatest person look disheveled and disoriented. This time, he had asked her to bring a white shirt, which she did. It turned out that white button-down shirts are not allowed at Rikers because higher-ranking corrections officers wear them as part of their uniforms and the jail wants no possibility that a prisoner could be mistaken for an officer.

Even if you read and try to follow the rules about what's allowed at the jail, these kinds of mix-ups happen frequently. The rules are complicated and hard to understand. Enforcement can also be capricious, and what's acceptable one time may not be the next time. Once, Eula Muhammad brought her son dress shoes to wear in court; they were rejected because of the metal shank inside the sole, which could be used as a weapon. It's frustrating, one of those endless small humiliations that can infuriate even the most even-keeled person.

When his mother told Muhammad that he couldn't have his white shirt, he lost his temper completely. Sitting in the crowded visitors room, he yelled and flailed until several officers had to escort him from the room. There were other incidents too. His mother was terrified. It took several months, but Muhammad finally talked to the psychologists. They found him incompetent to stand trial.

The court systems in New York and other big cities are appallingly slow. In her state of the judiciary speech, New York's chief judge, Janet DiFiore, talked about how bad court delays are for everybody involved, for "crime victims and their families, as they wait for justice to be done; prosecutors and their cases, as key witnesses move away, memories fade and evidence grows stale; and defendants, presumed innocent under the law, who must return to court over and over again or, too often, sit in jail waiting for their cases to be resolved."[1]

But the delays are worse for defendants with mental illness. A 2012 analysis by the Council of State Governments found that in New York City, people with mental illness stayed in jail on average almost *twice* as long as people without mental illness (112 days versus 69 days). Part of that is bail: only about 12 percent of defendants with mental illness were able to make bail compared with about 21 percent of those without mental illness. Even for those who were able to make bail, it took them much longer to do so than those without mental illness.[2] On television dramas, making bail takes only long enough to have a short scene of the defendant looking scared and out of place in an overcrowded holding cell. In real life, only a very small percentage of people are able to make bail at all, and an even smaller percentage are able to do so immediately. Even if a defendant can come up with the money, the logistics of paying it can also slow down the process.

Judges, prosecutors, and defense attorneys all attribute some delays for defendants with mental illness to a lack of alternatives to incarceration and a lack of *information* about those alternatives. This corroborates what I frequently heard: among other issues, finding a program that is able and willing to take a person with a particular constellation of issues can be extremely difficult.

The mental illness itself also contributes to the delays. In Muhammad's case at least four months were lost while he waited to have his mental health evaluated. And then, when he was finally found incompetent, it took another six months for him to be restored to sanity. The judge sent him to Kirby Forensic Psychiatric Center on Randalls Island. From what he can remember, the treatment focused mostly on what happens in the courtroom; there was little in the way of therapy.

Apart from the competency issues, Muhammad's case may have been complicated by the fact that he had previous convictions. As law professor John Pfaff writes, it's police who decide who gets into the system, but once somebody is in it, "prosecutors have complete control over which cases they file and which ones they dismiss." Furthermore, they can choose from a range of charges, charges that can have a significant impact on the outcome of the case and thus the person.[3]

The power of the prosecutor has been augmented by what Pfaff describes as "a growing array of often-overlapping charges from which to choose." Instead of simple assault (meaning one where there is bodily injury) and aggravated assault (one where there is serious bodily injury), New York now has approximately twenty-three different assault charges. In some places the precise charge the prosecutor chooses could more than *double* the sentence.[4] In Muhammad's case, the fact that his victim was over sixty-five and more than ten years older than he meant a more serious charge for which he could have faced seven years in prison.

For prosecutors, mental illness becomes a mitigating factor, though not necessarily to the benefit of the defendant. As one former district-attorney-turned-judge in Oklahoma told me, "The [district attorneys] don't want to hear about your client's mental illness. They want to get a conviction, a notch in the belt." "By the time we get them, they've raped someone," another prosecutor said to me. "The defense attorney is like 'But, come on, he has a mental illness,' but he's lit his mother on fire." He was exaggerating, certainly, but the question of dangerousness, whether perceived or legitimate, is a challenging one. For judges and prosecutors, it's a reason to be tougher on defendants with mental illness: nobody wants to wake up and find their case on the front page of the *New York Times*.

At the same time, even for the most well-meaning prosecutors, the options are somewhat limited. "If you're the restaurateur and same guy is sleeping within twenty yards of your front door, hassling customers, and you want the [police] to do something, they're going to remove that person," said Mike Herring, district attorney in Richmond, Virginia, because the only way police can do anything "is in the context of criminal intervention. Should [the defendant] be arrested, locked up, and detained? No, but if the city doesn't have a formalized diversion model, there's no alternative.... The challenge for us is the criminal justice system isn't set up to deal with mental illness. It's set up to punish or not. And once the court assumes jurisdiction, after conviction, the question is what do we do with them? Do we house them or try to address the trigger for the behavior? If we try to address the behavior for a poor, homeless, mentally ill defendant, however humane your thinking may be, trying to do it in the community is a prescription for failure because there is no stability."

Even when Kyle Muhammad's competency was restored and the case was restarted, it took more than a year and many, many hearings to resolve. Going to trial would have been a risky proposition for him. He faced a long sentence—not long perhaps by the double-digit standards of today, but certainly long enough to be extremely damaging and disruptive—and a jury would likely not have been sympathetic either toward him or toward his crime. Letting him take the stand would have been risky, as his behavior—even when he's stable—is unpredictable, and he's prone to random digressions.

Then there's the way he talks about the crime itself. I've spent hours talking to Kyle Muhammad, and I've heard several different explanations. He still insists, often with some agitation, that he is innocent, that it was just a mistake, that he honestly thought he knew the woman. He occasionally wonders aloud whether he might convince his attorney to reopen the case or if he could somehow acquire the video from surveillance cameras from nearby stores to prove his innocence. It's not malicious; I truly believe that some combination of his disease and a lack of understanding about the criminal justice system has made it difficult for him to understand.

There were discussions about what to do, ways to avoid the prison time. It took his attorney and a social worker months to negotiate placement for him. There were more discussions and delays, paperwork and negotiations. In the end the district attorney finally agreed to release him to the supervision of a Forensic Assertive Community Treatment (FACT) team in Harlem and into the Manhattan mental health court.

The Manhattan mental health court is only a few floors above the courtroom where Muhammad appeared all those times, but it is worlds away from it. The room is smaller and quieter. If the courtroom downstairs feels like a large, imposing church sanctuary, this is a small, intimate chapel. It is presided over by a Superior Court judge who had never had experience with mental health court before taking the job and who still works a regular courtroom the rest of the week. The participants—except for a handful being considered for the program—are free, so they come to court in street clothes. And the same people come back week after week, so there is a consistent, rotating cast of characters.

Mental health courts are known as "problem-solving courts." The idea started with drug courts in the 1980s and has spread. There are now, in addition to drug and mental health courts, domestic violence courts and veterans courts; Philadelphia even has a court specifically designed for people who are caught with small amounts of marijuana. The idea of problem-solving courts is to sidestep the traditional punitive criminal justice system in a supportive, encouraging environment designed to accommodate participants' specific needs. Participants in mental health court have to agree to go to treatment and stay off drugs. If they are successful, people often get the charges dropped or their records expunged. If they mess up—by not taking their medication or skipping appointments, for example—the judge can sanction them in various ways, including by sending them back to jail briefly or even kicking them out of the program.

Here, the judge and his clerks decide which people would make good candidates for the program: "We look at practical matters, like risk factors," he told me. "If somebody is connected with family, they're more likely to be stable, more like to have a strong support system. We're more willing to take a greater risk." Enrollment in mental health courts tends to be limited. For example, the Manhattan mental health court has about 50 clients at a time; by contrast, the diversion program in Miami sees 600 referrals each year and has a caseload of about 125 at any given time. On that scale, it would be very difficult to make even a dent in the number of people with mental illness who end up in New York City's criminal court system.

Around 10:30 every Friday morning, the judge, hair in a neat side swoop, black robe over his shirt and tie, walks into the courtroom of the Manhattan mental health court, and the bailiff calls the room to order. One by one, the judge calls participants up; they sit, usually quietly, while the caseworker and attorney update him. The judge holds a meeting with all the attorneys and social workers right before court begins, so this recitation is largely for the record. The judge asks how the client is doing. He often asks some follow-up questions— if a participant mentions a new apartment, he'll ask what it's like. The effect is avuncular if sometimes distracted. Occasionally he will warn people about their behavior. Only once did I see him send somebody back to jail, a man who had been caught bringing drugs into a shelter.

AS ONE OF THE CONDITIONS for joining the mental health court, Muhammad enrolled with a FACT team. Assertive Community Treatment (ACT) teams—a kind of "hospital without walls"—were developed in the 1970s to provide, on an outpatient basis, the kind of comprehensive care that people had previously received in state hospitals. Doctors see patients in clinics or at home, nurses make sure the patient takes his medication, and employment specialists help patients find work: there are housing specialists, substance use counselors, and more. But if ACT teams were fairly useful for keeping patients out of the hospital, they were less so at keeping them out of jail. FACT teams took the ACT team model and modified it for people with psychiatric issues and a criminal history. So in addition to helping with medical issues, it's also supposed to keep people like Kyle

Muhammad on the straight and narrow—identifying the things that get him sucked into the criminal justice system and reminding him how to avoid them.

Still, finding his feet after nearly two years in jail was difficult, one example after another of the barriers we set for people like Muhammad. First there was the housing issue. Although he is somewhat able to take care of himself, his doctors and his mother believed he needed to live in supportive housing. The wait in New York City, as elsewhere, is long. He could have moved in with his mother and sister, but that would have meant, according to the city bureaucracy, that he had a home, and he would have been sent to the end of the line for supportive housing. Instead, he spent months living in a homeless shelter for people with mental illness. The shelter was out of the way, a bus and a subway ride to almost anywhere in the city. Worse, like many shelters, this one insisted that residents leave between 7 A.M. and 4 P.M. He spent many days wandering the streets or sitting in the library with nothing to do and nowhere to go.

Money was a problem. Even though he'd been on disability for years, getting his checks started up again was a bureaucratic hassle. And finding a job proved harder than he'd expected. He'd wanted to work as a peer counselor, helping others with mental illness, a job he had held—and enjoyed—before he was locked up again. But because he has a criminal record, the state was required to sign off on any job he takes working with people with disabilities, something it took months to do. And he found that just about every potential employer he spoke to wanted an explanation of his criminal record.

But Muhammad persevered. He finally found an apartment in supportive housing. He graduated—in near-record time—from the mental health court. (In another ridiculous example of the little ways that the system fails, the day he graduated, Department of Corrections bureaucracy required him to be handcuffed and spend several hours—wearing a shirt, a tie, and dress pants—in one of the cells at the courthouse until the department could finish the paperwork to release him officially.) Muhammad is taking his medication and still sees a doctor regularly. He recently started a job as a caseworker, helping people with mental illness navigate the system. For now, at least, Muhammad has succeeded in beating the odds.

WE KNOW AND ACCEPT THAT cancer and other physical diseases sometimes recur. We have mostly come to accept that treating an addiction, whether to heroin or tobacco, is a process and that it often takes most people multiple tries to quit completely. (One exception to this is in the criminal justice system, which is still as harsh about relapses as it is about recidivism.) Yet a person with mental illness who ricochets repeatedly between inadequate health care and support in the community and the vortex of the criminal justice system is seen as a hopeless failure. But maybe it is not he, but we—society—that are to blame. If, as it is sometimes said, the definition of insanity is doing the same thing over and over again and expecting a different outcome, then there is little doubt that it is we, who continue to expect the nearly impossible from those least-equipped to handle it, are the crazy ones.

Conclusion

In retrospect, one wonders if it was the crime that got Isaiah Doyle sentenced to death or his behavior on the witness stand. His attorneys tried to convince him not to testify at all. They feared that anything he said would end up doing more harm than good. In the end, Doyle didn't take the stand until the sentencing phase of the trial, a day after the jury had found him guilty of killing a convenience store clerk during a 2005 robbery.

His attorneys were right to have been worried. He had spent much of the trial sleeping, sometimes snoring loudly. When he wasn't sleeping, he was disruptive, tearing up sheets of paper from the legal pads on the defense table, playing with evidence, and "laboriously copying out sections of a book onto multiple sheets of paper."[1] His mental state had deteriorated over the course of the trial; even during the trial, his attorneys noted that he was unable to provide them meaningful assistance.

His statement on the witness stand was predictably disastrous. On the night of the crime, Doyle and a friend robbed two convenience stores near New Orleans before coming to the third, where, after demanding Kool cigarettes and the money in the cash register, he shot and killed the clerk, the twenty-six-year-old daughter of Korean immigrants. According to the friend he was with on the night of the murder, Doyle was also high on a mix of cocaine, heroin, and Xanax.

"I wouldn't care what decision [the jurors] made," he said. "I have no conscious [sic]. I wouldn't care. I hate everybody that's up there right now, especially him over there [the jury foreman]. I wish I could cut his head off." He told the court that not only was the clerk's murder not an accident, but that he wasn't sorry for what he had done: "I would like to say that I have no sympathy or empathy for [the clerk] or her family....I have no conscious [*sic*]. So when I go back to the dorm and I lay down I don't think about it ever." He ended by directing his anger to the jury itself: "If I had a AK-47 I'd kill every last one of you all with no problem. I have no remorse for what I have done."[2]

It took the jury just two hours to decide that Isaiah Doyle should be put to death. According to newspaper reports from that day, Doyle showed no emotion as the verdict was read. His mother, who was in the courtroom that day, burst into tears and had to be helped from the room.

Lost on the jurors was that Doyle's chilling performance was almost certainly a further manifestation of the severe mental illness he had his entire life. As one of his attorneys told the court, Doyle "has a long history of mental problems that stretches from the time he was a baby until his sitting in the courtroom." The attorneys also noted that he had a developmental disability, had spent time in a psychiatric hospital as a teenager, and had substance use issues—he had overdosed three times in the years before the murder.[3]

The jury's decision to sentence him to death in spite of all that went against hundreds of years of history that said a person with severe mental illness shouldn't be put to death. In the same eighteenth-century treatise on English common law where he explains why a person must be sane to be put on trial, legal scholar William Blackstone argues that a person who is insane should also not be executed: "[I]f, after judgment, [the defendant] becomes of nonsane memory, execution shall be stayed: for peradventure, says the humanity of the English law, had the prisoner been of sound memory, he might have alleged something in stay of judgment or execution."[4]

In 1986 the US Supreme Court, in *Ford v. Wainwright*, upheld the notion that people with mental illness should not be subjected to capital punishment. Alvin Ford was a man from Florida who became very paranoid and was ultimately diagnosed with paranoid schizophrenia after his conviction in the 1970s of first-degree murder. The Court ruled that executing somebody who is too insane to understand why he is being put to death violates the Eighth Amendment: "It is no less abhorrent today than it has been for centuries to exact in penance the life of one whose mental illness prevents him from comprehending the reasons for the penalty or its implications," wrote Thurgood Marshall in the decision. Among other things, Marshall went on to say, there is little point to killing somebody who doesn't understand why he's being killed: "[T]he execution of an insane person simply offends humanity.... It provides no example to others, and thus contributes nothing to whatever deterrence value is intended to be served by capital punishment."[5] In practice, though, the Court left it up to the individual states to decide how insane is too insane to be killed. And unlike other areas of capital punishment, the law remains remarkably unclear on it. (The 2005 decision in *Roper v. Simmons* ruled it unconstitutional to execute juveniles, and the 2002 decision in *Atkins v. Virginia* deemed it unconstitutional to execute a person with developmental disabilities, although just how to define a developmental disability has also been left to the states to determine.) What remains is what one longtime capital defender told me, a standard of "too sick to execute" that is impossible to meet. Indeed, about half of the people executed between 2000 and 2015 had been diagnosed with a mental illness or substance use disorder at some time in their adult lives.

Many crimes that get defendants sentenced to death are grisly, so grotesque as to make the perpetrator seem almost inhuman. Isaiah Doyle's crime was terrible. But in stark contrast to those other capital cases, his hardly stands out. Certainly there are many in our prisons who have committed murder in the course of a robbery and were not sentenced to death.

It is hard to find more visceral proof of our ambivalence or, worse, antipathy toward people with severe mental illness than our continued readiness to sentence so many of them to death. The picture that accompanied every story about Doyle in the *New Orleans Times-Picayune* was his mug shot. It's a picture that speaks to our fear of young African American men: large indistinct tattoos on both sides of his neck, heavy-lidded eyes looking slightly sideways. But it's what he did in court—acting out, showing no remorse, and most of all, threatening the jury—that speaks to our culture's collective fear we have of people with mental illness: they will somehow attack us personally.

As with other questions relating to sick people in the criminal justice system, our way of approaching people with mental illness who have been sentenced to death is deeply contradictory. On the one hand, states (or, in some cases, the courts) are finally recognizing that, as with other parts of their prison populations, death row cohorts include growing numbers of people with mental illness. (The years that people now routinely spend, often in solitary confinement, waiting for their cases to be resolved cannot be good for their mental health.) But instead of addressing the cases themselves and whether the punishment is appropriate, states are simply expanding mental health services for the condemned. In 2014 California began construction on an inpatient psychiatric unit for men on death row. A judge also ruled that all 720 men on death row at San Quentin must be screened for mental illness. "This is the only place on Earth where you'd be talking about building a psychiatric hospital for condemned prisoners," one law professor told the *Los Angeles Times* when it was announced. "It is a measure of American greatness and American silliness at the same time." A cartoon that ran in the paper sums up the absurdity of the situation well. With the caption "Under court pressure, California is building a psychiatric care hospital at San Quentin prison to provide long-term mental health care for Death Row inmates," the cartoon depicts a classic psychiatrist's office where a man in prison scrubs, handcuffs, and leg shackles lies on an analyst's couch. Visible behind him are cell bars and a view of the electric chair. "Why so depressed?" the bearded therapist asks.[6] We are also a country that is willing to send people with mental illness to their death but insists on restoring them to competency first; a person on death row who attempts suicide will be patched up before he is killed by the state.

It sounds facile, but the most obvious way to stop executing people with mental illness—or threatening to execute them, for the average length of stay on death row is now at least twenty years—is to abolish the death penalty. In fact, although its end may come too late to save Isaiah Doyle or the many others with mental illness still on death row, it appears that it is finally on the wane in the United States. California has not executed anybody since 2006. Before Isaiah Doyle, nobody had been sentenced to die in Jefferson Parish in years. A look at the geography of death sentences makes clear that a very few jurisdictions—and their district attorneys and judges—are responsible for the vast majority of death sentences in the United States today. Barring abolishment, a US Supreme Court decision that clearly outlines the parameters for giving the death penalty to a person with mental illness—much as it did for juveniles—would be a relatively easy fix, although there would presumably still be arguments about what constitutes sick enough and trying to decide who is, in fact, sick versus who is malingering. (The prosecutors in Isaiah Doyle's criminal case continued to argue to the end that he was "crazy like a fox.")

Of course, as disturbing as their cases often are, the people with mental illness on death row remain only a small part of the large and growing population of people with mental illness who we routinely lock up. But the death penalty cases are important in another crucial aspect: in their extreme punishment, sanctioned by juries, they provide powerful evidence of our views about mental illness and crimes more generally. As Austin Sarat, a professor at Amherst College who has studied the death penalty extensively, told me, "The issues in capital cases are different only in degree, not in kind. The same kind of problems that plague the mentally ill throughout the criminal justice system show in the death penalty system."

Finding a way to stop the incredible growth in the number of people with mental illness we shunt into the criminal justice system is obviously complicated. The approaches outlined in the last chapters of the book are certainly moves in the right direction: training police to respond in a more sympathetic, health-care–oriented way; building diversion programs to get people out of the system when they do get caught up in it; or making it easier for people to get mental health care. Should those steps fail and people end up in the criminal justice system anyway, it's clear that jails and prisons need to be better equipped to take care of those people, whether by creating housing that allows them to stay apart from the general population or by hiring more health care workers.

What really needs to happen, though, is what psychiatrist George Stevenson called for more than a half century ago in *the New York Times:* a new way of treating people with mental illness. Both the *official* mental health care system and the *de facto* one, the criminal justice system, need to be completely overhauled. On the one hand, our awareness of the shortcomings in both suggests that the chances for comprehensive reform are higher than they have been in years. At the same time, there are also worrying signs that, instead of taking on this difficult task, we are getting further mired in the status quo and setting ourselves up to repeat the mistakes of the past once again.

This isn't the first time we have been on the cusp of dramatic reform. In the mid-1940s, driven in part by the news and other reports coming out of psychiatric hospitals, states began a frantic drive to *fix* the mental health care system. In 1945, for example, New York ordered its hospitals to hire more psychiatrists and other mental health staff and to provide more treatment to their patients. It also commissioned a study by Columbia University to look at all the New York hospitals. Kansas, California, Missouri, Maryland, and other states examined their mental health care systems and found them lacking. A 1950 study by the Council of State Governments recommended, among other solutions, the construction of new facilities to help reduce overcrowding in hospitals.[7] All of these reforms make considerable sense, even today. Had we resolved the problems then, it's possible we might not be where we are now.

We have begun to understand, again, that jails and prisons are not appropriate places for dealing with mental illness. Yet the push continues to medicalize criminal justice in response to the criminalization of mental illness, often at the expense of diverting people out of the criminal justice system or of keeping them out of there from the beginning. One of the latest developments on that front—and the most expensive—was the offer from the Alabama Department of Corrections, in response to the class-action lawsuit over its treatment of prisoners, to find millions of dollars to build four new prisons, facilities that would allow the state to provide better mental health care to its prisoners. New York City has begun to talk seriously about closing Rikers Island, but only to replace it with new jails. We have known for more than two hundred years that keeping people with mental illness locked up in jails and prisons does little but make them worse. We know how to lock up masses of people. Now we need to figure out how to treat them.

Epilogue

WHENEVER I TELL PEOPLE I am writing about mental illness, they always ask about my connection to the subject. Unlike many other issues that have featured prominently in my work as a journalist, among them immigration and criminal justice, people tend to assume I must have a personal tie to mental illness. Sometimes it seems like the assumption is that only somebody who did would be interested in *those* people. Then again, as I've discovered, most of us do have some connection to mental illness—a distant aunt, a neighbor, an old friend. I am no exception.

It's a story I don't often tell, even when I'm asked that question, in part because it's something of a conversation stopper. But I thought about it a great deal as I researched this book.

I DON'T KNOW ANYMORE IF my knees really buckled when I heard the news. Or if that's just how I remember it now. In my sheltered world, parents didn't die. They certainly didn't get murdered. And especially not at the hands of their brilliant and much-loved college student son, home for Christmas break of his senior year. Matthew had been a year ahead of me at our public high school, a competitive suburban one where the question was not whether you'd go to college, but rather which of the country's top institutions you'd end up in. His younger sister was in my class and was—and still is—a close friend. I knew their parents, too: their chemist father, who was a colleague of my own scientist father, and their mother, who sold antique prints.

Even in a place where many kids had special talents, Matthew stood out. He was not only exceptionally smart; he was also a precocious artist. While we were all still in high school, he was already selling his paintings: realist cityscapes, landscapes inspired by the countryside where the family had a rustic cabin, and impressions of the Atlantic coast, where they often went on vacation. He was creative in other ways, too: he once wrote and recorded an entire musical; he designed elaborate sets for school plays and the local summer stage. But Matthew was no brooding artist type. He was gregarious, funny, and poised, as comfortable talking to parents and teachers as he was to his friends. We all admired him and his unique sensibility; his sister adored him. Sweet-tempered and gentle, there was no indication that he used drugs or alcohol. After high school, he went on to a fancy liberal arts college where he majored in studio art and got A's.

He had never shown any signs of mental illness before, nor had he been violent. In retrospect, though, maybe there were signs that he wasn't himself that Christmas. He had spent the fall semester studying abroad in Paris, and in letters home—this was before e-mail and Skype—he'd complained of strange dreams. At home over winter break, he'd been moody, arguing with his family about the feminist academic Camille Paglia and being weirdly obsessed with the lyrics of the singer/songwriter Sting. At the time, it had seemed nothing more than irritating, the bombastic thoughts of a young man who'd been immersed in challenging new ideas and was, perhaps, trying to figure out what he would do when he graduated.

Then one morning in early January, Matthew took a hammer and bludgeoned his mother to death. He later told psychiatrists and his surviving family that he'd been in the thrall of terrifying delusions about an impending apocalypse. The only way to save his mother, he believed, was to kill her.

His father was at work; his sister was back at her own college. Matthew had had plans that day to visit a museum with our old high school art teacher, Mr. Johnson. When Mr. Johnson arrived at the modest house, he found Matthew's mother unconscious and bleeding in the entryway and Matthew wandering around, speaking incoherently and seemingly oblivious to what he had just done. Mr. Johnson called 911. By the time Matthew's father arrived home, the EMTs were attending his wife, and the police had surrounded Matthew, who was quoting lines from *The Tempest*. At the local hospital, Matthew's mother was declared dead. He was taken to the state forensic hospital.

The next day, his father hired a criminal defense attorney to represent him. At a hearing before the judge, Matthew was asked if he understood the nature of the charges against him and was quickly declared "not criminally responsible," that state's version of not guilty by reason of insanity. (The state dropped the murder charge, but the judge did not acquit him completely.) Matthew was committed to the same forensic hospital where he had been sent immediately after the incident. It has been difficult for doctors to determine precisely what disorder would have caused him to become so psychotic. His diagnosis has shifted over the years, first from schizophrenia to schizoaffective disorder—which has symptoms of both schizophrenia, such as hallucinations and delusions, and mood disorders, such as mania and depression. Later still, it was changed to bipolar disorder.

After he spent five years in the hospital, psychiatrists eventually decided Matthew was well, and he was released to live in the community, first in a halfway house and later on his own. Along the way, he finished the requirements for his degree and graduated from college. Today, some two decades later, he lives on his own, working various jobs to support his painting and showing his work in local galleries. He still sees a psychiatrist every month and takes medication to treat what is now believed to be bipolar disorder. He hasn't been violent, nor has he been a threat to anyone. Apart from some nasty side effects from some of his medications, he's been healthy.

Unlike so many other people with mental illness who commit horrific violent crimes or even far less awful nonviolent crimes, Matthew never went to prison. It is thanks, in no small measure, to his father, who, despite having lost so much, fought for him throughout his case and continues to this day to support him. His family's relative wealth meant access to paid legal representation. (There are many excellent public defenders, but as with so many things, having money means more choices.)

The fact that Matthew did what he did in a very liberal county of a liberal state likely contributed to the favorable outcome as well. That he is white undoubtedly helped, as did his education and his clean-cut good looks. The result is that Matthew has been able to lead a fairly normal life since that terrible day.

Is this the right outcome? *I* think so—even though I continue to be haunted by what happened and disturbed by how much this story contrasts with the fate of so many others I have seen. And the outcome has not just helped Matthew but has also offered some measure of consolation to his father. I know a lot of people won't agree. Maybe he shouldn't be in prison, people have said to me, but is it really safe for him to be living in the community? And does he "deserve" to have a normal life after what he did? His father tells me he is "back to his old self." (I haven't seen him since before this happened; his father asked me not to contact Matthew about this book, and I haven't.) It's been more than twenty years, and he hasn't given the slightest sign that he would ever do something like it again (although, as people have frequently pointed out to me, there was no indication the first time either).

But it is precisely the extremity of his case—and my complicated feelings about it—that suggest to me a different, perhaps more universal lesson. If such a path of rehabilitation is possible for a person with mental illness who commits an act so violent and so heinous, it gives me hope that one day we can also change the outcomes for the tens of thousands of others with mental illness, most of them charged with or convicted of far lesser crimes—people who are now stuck in our jails and prisons. If we do not try, we will not only have failed these people and their families. We will have failed ourselves.

Acknowledgments

I could not have researched and written this book without the help and generosity of many people.

I owe a great deal to reporters around the country who have done valuable work on this subject and who often have been exceptionally generous with their time, their knowledge and their sources. In particular, Beth Shelburne in Alabama and Jaclyn Cosgrove in Oklahoma went out of their way to help me and vouch for me among their many sources.

Legal experts provided crucial insights into the workings of police departments, courts, jails, prisons, and other aspects of the criminal justice system. Lawyers were essential in connecting me with several of the people whose stories and experiences became central to my own investigation. Thank you to Maria Morris and Jackie Aranda at the Southern Poverty Law Center, who told me about Jamie Wallace, and helped me understand the acute challenges confronting Alabama's prison system. Jill Webb and the late Rob Nigh in Tulsa took the time to tell me about their long experience working with clients with mental illness, and to connect me to people in Oklahoma. Claudia Montoya at the Legal Aid Society, and Scott Hechinger, Colleen King, and Joyce Kendrick at the Brooklyn Defender Services talked me through the intricacies of New York City's criminal justice system, as did Jennifer Parish, of the Urban Justice Center, who also introduced me to Eula Muhammad. Jonathan Safran and Alan Mills in Chicago directed me to people and documents I wouldn't have found otherwise. Fred Cohen shared his experiences observing in prisons. Michael Bien in San Francisco and Denny LeBoeuf and Richard Bourke in New Orleans showed me the extent to which mental illness has become a defining feature of death row populations. Valentina Morales helped me understand how attorneys can affect the process of involuntary commitments. Michael Perlin patiently answered my numerous questions about competency to stand trial, and connected me to many people who work in the field. Randy Berg, Molly Paris, and Dave Boyer were among those who provided crucial orientation about the Florida prison system. At the ACLU, David Fathi and Amy Fettig, along with a number of others at both the national office and local affiliates, were very helpful. Glenn Abolafia allowed me unparalleled access to his client, the man I call Kyle Muhammad. Matt Topic and Andy Celli both went above and beyond to provide actual legal help for me.

I have spent more time over the last several years than I ever anticipated thinking about policing and talking to police officers. Mike Woody in Ohio and Sam Cochran in Memphis helped me understand the CIT system; Amy Watson in Chicago gave me an academic take on it. Seth Stoughton at the University of South Carolina and David Klinger at the University of Missouri–St. Louis supplied a deeper and more nuanced understanding of law enforcement. Lieutenant Chuck Miner at the University of Minnesota Police Department obligingly tracked down information about Edgar Coleman. Numerous officers across the country allowed me to come along for the ride, an experience that was always eye-opening, even when the shift was uneventful. Special mention goes to Jamie Lambert in Memphis, who continued answering my questions even after I left town.

Numerous people who work in corrections were kind enough to take me deep into their own professional world. There are too many to name, but Christy Sturtevant and Lisa Murray were especially helpful in Florida. Warden Debbie Aldridge allowed me to visit the Mabel Bassett Correctional Center in Oklahoma. In Chicago, Sheriff Tom Dart answered my many questions and made it possible for me to visit his jail more than once. In Los Angeles County, I am grateful to Chief David Fender, Captain Shaun Mathers, Lieutenant Damon Jones, Deputy Jorge Zavala and, especially, Lieutenant Mike Burse, who believed in the book enough to give me the extraordinary access I needed.

Many judges welcomed me into their courtrooms, among them Matthew D'Emic of the Brooklyn Mental Health Court, Juan Merchan of the Manhattan Mental Health Court, and Arthur Engoron of the New York Supreme Court in Manhattan. Judge Steve Leifman, in Florida, submitted to my questions multiple times.

Medical and mental health experts provided essential orientation about the treatment of mental illness and the panoply of medical issues that arise in the correctional system. Among them, Mark Ghaly and Jackie Clark-Weissman offered important information about medical care behind bars. Doctors John Kane and Leo Lopez explained the inner workings of psychiatric care in the civilian world. Steve Norwood was an excellent guide to community mental healthcare in Oklahoma. Bandy X. Lee brought the challenges of providing mental healthcare in jails and prisons sharply into focus. The writings of Craig Haney were very useful, as was a long conversation I had with him. Denis Zavodny was an excellent guide to restoration to competency, and generously introduced me to numerous people involved in that process. Victoria Roberts let me sit in on her competency programs at the Fulton County Jail. Princewell Onwere described the unique challenges of practing psychiatry in prison. Elizabeth Ford and Homer Venters were both helpful in understanding correctional healthcare in general and in New York in particular. Ted Willbright shared his long experience working with people in the court system in New York City. Leon Evans in San Antonio showed me some of the ways that mental healthcare and criminal justice are increasingly part of the same big system. Elli Petacque Montgomery let me tag along with her more than once as she made the rounds in the Cook County Jail, and beautifully explained her work along the way. That I was able to benefit from so many of these people owes much to the help of their colleagues who paved the way to them. Marisol Lucio in San Antonio, Cindy Schwartz in Miami, and Kirsten Bokenkamp in Alabama stand out in that regard.

I'm grateful to the many people—and their families—who shared their stories with me, including Mora Wilkevicz, DJ Walker, and Lois Pullano in Michigan, Bryan Sanderson and Yvonne Roberts in Virginia, and Gemma Pena in Florida. Windy Hempstead connected me to countless families of people incarcerated in Florida and elsewhere. Amy McClellan was also very welcoming there. Jackie and Roger Mashore, Jean Williams, and numerous other families in Oklahoma told me their heartbreaking yet often inspiring stories. Belinda Wallace and Christopher Wallace in Alabama were exceedingly generous in filling in crucial details about Jamie Wallace. Dolores Canales helped me understand the California prison system, and generously shared with me her many contacts. Mary Errigo Wilsey told me the tragic story of her son, Keith Vidal. Brian Nelson shared not only his own story, but connected me to fellow survivors of solitary confinement across the country. I'm also grateful to those who asked to remain anonymous, but who nevertheless provided valuable information.

On the editorial front, thanks go to *Marketplace* and NPR, which aired some of the stories that ended up in this book. Amy Rosenberg saved me from many errors. Jessica Nash provided expert advice about the publishing business. I'm grateful to my editors at Basic Books, Ben Platt, who understood and embraced the vision for the book, and Brian Distelberg, who enthusiastically saw the project through. Publisher Lara Heimert has been excited about it from the beginning. Michelle Welsh-Horst has patiently guided it through the production process. Kait Howard, Allie Finkel, and the whole marketing and publicity teams at Basic have been outstanding. None of this would have happened if it weren't for my terrific agent, Gillian MacKenzie.

The Soros Justice Fellowship from the Open Society Foundation provided generous funding for the research that became the core of this book. At the Foundation, Adam Culbreath and Chrissy Voight go above and beyond for fellows and former fellows—many of whom appear elsewhere in these acknowledgements. Many other people provided invaluable support at every stage of the way. Peter Wagner and Peter Martel were among those who answered my endless questions about the criminal justice system, and, when they didn't have the answers, connected me with those who did. Jill Patterson made connections in the world of the death penalty, and offered plenty of encouragement. Mark Byers filled in the blanks in my religious education. Ann Seymour and Ellery Seymour did crack archival research for me in Memphis. Liesel Allen-Yeager did court research in Los Angeles. Molly Schnick is my social media guru.

Among those who read some or all of my manuscript—sometimes more than once—and offered valuable feedback are Susan Mizner, Maureen Barden, Peter Eliasberg, Anne Parsons, Esther Lim, Jean Casella, Amy Lehrner, Sarah Vinson, Andrew Blackwell, and Josh Roth. Andrea Crawford went above and beyond on this and every other front. The mistakes, of course, are my own.

Many dear friends provided housing and food, not to mention encouragement, among them Brian Watt and Daisy Nguyen in Los Angeles, and Shelby Ottensmeyer Mitchell and her family in the Chicago area. Amy Cheung let me use her studio in the East Village and Dean Cox in Sweden and Mike Eakin and Janet Schumacher in Canada provided mini writer's retreats. Valeria Ramirez Stiller, Eryn Mathewson, and Tiana Cruz kept things running on the home front. Many friends helped keep me sane, including Tali Shafrir-Shalit, Karen Leo, Michelle Brown, and Laura Phang.

I was especially lucky to benefit from family members with legal and medical expertise, including Jesse Roth, Marion Eakin, Alana Roth, and Alex Roth. Special mention goes to Peter Laufer and Sheila Swan Laufer, John and Sybil Eakin, and of course Susan and Jesse Roth. Most of all thank you to Leo, Eva, and Hugh. If my readers end up understanding half as much as you do about mental illness and the criminal justice system, I will consider my job done.

Notes

Introduction

1. Ken Kesey, *One Flew Over the Cuckoo's Nest* (New York: Penguin, 2002), 9.
2. Ibid., 15.
3. Richard G. Frank and Sherry A. Glied, *Better but Not Well: Mental Health Policy in the United States* (Baltimore: Johns Hopkins University Press, 2006), 126.
4. E-mail exchange with Michigan Department of Corrections. See also www .michigan.gov/corrections/0,4551,7–119–1441_1513—,00.html.
5. Iowa Department of Corrections, Mental Health Information Sharing Program, January 2017, http://idph.iowa.gov/Portals/1/Meetings/MeetingFiles /OtherFiles/95/8d8a73aa-da57-475e-b44f-77c91800cbd0.pdf.
6. Frank R. Baumgartner et al., *Deadly Justice: A Statistical Portrait of the Death Penalty* (New York: Oxford University Press, 2018), 238.
7. Doris J. James and Lauren E. Glaze, "Mental Health Problems of Prison and Jail Inmates," US Bureau of Justice Statistics, revised December 14, 2006.
8. Jennifer Bronson and Marcus Berzofsky, "Indicators of Mental Health Problems Reported by Prisoners and Jail Inmates, 2011–12," US Bureau of Justice Statistics, June 2017.
9. E-mail exchange with New York City Department of Corrections. See also Mayor's Task Force on Behavioral Health and the Criminal Justice System Action Plan 2014, 5, www1.nyc.gov/assets/criminaljustice/downloads/pdfs /annual-report-complete.pdf.
10. Sentencing Project, "Criminal Justice Facts," www.sentencingproject.org /criminal-justice-facts. These data are based on projections made by the US Bureau of Justice Statistics in 2001. Among other things, incarceration rates and racial disparities have both dropped slightly since then, but these remain the best projections available.
11. Jeffrey Draine et al., "Role of Social Disadvantage in Crime, Joblessness and Homelessness Among Persons with Serious Mental Illness," *Psychiatric Services* 53, no. 5 (2002): 565–573.

12. "Fatal Force," *Washington Post,* https://www.washingtonpost.com/graphics /national/police-shootings-2016.

13. "Improving Outcomes for People with Mental Illnesses Involved with New York City's Criminal Court and Corrections System," Council of State Governments Justice Center, December 2012, 3, https://csgjusticecenter.org/mental-health /publications/improving-outcomes-for-people-with-mental-illnesses-involved -with-new-york-citys-criminal-court-and-correction-systems; Doris J. James and Lauren E. Glaze, "Mental Health Problems of Prison and Jail Inmates," US Bureau of Justice Statistics Special Report, September 2006, revised December 2006, 8, https://www.bjs.gov/content/pub/pdf/mhppji.pdf.

14. J. R. Goss et al., "Characteristics of Suicide Attempts in a Large Urban Jail System with an Established Suicide Prevention Program," *Psychiatric Services* 53, no. 5 (2002): 574–579.

15. Kesey, *One Flew,* 13–14.

16. Pew Charitable Trusts, "The Effects of Changing Felony Theft Thresholds: More Evidence That Higher Values Have Not Led to Increased Property Crime or Larceny Rates," April 12, 2017, www.pewtrusts.org/en/research-and -analysis/issue-briefs/2017/04/the-effects-of-changing-felony-theft -thresholds.

17. "State Marijuana Laws in 2017 Map," www.governing.com/gov-data/state -marijuana-laws-map-medical-recreational.html.

18. Jerome Mertens et al., "Differential Responses to Lithium in Hyperexcitable Neurons from Patients with Bipolar Disorder," *Nature,* October 28, 2015, 95–99.

19. Aswin Sekar et al., "Schizophrenia Risk from Complex Variation of Complement Component 4," *Nature,* February 11, 2016, 177–183.

Author's Note

1. *Diagnostic and Statistical Manual of Mental Disorders,* 5th ed. (Washington, DC: American Psychiatric Association, 2013), 160–161.

2. National Institute of Mental Health, "Major Depression Among Adults," https://www.nimh.nih.gov/health/statistics/prevalence/major-depression -among-adults.shtml.

3. *Diagnostic and Statistical Manual,* 123–127.

4. National Institute of Mental Health, "Bipolar Disorder Among Adults," https://www.nimh.nih.gov/health/statistics/prevalence/bipolar-disorder -among-adults.shtml.

5. *Diagnostic and Statistical Manual,* 87–111; National Institute of Mental Health, "Schizophrenia," https://www.nimh.nih.gov/health/statistics/prevalence/schizo phrenia.shtml.

6. E-mail exchange with Levi Fishman, associate director, Public Affairs Correctional Health Services NYC Health + Hospitals, August 18, 2017.

Chapter 1 Jail Is the Only Safe Place

1. Jamie Fellner, "A Corrections Quandary: Mental Illness and Prison Rules," *Harvard Civil Rights–Civil Liberties Law Review* 41, no. 2 (2006): 391–412.
2. I tried to obtain the records of Sanderson's incarceration in South Carolina and was told that they had been destroyed. However, other records and interviews with his mother did confirm the story he told me.
3. Sabriya Rice, "State Increasingly Trying to Protect Health-Care Workers from Violence," *Modern Healthcare*, February 14, 2014, www.modernhealthcare.com /article/20140214/NEWS/302149971.
4. This tool is known as the Sequential Intercept Model and was developed by Mark Munetz and Patricia Griffin. For further information, see *The Sequential Intercept Model and Criminal Justice*, ed. Patricia A. Griffin et al. (New York and Oxford: Oxford University Press. 2015).
5. The Bible has numerous references to plucking out eyes. In Matthew 18:9, for example, Jesus says, "And if your eye causes you to stumble, tear it out and throw it away; it is better for you to enter life with one eye than to have two eyes and to be thrown into the hell of fire."

Chapter 2 The Largest Psych Ward in America

1. Bob Herman, "Los Angeles Goes After Patient-Dumping for a Third Time," *Modern Healthcare*, August 14, 2014, www.modernhealthcare.com/article /20140828/NEWS/308289960.
2. Council of State Governments, "Improving Outcomes for People with Mental Illnesses Involved with New York City's Criminal Court and Corrections Systems," December 2012, https://csgjusticecenter.org/wp-content/uploads /2013/05/CTBNYC-Court-Jail_7-cc.pdf.
3. US Department of Justice, letter to Anthony Peck, Esq., and Stephanie Jo Regan, Esq., RE: Mental Health Care and Suicide Prevention Practices at Los Angeles County Jails, June 4, 2014, 13.
4. Sarah L. Desmarais et al., "Community Violence Perpetration and Victimization Among Adults with Mental Illnesses," *American Journal of Public Health*, December 2014.
5. Los Angeles County Sheriff's Department, *Custody Division Year End Review 2015*, 3, www.la-sheriff.org/s2/static_content/info/documents/PMB_YER2015 .pdf.
6. US Department of Justice, letter, 15.
7. Ibid.
8. *Psychiatric Services in Correctional Facilities*, 3rd ed. (Arlington, VA: American Psychiatric Association, 2016), 5.
9. Alexander L. Bednar, "HIPAA'S Impact on Prisoners' Rights to Healthcare," 2003, https://www.law.uh.edu/healthlaw/perspectives/Privacy/030128HIPAAs .pdf; Wesley D. Bizzell, "The Protection of Inmates' Medical Records: The

Challenge of HIPAA Privacy Regulations," *CorrectionsOne.com*, February 24, 2003, www.corrections.com/articles/11103-the-protection-of-inmates-medical -records-the-challenge-of-hipaa-privacy-regulations.

10. Doris J. James and Lauren E. Glaze, "Mental Health Problems of Jail and Prison Inmates," US Bureau of Justice Statistics, September 2006.

11. Robert C. Schwartz and David M. Blankenship, "Racial Disparities in Psychotic Disorder Diagnosis: A Review of Empirical Literature," *World Journal of Psychiatry*, December 22, 2014, 133–140.

12. US Department of Justice, letter, 9.

13. Ibid., 15.

14. Ibid., 24.

Chapter 3 The Asylum Fallacy

1. Lionel S. Penrose, "Mental Disease and Crime: Outline of a Comparative Study of European Statistics," *British Journal of Medical Psychology* 18, no. 1 (1939): 1–15.

2. Richard G. Frank and Sherry A. Glied, *Better but Not Well: Mental Health Policy in the United States* (Baltimore: Johns Hopkins University Press, 2006), 123–127.

3. Marc Mauer, *Race to Incarcerate* (New York: New Press, 2006), 20.

4. Anne Parsons, "From Asylum to Prison: The Story of Lincoln, Illinois," *Journal of Illinois History* 15 (Winter 2011).

5. Frank and Glied, *Better but Not Well*, 123–124.

6. Steven Raphael and Michael A. Stoll, "Assessing the Contribution of the Deinstitutionalization of the Mentally Ill to Growth in the U.S. Incarceration Rate," *Journal of Legal Studies* 42, no. 1 (2013): 200.

7. Henry J. Steadman et al., "The Impact of State Mental Hospital Deinstitutionalization on United States Prison Populations, 1968–1978," *Journal of Criminal Law and Criminology* 75, no. 2 (1984): 474–490.

8. Benjamin Franklin, "Some Account of the Pennsylvania Hospital, [May 28, 1754]," *The Papers of Benjamin Franklin*, vol. 5, *July 1, 1753, Through March 31, 1755*, ed. Leonard W. Labaree (New Haven, CT: Yale University Press, 1962), 283–330.

9. Ibid.

10. Ibid.

11. Kristen A. Graham, *A History of the Pennsylvania Hospital* (Charleston, SC: History Press, 2008), 20, 38–39.

12. www.liquisearch.com/eastern_state_hospital_virginia/francis_fauquier_and _the_enlightenment.

13. Shomer S. Zwelling, *Quest for a Cure: The Public Hospital in Williamsburg, Virginia, 1773–1885* (Williamsburg, VA: Colonial Williamsburg Foundation, 1985), 3–5.

14. Norman Dain, *Disordered Minds: The First Century of Eastern State Hospital in Williamsburg, Virginia, 1766–1866* (Williamsburg, VA: Colonial Williamsburg Foundation, 1971), 17–18.

15. Ibid., 17–19.

16. Zwelling, *Quest for a Cure*, 14–15.

17. Gerald Grob, *The Mad Among Us: A History of the Care of America's Mentally Ill* (New York: Free Press, 1994), 15.

18. Dain, *Disordered Minds*, 22–23; Zwelling, *Quest for a Cure*.

19. Zwelling, *Quest for a Cure*.

20. www.uphs.upenn.edu/paharc/features/brush.html.

21. David J. Rothman, "Perfecting the Prison: United States, 1789–1865," in *The Oxford History of the Prison: The Practice of Punishment in Western Society*, ed. Norval Morris and David J. Rothman (Oxford and New York: Oxford University Press, 1995), 101.

22. https://www.easternstate.org/sites/easternstate/files/inline-files/ESP-history-overview.pdf.

23. Mauer, *Race to Incarcerate*.

24. Grob, *The Mad Among Us*, 43.

25. *Fourteenth Annual Report of the Board of Managers of the Prison Discipline Society, Boston, May 1839* (Boston: published at the Society's Rooms, 1839).

26. Already in the nineteenth century, most prisoners and state hospital patients were poor first- or second-generation immigrants. In *Conscience and Convenience: The Asylum and Its Alternatives in Progressive America*, David Rothman writes that 50 percent of the patients at the asylum in Worcester, Massachusetts, were immigrants or children of immigrants; at McLean, barely 10 percent were. At the asylum on Blackwell's Island in New York City, the figure was 86 percent, while the private Bloomingdale asylum had only 31 percent.

27. Alex Beam, *Gracefully Insane: Life and Death Inside America's Premier Mental Hospital* (New York: PublicAffairs, 2001), 21.

28. Ibid., 22.

29. Ibid.

30. Margaret Fuller, *Essays on American Life and Letters* (New Haven, CT: Yale University Press, 1978), 278.

31. Judith Mattson Bean and Joel Myerson, eds., *Margaret Fuller, Critic: Writings from the New-York Tribune, 1844–1846* (New York: Columbia University Press, 2000), 101.

32. Dorothea Dix, "'I Tell What I Have Seen'—The Reports of Asylum Reformer Dorothea Dix," https://www.ncbi.nlm.nih.gov/pmc/articles/PMC1470564.

33. Dorothea Dix, *On Behalf of the Insane Poor* (Honolulu: University Press of the Pacific, 2001).

34. Grob, *The Mad Among Us*, 24.

35. Ibid., 42.

36. Charles Dickens, *American Notes for General Circulation* (London: Chapman and Hall, 1842), 1:109–110.

37. Grob, *The Mad Among Us*, 67.

38. Mary Jane Ward, *The Snake Pit* (New York: Random House, 1946), 157.

39. Grob, *The Mad Among Us*, 49.

40. Ibid., 106.

41. David Rothman, *Conscience and Convenience: The Asylum and Its Alternatives in Progressive America* (New York: Transaction, 2002), 29.

42. Grob, *The Mad Among Us*, 48.

43. Frank and Glied, *Better but Not Well*, 124.

44. Marle Woodson, *Behind the Door of Delusion* (New York: Macmillan, 1932), 209.

45. Gerald Grob, *From Asylum to Community: Mental Health Policy in Modern America* (Princeton, NJ: Princeton University Press, 1991), 72.

46. Mike Gorman, "Misery Rules in State Shadowland," *Daily Oklahoman*, September 22, 1946.

47. Albert Q. Maisel, "Most U.S. Mental Hospitals Are a Shame and a Disgrace," *Life*, 1946, https://mn.gov/mnddc/parallels2/prologue/6a-bedlam/bedlam-life1946.pdf.

48. Ibid.

49. Grob, *From Asylum to Community*, 71.

50. Group for the Advancement of Psychiatry, "Public Psychiatric Hospitals," report no.5, April 1948, http://gap-dev.s3.amazonaws.com/documents/assets/000/000/154/original/reports_public_psychiatric_ho.pdf?1429591315.

51. Ward, *The Snake Pit*, 91–92.

52. Maisel, "Most U.S. Mental Hospitals."

53. George S. Stevenson, "Needed: A Plan for the Mentally Ill. Plea for an Enlightened System of Public Psychiatry to Remove a Blight on Society," *New York Times*, July 27, 1947.

54. Robert Whitaker, *Mad in America: Bad Science, Bad Medicine, and the Enduring Treatment of the Mentally Ill* (New York: Basic, 2002), 144–145.

55. Andrew Scull, *Madness in Civilization: A Cultural History of Insanity* (Princeton, NJ: Princeton University Press, 2015), 380.

56. Whitaker, *Mad in America*, 144–145.

57. Ibid., 150–151.

58. Scull, *Madness in Civilization*, 367.

59. *Mental Health and the Role of States: A Report from the Pew Charitable Trusts and the John D. and Catherine T. MacArthur Foundation*, 2015, 6, www.pewtrusts.org/~/media/assets/2015/06/mentalhealthandroleofstatesreport.pdf.

60. US Department of Health and Human Services, Mental Health United States 2010, SAMHSA, 32, www.samhsa.gov/data/sites/default/files/MHUS2010/MHUS2010/MHUS-2010.pdf.

61. Grob, *The Mad Among Us*, 233.

62. https://www.jfklibrary.org/Asset-Viewer/Archives/JFKPOF-047-045.aspx.

63. https://www.ssa.gov/OP_Home/ssact/title19/1905.htm.

64. https://www.medicaid.gov/medicaid/benefits/bhs/index.html.

65. Frank and Glied, *Better but Not Well*, 126.

66. www.cookcountysheriff.com/MentalHealth/MentalHealth_main.html.

67. Abby Sewell, "Mentally Ill Inmates Are Swamping the State's Prisons and Jails," *Los Angeles Times*, June 19, 2016, www.latimes.com/local/california/la-me-mentally-ill-inmate-snap-story.html.

68. www1.nyc.gov/site/criminaljustice/work/bhtf.page.

69. Ibid.

70. David Garland, *The Culture of Control: Crime and Social Order in Contemporary Society* (Chicago: University of Chicago Press, 2001), 9.

71. Richard A. Oppel, Jr., "States Trim Penalties and Prison Rolls, Even as Sessions Gets Tough," *New York Times*, May 18, 2017.

72. Joel E. Miller, "Too Significant to Fail: The Importance of State Behavioral Health Agencies in the Daily Lives of Americans with Mental Illness, for Their Families, and for Their Communities," National Association of State Mental Health Program Directors, 2012, www.nasmhpd.org/sites/default/files/Too%20Significant%20To%20Fail%287%29.pdf.

73. Albert Deutsch, *Shame of the States* (New York: Harcourt Brace, 1948), 93.

Chapter 4 Jail as Hospital

1. CBS, *60 Minutes*, May 21, 2017, https://www.cbsnews.com/news/cook-county-jail-sheriff-tom-dart-on-60-minutes.

2. Tom Dart, "A Mental Health Template for American Jails: Saving Lives and Money Through Commonsense Reform," July 2016, www.cookcountysheriff.org/pdf/MentalHealthTemplate_072116.pdf.

3. "Mayor de Blasio to Triple Intensive-Care Mental Health Units on Rikers Island," press release, April 26, 2016, www1.nyc.gov/office-of-the-mayor/news/394-16/mayor-de-blasio-triple-intensive-care-mental-health-units-rikers-island.

4. www1.nyc.gov/site/criminaljustice/work/bhtf.page.

5. "Mayor de Blasio to Triple."

6. Marianna Napoles, "Mental Hospital Planned for CIM," *Chino Champion*, April 1, 2017.

7. *Monroe Correctional Complex Special Offender Unit Officer Orientation Handbook*, https://www.law.umich.edu/special/policyclearinghouse/Documents/WA%20-%20Monroe%20Corr.%20Complx%20Orientation%20Manual%201980.pdf.

8. Emily Lane, "Plans Call for New Jail Building, 89 New Beds to House New Orleans' Mentally Ill Inmates," *Times Picayune*, January 5, 2017, www.nola.com/crime/index.ssf/2017/01/plans_revealed_for_new_jail_bu.html.

9. Wendy Culverwell, "Benton County Wants $5M Jail Unit for Mentally Ill Inmates," *Tri-City Herald*, April 1, 2017, www.tri-cityherald.com/news/local/article142224979.html.

10. American Medical Association, House of Delegates Proceedings, Annual Session, 1930, 41, http://ama.nmtvault.com/jsp/viewer.jsp?doc_id=ama_arch%2FHOD00001%2F00000021&query1=&recoffset=0&collection_filter=All&collection_name=1ee24daa-2768-4bff-b792-e4859988fe94&sort_col=publication%20date&CurSearchNum=-1.

11. B. Jaye Anno, "Correctional Health Care: Guidelines for the Management of an Adequate Delivery System," National Commission on Correctional Health Care, December 2001, http://static.nicic.gov/Library/017521.pdf.

12. US Department of Justice, "Survey of Inmates of Local Jails, 1972," http://files
.eric.ed.gov/fulltext/ED099549.pdf.

13. Estelle v. Gamble, 429 U.S. 97 (No. 75-929), opinion of Thurgood Marshall,
104, https://www.law.cornell.edu/supremecourt/text/429/97#writing-USSC
_CR_0429_0097_ZO.

14. *Psychiatric Services in Correctional Facilities*, 3rd ed. (Arlington, VA: American
Psychiatric Association, 2016), 3.

15. Ibid.

16. Ibid., 35.

17. Robert M. A. Hirschfeld et al., *Practice Guidelines for the Treatment of Patients
with Bipolar Disorder*, 2nd ed., 2002, http://psychiatryonline.org/pb/assets
/raw/sitewide/practice_guidelines/guidelines/bipolar.pdf.

18. Marvin Zalman, "Prisoners' Rights to Medical Care," *Journal of Criminal Law,
Criminology and Police Science* 63, no. 2 (1972): 185–199.

19. Douglas Shenson, Nancy Dubler, and David Michaels, "Jails and Prisons:
The New Asylums?" *American Journal of Public Health* 80, no. 6 (1990): 655–656.

20. Associated Press, "Union Claims Prison Employees Pressured to Fake Suicide-
Watch Records at Stockton Medical Facility," July 31, 2014, http://sanfrancisco
.cbslocal.com/2014/07/31/union-claims-prison-employees-pressured-to-fake
-suicide-watch-records-at-stockton-medical-facility.

21. Lane, "Plans Call for New Jail Building."

Chapter 5 Destined to Fail

1. Roughly a third: 40 percent of those in jail and 30 percent of those in prison. See
Andrew P. Wilper et al., "The Health and Healthcare of US Prisoners: Results
of a Nationwide Survey," *American Journal of Public Health* 99 (April 2009):
666–672.

2. Doris J. James and Lauren E. Glaze, "Mental Health Problems of Prison
and Jail Inmates," US Bureau of Justice Statistics Special Report, September
2006, 1.

3. Oklahoma Justice Reform Task Force Final Report, February 2017, 7, https://
s3.amazonaws.com/content.newsok.com/documents/OJRTFFinalReport%20
(1).pdf.

4. Ibid., 12.

5. Jennifer Palmer, "Adding Beds Isn't Enough to Address Oklahoma Prison
Overcrowding, Experts Say," *Oklahoman*, October 25, 2015, http://newsok
.com/article/5455820.

6. Craig Haney, "The Wages of Prison Overcrowding: Harmful Psychological
Consequences and Dysfunctional Correctional Reactions," *Washington University Journal of Law and Policy* 22, no. 1 (2006): 265–293.

7. Brown, Governor of California, et al. v. Plata, Supreme Court of the United
States, October Term 2010, 11, www.cdcr.ca.gov/News/docs/USSC-Plata
-opinion09-1233.pdf.

8. Ibid.

9. Ralph Coleman, et al. v. Arnold Schwarzenegger, et al., no. CIV S-90-0520 LKK JFM P, Three Judge Court Opinion and Order, August 4, 2009, www .cand.uscourts.gov/filelibrary/204/Opinion%20and%20Order.pdf.

10. Ibid.

11. "Supplemental Expert Report of Pablo Stewart MD," 4, http://rbgg.com/wp -content/uploads/_Stewart,%20Pablo%20MD,%20Supp%20Report%20 %283221%29,%2010-30-08,%20OCR.PDF.

12. E. Ann Carson and Elizabeth Anderson, "Prisoners in 2015," US Department of Justice, Bureau of Justice Statistics, Office of Justice Programs, 16, https:// www.bjs.gov/content/pub/pdf/p15.pdf.

13. Hannah Sabata et al. v. Nebraska Department of Correctional Services, Class Action Complaint for Injunctive and Declaratory Relief, August 16, 2017, https:// www.aclunebraska.org/sites/default/files/sabata_v_ndoc_complaint.pdf.

14. Mary Jane Ward, *The Snake Pit* (New York: Random House, 1946), 253–254.

15. Victor Parsons et al. v. Charles Ryan et al., no. CV 12-00601-PHX-DKD, filed in United States District Court, District of Arizona, August 29, 2014, declaration of Pablo Stewart, MD, 9, https://www.aclu.org/legal-document /parsons-v-ryan-stewart-expert-report.

16. Ibid., 20–22.

17. Sarah Mueller, "Florida Senators Call Staffing Shortages in State Prisons a Crisis," WUSF News, March 17, 2017, http://wusfnews.wusf.usf.edu/post /florida-senators-call-staffing-shortages-state-prisons-crisis#stream/0.

18. Andrew Knittle, "Oklahoma Corrections Department Officials Say Prison Doctors Aren't Shackled by Past Problems," *Daily Oklahoman*, September 27, 2016.

19. Danny Robbins, "Georgia Hires Prison Doctors with Troubled Pasts," *Atlanta Journal-Constitution*, December 13, 2014.

20. Sasha Abramsky and Jamie Fellner, *Ill-Equipped: U.S. Prisons and Offenders with Mental Illness*, Human Rights Watch, October 2003, https://www.hrw .org/reports/2003/usa1003/usa1003.pdf.

21. Tara F. Bishop et al., "Population of US Practicing Psychiatrists Declined, 2003–13, Which May Help Explain Poor Access to Mental Health Care," *Health Affairs*, July 2016.

22. Don Thompson, "Some California Prison Doctors Could Get Big Raise: Doctors Who Work in Certain California State Prisons Could Be in Line for a Big Raise," Associated Press, March 2, 2017, https://www.usnews.com/news/best-states/cali fornia/articles/2017-03-02/some-california-prison-doctors-could-get-big-raise.

23. Adam Ashton, "New Contract Raises Pay by 24 Percent for California Prison Doctors," *Sacramento Bee*, March 2, 2017, www.sacbee.com/news /politics-government/the-state-worker.

24. Greg Trotter, "Cook Jail Seeking to Attract More Psychiatrists to Staff," *Chicago Tribune*, July 10, 2015.

25. Steve Bousquet, "If You're a Florida State Employee, Do You Know How Much Your Raise Will Be?" *Miami Herald,* June 14, 2017, www.miamiherald.com /news/local/community/miami-dade/article156155204.html.

26. Pew Charitable Trust and John D. and Catherine T. MacArthur Foundation, *State Prison Health Care Spending: An Examination, 2014,* 3, www.pewtrusts .org/~/media/assets/2014/07/stateprisonhealthcarespendingreport.pdf.

27. B. Jaye Anno, "Prison Health Services: An Overview," *Journal of Correctional Healthcare* 10, no. 3 (2004): 287–301.

28. Lauren Galik, Leonard Gilroy, and Alexander Volokh, "Annual Privatization Report: 2014 Criminal Justice and Corrections," Reason Foundation, 2004, 21, http://reason.org/files/apr-2014-criminal-justice.pdf.

29. Beth Kutscher, "Rumble Over Jailhouse Healthcare: As States Broaden Outsourcing to Private Vendors, Critics Question Quality of Care and Cost Savings," *Modern Healthcare,* August 31, 2013, www.modernhealthcare.com /article/20130831/MAGAZINE/308319891.

30. Maura Ewing, "The Corizon CEO on Losing Its Contract with Rikers," *Marshall Project,* June 16, 2015, https://www.themarshallproject.org/2015/06/16 /ceo-of-private-medical-provider-corizon-on-losing-its-contract-with-rikers# .3G5CftlJG.

31. "Request for Proposal: Alabama Department of Corrections Mental Health Services, 2013," 27, www.documentcloud.org/documents/1263950-adoc-medical -services-rfp-2013.html#document/p4.

32. www.mhm-services.com.

33. McCreary et al. v. The Federal Bureau of Prisons et al., Class Action Complaint in the United States District Court for the Middle District of Pennsylvania, filed June 9, 2017.

34. Expert report of Kathryn A. Burns, MD, MPH, mental health expert, Dunn v. Dunn, submitted July 5, 2016, 37, https://www.splcenter.org/sites/default /files/documents/doc._555-5_-_expert_report_of_dr._kathyrn_a._burns.pdf.

35. *Psychiatric Services in Correctional Facilities,* 3rd ed. (Arlington, VA: American Psychiatric Association, 2016).

36. Allen J. Beck and Laura M. Maruschak, "Mental Health Treatment in State Prisons, 2000," Bureau of Justice Statistics Special Report, July 2001.

37. James and Glaze, "Mental Health Problems."

38. Department of Justice Civil Rights Division, letter to the Honorable Carlos A. Gimenez, Mayor, Miami-Dade County, Re: Investigation of the Miami-Dade County Jail, August 24, 2011, https://www.justice.gov/sites/default/files/usao -sdf1/legacy/2012/12/31/110829-01.FindingsLetter.pdf.

39. "Analysis: Large Part of Prison Rx Spending Goes Toward Anti-Psychotics," *California Healthline,* May 1, 2013, http://californiahealthline.org/morning-breakout /analysis-large-part-of-prison-rx-spending-goes-toward-anti-psychotics.

40. Don Thompson, "California Spends Big on Anti-Psychotics," *Associated Press,* May 1, 2013.

41. Council of State Governments, *Criminal Justice/Mental Health Consensus Project*, June 2002, 136, https://www.ncjrs.gov/pdffiles1/nij/grants/197103.pdf.

Chapter 6 Sanctioned Torture

1. Elizabeth Ford, *Sometimes Amazing Things Happen: Heartbreak and Hope on the Bellevue Hospital Psychiatric Prison Ward* (New York: Regan Arts, 2017).
2. Trial testimony by Raymond Castro, former corrections officer, United States of America v. Terrence Pendergrass, December 10, 2014.
3. United States of America v. Terrence Pendergrass, sealed complaint, Southern District of New York, 3, https://www.justice.gov/sites/default/files/usao-sdny/legacy/2015/03/25/Pendergrass%2C%20Terrence%20Complaint.pdf.
4. Michael Schwirtz, "$2.25 Million Settlement for Family of Rikers Inmate Who Died in Hot Cell," *New York Times*, October 31, 2014.
5. Patrick Wilson, "McAuliffe Calls Jail Death of Jamycheal Mitchell 'Beyond Comprehension,'" *Virginian-Pilot*, March 31, 2016, http://pilotonline.com/news/government/politics/virginia/mcauliffe-calls-jail-death-of-jamycheal-mitchell-beyond-comprehension/article_ace90d0d-8579-5769-afaf-bc603be10dc9.html.
6. Roxanne Adams, Administrator of the Estate of Jamycheal M. Mitchell, Deceased, Plaintiff, v. Naphcare, et al., United States District Court for the Eastern District of Virginia (Norfolk Division), Case 2:16-cv-00229-RBS-LRL.
7. Julie K. Brown, "Behind Bars, a Brutal and Unexplained Death," *Miami Herald*, May 17, 2014, www.miamiherald.com/news/local/community/miami-dade/article1964620.html.
8. Julie K. Brown, "Graphic Photos Stir Doubts About Darren Rainey's 'Accidental' Prison Death," *Miami Herald*, May 6, 2017, www.miamiherald.com/news/local/community/miami-dade/article149026764.html.
9. For a number of reasons, there is no precise count of people in solitary confinement in the US criminal justice system. Eighty thousand is a frequently cited number; it comes from a 2005 census done by the US Bureau of Justice Statistics. See James J. Stephan, "Census of State and Federal Correctional Facilities, 2005," US Bureau of Justice Statistics, October 2008. More recently, the Yale Law School, along with the Association of State Correctional Administrators, conducted a survey that concluded somewhere between 80,000 and 100,000 people were in solitary in 2014, a number that does not include local jails, juvenile facilities, or military or immigration detention. See "Time-in-Cell: The ASCA-Liman 2014 National Survey of Administrative Segregation in Prison," August 2015, https://law.yale.edu/system/files/documents/pdf/asca-liman_administrative_segregation_report_sep_2_2015.pdf.
10. American Civil Liberties Union Texas, *A Solitary Failure: The Waste, Cost, and Harm of Solitary Confinement*, February 2015, 11, https://www.aclutx.org/sites/default/files/field_documents/SolitaryReport_2015.pdf.
11. Charles Dickens, *American Notes for General Circulation* (London: Chapman and Hall, 1842), 1:242.

12. Keramet Reiter, *23/7: Pelican Bay Prison and the Rise of Long-Term Solitary Confinement* (New Haven, CT: Yale University Press, 2016), 24.

13. Testimony of Professor Craig Haney, Senate Judiciary Subcommittee on the Constitution, Civil Rights, and Human Rights Hearing on Solitary Confinement, June 19, 2012, 6, https://www.judiciary.senate.gov/imo/media/doc/12-6-19HaneyTestimony.pdf.

14. Dickens, *American Notes*, 239.

15. Jeffrey L. Metzner and Jamie Fellner, "Solitary Confinement and Mental Illness in US Prisons: A Challenge for Medical Ethics," *Journal of the American Academy of Psychiatry and the Law* 38, no. 1 (2010), https://www.hrw.org/news/2010/03/01/solitary-confinement-and-mental-illness-us-prisons-challenge-medical-ethics#_edn8.

16. Fatos Kaba et al., "Solitary Confinement and Risk of Self-Harm Among Jail Inmates," *American Journal of Public Health*, March 2014, http://ajph.aphapublications.org/doi/full/10.2105/AJPH.2013.301742.

17. Disability Rights Network of Pennsylvania v. Wetzel, 1:13-cv-00635-JEJ (M.D. Pa.), 16–17, https://www.clearinghouse.net/detail.php?id=12719.

18. Haney testimony, 9.

19. Expert report of Kathryn Burns, for the Southern District of Illinois East St. Louis Division, Brian Nelson and Robert Boyd, Defendants.

20. Juan Méndez, Interim Report Prepared by the Special Rapporteur of the Human Rights Council on Torture and Other Cruel, Inhuman, or Degrading Treatment or Punishment, presented to the United Nations on August 5, 2011.

21. Michael Schwirtz, "$2.5 Million Settlement for Family of Rikers Inmate Who Died in Hot Cell," *New York Times*, October 31, 2014, https://www.nytimes.com/2014/11/01/nyregion/settlement-for-family-of-rikers-inmate-who-died-in-overheated-cell.html?_r=0.

22. US Department of Justice, Office of the Inspector General, Review of the Federal Bureau of Prisons' Use of Restrictive Housing for Inmates with Mental Illness, July 2017, https://www.themarshallproject.org/documents/3893449-Review-of-the-Federal-Bureau-of-Prisons-Use-of#.3Q_pz31aUP.

23. Testimony by Jack Beck, Director, Prison Visiting Project, the Correctional Association of New York, Before the Hearing of the Assembly's Corrections and Mental Health Committees, Mental Health Services in NY Prisons, December 6, 2011, www.correctionalassociation.org/wp-content/uploads/2012/05/12-6-2011_beck-testimony-mental-health1.pdf.

24. New York Consolidated Laws, Correction Law 401, Section 3.

25. Ibid.

26. Craig Haney, *Reforming Punishment: Psychological Limits to the Pain of Imprisonment* (Washington, DC: American Psychological Association, 2006), 199.

27. Sarah Glowa-Kollisch et al., "Data-Driven Human Rights: Using Dual Loyalty Trainings to Promote the Care of Vulnerable Patients in Jail," *Health and Human Rights* 17, no. 1 (2015): 124–135.

28. Ibid.

29. Ross MacDonald, Amanda Parsons, and Homer D. Venters, "The Triple Aims of Correctional Health: Patient Safety, Population Health, and Human Rights," *Journal of Health Care for the Poor and Underserved* 24 (2013): 1226–1234.

30. Ibid.

Chapter 7 Better Off Dead

1. Edward Braggs et al. v. Jefferson S. Dunn, the District of the United States for the Middle District of Alabama, Northern Division, Liability Opinion and Order as to Phase 2A Eighth Amendment Claim, June 27, 2017, 24.

2. www.doc.state.al.us/docs/AdminRegs/AR633.pdf, 6.

3. Joshua Dunn et al. v. Jefferson Dunn, expert report of Professor Craig Haney, PhD, JD, 68–69, https://www.splcenter.org/sites/default/files/documents/doc._555–6_-_expert_report_of_dr._craig_haney.pdf.

4. Dunn v. Dunn, Civil Action No. 2:14-cv-00601-WKW-TFM, First Amended Complaint, 26, https://www.splcenter.org/sites/default/files/d6_legacy_files /downloads/case/first_amended_complaint.pdf.

5. Expert report of Kathryn A. Burns, MD, MPH, Mental Health Expert, Dunn v. Dunn, submitted July 5, 2016, 30, https://www.splcenter.org/sites/default /files/documents/doc._555-5_-_expert_report_of_dr._kathyrn_a._burns.pdf.

6. "Justice Department Announces Statewide Investigation into Conditions in Alabama's Prisons for Men," October 6, 2016, https://www.justice.gov/opa /pr/justice-department-announces-statewide-investigation-conditions -alabama-s-prisons-men.

7. www.preventsuicide.com/#!suicide-prevention-products/ctcv.

8. https://www.grainger.com/category/penal-system-fixtures/toilets-urinals /plumbing/ecatalog/N-ab6.

9. Ashoor Rasho, et al. v. Director John R. Baldwin et al., Plaintiff's Motion to Enforce the Settlement Agreement, October 10, 2017.

10. Dunn v. Dunn, testimony of Jamie Wallace, 9.

11. Ibid., 77.

12. "State Mental Health Agency (SMHA) Per Capita Mental Health Services Expenditures," Henry J. Kaiser Family Foundation, http://kff.org/other/state -indicator/smha-expenditures-per-capita/?currentTimeframe=0&selectedDistri butions=smha-expenditures-per-capita&selectedRows=%7B%7D.

13. www.mentalhealthamerica.net/issues/ranking-states.

14. Eric Velasco, "Son Admits Killing Mom, Officer Says Graysville Teen Goes to Grand Jury," *Birmingham News,* April 29, 2009.

15. Jamie Wallace suicide report, MHM Services Inc., CQI Major Occurrence Report, December 15, 2016 (1038–1055), 46.

16. Ibid., 60.

17. www.doc.state.al.us/docs/AdminRegs/AR632.pdf, 3.

18. I tried several times to contact his criminal defense attorney, but he did not want to talk to me. He did talk to a local television reporter, telling her he believes that he failed by allowing Wallace to take the plea. But he also holds the prison responsible for what happened: "I blame myself in a lot of ways for his ultimate demise, but he could have been protected more if he were in the right facility." See Beth Shelburne, "What Happened to Jamie Lee Wallace?" WBRC Fox 6 News, July 5, 2017.

Chapter 8 *Guilty by Reason of Insanity*

1. Gary B. Melton et al., *Psychological Evaluations for the Courts: A Handbook for Mental Health Professionals and Lawyers*, 4th ed. (New York: Guilford, 2017).
2. Richard J. Bonnie, John C. Jeffries, Jr., and Peter W. Low, *A Case Study in the Insanity Defense: The Trial of John W. Hinckley, Jr.*, 3rd ed. (New York: Thomson/Foundation, 2008), 139.
3. Melton et al., *Psychological Evaluations for the Courts*, 4–5.
4. Bonnie, Jeffries, and Low, *A Case Study in the Insanity Defense*, 10.
5. Ibid., 9–11.
6. Steven V. Roberts, "High US Officials Express Outrage, Asking for New Laws on Insanity Plea," *New York Times*, June 23, 1982.
7. Christopher Slobogin, *Minding Justice: Laws That Deprive People with Mental Disability of Life and Liberty* (Cambridge. MA: Harvard University Press, 2006), 98–99.
8. Christopher Slobogin, "The Guilty but Mentally Ill Verdict: An Idea Whose Time Should Not Have Come," *George Washington Law Review* 53, nos. 3–4 (1985): 494–526.
9. Ann O'Neill, "Theater Shooter Holmes Gets 12 Life Sentences, Plus 3,318 Years," CNN, August 27, 2015, www.cnn.com/2015/08/26/us/james-holmes -aurora-massacre-sentencing/index.html.
10. "Theater Shooting Victims."
11. William Blackstone, *Blackstone's Commentaries on the Laws of England. Book the Fourth—Chapter the Second: Of Persons Capable of Committing Crimes*, 24, http://avalon.law.yale.edu/18th_century/blackstone_bk4ch2.asp.
12. Steve Poole, *The Politics of Regicide in England, 1760–1850: Troublesome Subjects* (Manchester and New York: Manchester University Press, 2000), 91–92.
13. *Old Bailey Proceedings Online*, www.oldbaileyonline.org, version 7.2, October 23, 2017, April 1790, trial of John Frith (t17900417-1).
14. Dusky v. United States, 362 U.S. 402 (1960), https://supreme.justia.com/cases /federal/us/362/402/case.html.
15. Justice Policy Institute, *When Treatment Is Punishment: The Effects of Maryland's Incompetency to Stand Trial Policies and Practices*, October 2011, www.justice policy.org/uploads/justicepolicy/documents/jpi_when_treatment_is_punish ment_national_factsheet.pdf.
16. www.dbhds.virginia.gov/library/forensics/ofo-restorationmanual.pdf.

17. Michael Braga, Anthony Cormier, and Leonora LaPeter Anton, "Definition of Insanity: Florida Spends Millions Making Sure the Mentally Ill Go to Court and Gets Nothing for It," *Tampa Bay Times*, December 18, 2015, www.tampabay .com/projects/2015/investigations/florida-mental-health-hospitals/competency.
18. "Trial and Error," *Tampa Bay Times Herald Tribune*, December 8, 2015, www.tampabay.com/projects/2015/investigations/florida-mental-health -hospitals/competency-game-show-video.
19. Braga, Cormier, and LaPeter Anton, "Definition of Insanity."
20. Abby Sewell, "Defendants Declared Mentally Incompetent Face Lengthy Delays in Jails," *Los Angeles Times*, April 1, 2015.
21. Vaidya Gullapalli, "Judged Incompetent to Stand Trial, People with Mental Illness Still Languish in Pennsylvania Jails," *Solitary Watch*, November 19, 2015, http://solitarywatch.com/2015/11/19/judged-incompetent-to-stand-trial -people-with-mental-illness-still-languish-in-pennsylvania-jails.
22. https://www.aclupa.org/news/2016/01/27/aclu-pa-settles-lawsuit-over -unconstitutional-delays-treatme.
23. "Federal Judge in Seattle Orders End to Long Jail Holds for Mentally Ill," Reuters, April 3, 2015, www.reuters.com/article/us-usa-washington -inmates-idUSKBN0MU09020150403.
24. Martha Bellisle, "Report: Washington State Jails Spend Millions Housing Mentally Ill," Associated Press, April 19, 2016, www.opb.org/news/article /ap-report-washington-state-jails-mentally-ill-spending.

Chapter 9 Inside Out

1. Jaclyn Cosgrove, "Epidemic Ignored: Oklahoma Treats Its Mental Health System Without Care," *Oklahoman*, http://newsok.com/article/5474415.
2. http://kfor.com/2015/05/20/exclusive-inside-the-oklahoma-hospital-for-the -insane.
3. Richard G. Frank and Sherry A. Glied, *Better but Not Well: Mental Health Policy in the United States Since 1950* (Baltimore: Johns Hopkins University Press, 2006), 70–90.
4. "Results from the 2015 National Survey on Drug Use and Health: Detailed Tables," Substance Abuse and Mental Health Services Administration, Center for Behavioral Health Statistics and Quality, September 8, 2016, https:// www.samhsa.gov/data/sites/default/files/NSDUH-DetTabs-2015/NSDUH -DetTabs-2015/NSDUH-DetTabs-2015.pdf.
5. Dominic A. Sisti, Andrea G. Segal, and Ezekiel J. Emmanuel, "Improving Long-Term Psychiatric Care: Bring Back the Asylum," *Journal of the American Medical Association* 313, no. 3 (2015): 243–244.
6. Eric Dexheimer, "Defendants Fill, Linger in State's Mental Health Facilities," *American-Statesman*, May 27, 2012, www.statesman.com/news/news /special-reports/defendants-fill-linger-in-states-mental-health-f-1/nRn4m.

7. Robert Creigh Deeds, administrator of the estate of Austin Creigh Deeds, deceased v. Commonwealth of Virginia, et al., filed in the Circuit Court for the County of Bath, March 12, 2014.

8. W. Lawrence Fitch, *Assessment #3: Forensic Mental Health Services in the United States*, National Association of State Mental Health Program Directors, 2014, 12, https://www.nasmhpd.org/sites/default/files/Assessment%203%20-%20 Updated%20Forensic%20Mental%20Health%20Services.pdf.

9. Ted Lutterman, "Virginia's State Mental Health System: National Comparisons and Trends in State Mental Health Systems," National Association of State Mental Health Program Directors Research Institute, September 9, 2014, http://dls.virginia.gov/GROUPS/MHS/va%20system.pdf.

10. Edgar Walters, "State Spending More on Mental Healthcare, but Waitlist Grows," *Texas Tribune*, May 1, 2016, www.texastribune.org/2016/05/01/despite -state-spending-dearth-pysch-hospital-beds.

11. A legal settlement in 2011 forced the state to streamline the process of evaluating defendants for competency to stand trial; the process now takes about a month, but it previously took more than three months. See Colorado Department of Human Services Office of Behavioral Health, "Needs Analysis: Current Status, Strategic Positioning, and Future Planning," April 2015, 9, www .ahpnet.com/AHPNet/media/AHPNetMediaLibrary/White%20Papers /OBH-Needs-Analysis-Report2015-pdf.pdf.

12. Doris J. James and Lauren E. Glaze, "Mental Health Problems of Prison and Jail Inmates," US Bureau of Justice Statistics Special Report, September 2006, 9.

13. Oklahoma Department of Mental Health and Substance Abuse Services, "Fiscal Year 2016 Budget Request," January 2015, https://www.ok.gov/odmhsas /documents/FY16%20Budget%20Narrative%20-%20Updated.pdf.

14. Jaclyn Cosgrove, "Oklahoma Ranks Low in Mental-Health Funding," September 26, 2015, http://newsok.com/article/5449521.

15. Frank and Glied, *Better but Not Well*, 6.

16. Oklahoma Department of Mental Health and Substance Abuse Services, "Fiscal Year 2016 Budget Request."

17. *The Psychiatric Shortage: Causes and Solutions* (Washington, DC: National Council for Behavioral Health, 2017), 12.

18. Beth Han et al., *Data Review Receipt of Services for Behavioral Health Problems: Results from the 2014 National Survey on Drug Use and Health*, September 2015, https://www.samhsa.gov/data/sites/default/files/NSDUH-DR-FRR3-2014 /NSDUH-DR-FRR3-2014/NSDUH-DR-FRR3-2014.htm.

19. The Paul Wellstone and Pete Domenici Mental Health Parity and Addiction Equity Act of 2008 (MHPAEA) required group health plans to treat mental health care the same as they do physical care, namely by not imposing lifetime caps on mental health care that were more limiting than those on medical or surgical care. The act, which initially only applied to group health plans, was later amended to apply to individual insurance as well. For more

information, see https://www.cms.gov/cciio/programs-and-initiatives/other -insurance-protections/mhpaea_factsheet.html.

20. *Interim Report of the President's New Freedom Commission on Mental Health,* President's New Freedom Commission on Mental Health, 2002, http://gov info.library.unt.edu/mentalhealthcommission/reports/Interim_Report.htm# P75_10348.

21. Liz Szabo, "Cost of Not Caring: Nowhere to Go," *USA Today,* May 12, 2014.

22. L. Aron et al., *Grading the States 2009: A Report on America's Health Care System for Adults with Serious Mental Illness,* National Alliance on Mental Illness, 2009, www.nami.org/getattachment/About-NAMI/Publications/Reports/NAMI _GTS2009_FullReport.pdf.

23. "Mental Health and the Role of States: A Report from the Pew Charitable Trusts and the John D. and Catherine T. MacArthur Foundation," 2015, 3, www .pewtrusts.org/~/media/assets/2015/06/mentalhealthandroleofstatesre port.pdf.

24. https://www.nami.org/getattachment/About-NAMI/Publications/Reports /NAMIStateBudgetCrisis2011.pdf.

25. Tara F. Bishop et al., "Population of US Practicing Psychiatrists Declined, 2003–13, Which May Help Explain Poor Access to Mental Health Care," Health Affairs, July 2016, http://content.healthaffairs.org/content/35/7/1271 .abstract.

26. Carol Peckham, Medscape Physician Compensation Report 2016, Medscape, April 1, 2016, www.medscape.com/features/slideshow/compensation/2016 /public/overview#page=2.

27. www.modernhealthcare.com/article/20150704/MAGAZINE/307049979.

28. Board of Mental Health and Substance Abuse Services meeting, January 24, 2014, https://www.ok.gov/odmhsas/documents/BM%20January24%202014 .pdf. See also Clifton Adcock, "Oklahoma's Mental-Health System Has Strict Criteria to Get Treatment," Oklahoma Watch, June 21, 2015, http://newsok .com/article/5428983.

Chapter 10 The Cycle

1. Ross MacDonald et al., "The Rikers Island Hot Spotters: Defining the Needs of the Most Frequently Incarcerated," *American Journal of Public Health* 105, no. 11 (2015): 2262–2268.

2. Amy Blank Wilson et al., "Examining the Impact of Mental Illness and Substance Use on Recidivism in a County Jail," *International Journal of Law and Psychiatry* 34 (2011): 264–268.

3. MacDonald et al., "The Rikers Island Hot Spotters."

4. The book was published under his legal name, not Kyle Muhammad.

5. Gerald Grob, *Mental Illness and American Society, 1875–1940* (Princeton, NJ: Princeton University Press, 1983), 9.

6. Ibid., 288.

7. Marc Abramson, "The Criminalization of Mentally Disordered Behavior: Possible Side-Effect of a New Mental Health Law," *Hospital and Community Psychiatry* 23, no. 4 (1972): 101–105.

8. Mary Jane Ward, *The Snake Pit* (New York: Random House, 1946), 136.

9. Jillian K. Peterson et al., "How Often and How Consistently Do Symptoms Directly Precede Criminal Behavior Among Offenders with Mental Illness?" *Law and Human Behavior* 38, no. 5 (2014): 439–449.

10. William H. Fisher et al., "Patterns and Prevalence of Arrest in a Statewide Cohort of Mental Health Care Consumers," *Psychiatric Services* 57, no. 11 (2006): 1623–1628.

11. Allison G. Robertson et al., "Patterns of Justice Involvement Among Adults with Schizophrenia and Bipolar Disorder: Key Risk Factors," *Psychiatric Services* 65, no. 7 (2014): 931–938.

12. Greg Greenberg et al., "Criminal Justice Involvement Among People with Schizophrenia," *Community Mental Health Journal* 47 (2011): 727–736.

13. National Alliance on Mental Illness, *Road to Recovery: Employment and Mental Illness*, July 2014, https://www.nami.org/work.

Chapter 11 Shooting the Victim

1. Christina Haley, "EMTs Testify in Day Four of Bryon Vassey Trial," *Port City Daily*, April 23, 2016.

2. "Database of Police Shootings," *Washington Post*, https://www.washingtonpost.com/graphics/national/police-shootings.

3. Jennifer Wadsworth, "Every San Jose Police Shooting in 2017 Has Involved Suspect with a History of Mental Illness," *San Jose Inside*, May 30, 2017, www.sanjoseinside.com/2017/05/30/every-san-jose-police-shooting-in-2017-has-involved-suspects-with-a-history-of-mental-illness.

4. "Deadly Force: Police and the Mentally Ill," *Portland Press Herald*, February 2012, www.pressherald.com/interactive/maine_police_deadly_force_series_day_2.

5. Alex Emslie and Rachael Bale, "More Than Half of Those Killed by San Francisco Police Are Mentally Ill," *KQED News*, September 30, 2014, http://ww2.kqed.org/news/2014/09/30/half-of-those-killed-by-san-francisco-police-are-mentally-ill.

6. Skyler Swisher, "Fatal Encounters: Instead of Helping, Police Sometimes Shoot the Mentally Ill," *Daytona Beach News-Journal*, 2015, http://creative.news-journalonline.com/shotsfired/lethal.html.

7. https://assets.documentcloud.org/documents/3146953/Living-With-Schizophrenia-by-Deborah-Danner.pdf.

8. "Cherokee County Teen Shot by Police Sniper, Parents Speak Out," CBS46.com, October 25, 2012, www.cbs46.com/story/19917831/teen-shot-by-police-sniper-parents-talk-only-to-cbs-atlanta-news.

9. Jonathan Edwards, "Norfolk Officers Testify That David Latham Never Threatened Them Before He Was Shot, Killed," *Virginian-Pilot*, September 28, 2016.

10. Lynn Thompson, "Seattle Police Fatally Shoot Black Seattle Mother; Family Demands Answers," *Seattle Times,* June 18, 2017.

11. "Database of Police Shootings."

12. Cindy Rodriguez, "New York's Kindest," WNYC Radio, December 23, 2015, www.wnyc.org/story/new-yorks-kindest.

13. Darren DaRonco and Carli Brosseau, "Many in Mental Crisis Call Tucson Police: Health Agency to Help TPD Prioritize Queries Starting This Summer," *Arizona Daily Star,* April 14, 2013, http://tucson.com/news/local/crime /many-in-mental-crisis-call-tucson-police/article_a03800d9-6608-5907-9fc4 -74ad7f9c441a.html.

14. Written testimony of Alfonza Wysinger, First Deputy Superintendent, Chicago Police Department, Before the Senate Judiciary Subcommittee on the Constitution, Civil Rights, and Human Rights, "Law Enforcement Responses to Disabled Americans: Promising Approaches for Protecting Public Safety Hearing," April 29, 2014, www.judiciary.senate.gov/imo/media/doc/04-29-1WysingerTestimony.pdf.

15. Norman Dain, *Disordered Minds: The First Century of Eastern State Hospital in Williamsburg, Virginia, 1766–1866* (Williamsburg, VA: Colonial Williamsburg Foundation, 1971), 17.

16. Oklahoma Department of Mental Health and Substance Abuse Services, "Fiscal Year 2016 Budget Request," January 2015, https://www.ok.gov/odmhsas /documents/FY16%20Budget%20Narrative%20-%20Updated.pdf.

17. J. Ruiz and C. Miller, "An Exploratory Study of Pennsylvania Police Officers' Perceptions of Dangerousness and Their Ability to Manage Persons with Mental Illness," *Police Quarterly* 7, no. 3 (2004): 359–371.

18. Linda Teplin and Nancy S. Pruett, "Police as Streetcorner Psychiatrist: Managing the Mentally Ill," *International Journal of Law and Psychiatry* 14 (1992): 139–156.

19. Egon Bittner, "Police Discretion in Emergency Apprehension of Mentally Ill Persons," *Social Problems* 14, no. 3 (1967): 278–292.

20. "Assistant Attorney General for the Civil Rights Division Thomas E. Perez Speaks at the City of Portland, Ore. Press Conference," September 13, 2012, www.justice.gov/opa/speech/assistant-attorney-general-civil-rights-division -thomas-e-perez-speaks-city-portland-ore.

21. Jasmine Turner, "Bryon Vassey Takes the Stand in Day 11 of the Trial," WECT, May 3, 2016, www.wect.com/story/31874924/bryon-vassey-takes-the -stand-in-day-11-of-trial.

22. Force Review Board Findings 2017-219301 spdblotter.seattle.gov/wp-content /uploads/2017/12/SPD-Force-Review-Board-Officer-Involved-Shooting.pdf

23. Ashley Luthern, "City of Milwaukee Reaches Tentative $2.3 Million Settlement in Dontre Hamilton Case," *Milwaukee Journal Sentinel,* May 9, 2017.

24. Jonathan Edwards and Eric Hartley, "Norfolk Family Agrees to Settle for $1.5 Million After Officer Killed Mentally Ill Relative," *Virginian-Pilot,* October 4, 2017.

Chapter 12 The Good-Cop Solution

1. Steve Osborne, *True Tales from the Life of a New York City Cop* (New York: Doubleday, 2015), 34.
2. Amy C. Watson and Anjali J. Fulambarker, "The Crisis Intervention Team Model of Police Response to Mental Health Crises: A Primer for Mental Health Practitioners," *Best Practices in Mental Health* 8, no. 2 (2012): 71.
3. Barbara A. Burch and Celeste Williams, "Fatal Police Fire Hits Man 10 Times: Stabbing Report Sparks Disputed Confrontation," *Commercial Appeal,* September 25, 1987.
4. John Beifuss, "Police-Citizen Link Rattled by Killing: Holt Will Hear Silent Partners," *Commercial Appeal,* October 1, 1987.
5. https://www.bjs.gov/index.cfm?ty=tp&tid=71.
6. Egon Bittner, "Police Discretion in Emergency Apprehension of Mentally Ill Persons," *Social Problems* 14, no. 3 (1967): 278–292.

Chapter 13 Disorder in the Court

1. James C. McKinley, Jr., "New York's Top Judge Picks Bronx as Site to Detail Courts' Flaws and Gains," *New York Times,* February 22, 2017.
2. https://csgjusticecenter.org/wp-content/uploads/2013/05/CTBNYC-Court -Jail_7-cc.pdf.
3. John F. Pfaff, *Locked In: The True Causes of Mass Incarceration and How to Achieve Real Reform* (New York: Basic, 2017), 133.
4. Ibid., 130–131.

Conclusion

1. State of Louisiana v. Isaiah Doyle, Omnibus Motion for a New Trial, for Arrest of Judgment, to Bar the Death Penalty and for Relief from Discrimination in Jury Selection, July 25, 2011.
2. Ibid.
3. Paul Purpura, "Harvey Man Guilty of First-Degree Murder for Killing Store Clerk in Marrero Robbery," *Times-Picayune,* March 24, 2011.
4. William Blackstone, *Blackstone's Commentaries on the Laws of England. Book the Fourth—Chapter the Second: Of Persons Capable of Committing Crimes,* 24, http:// avalon.law.yale.edu/18th_century/blackstone_bk4ch2.asp.
5. Ford v. Wainwright, 477 U.S. 399 (No. 85–5542), https://www.law.cornell.edu /supremecourt/text/477/399#writing-USSC_CR_0477_0399_ZO.
6. www.latimes.com/opinion/opinion-la/la-ol-rall-san-quentin-death-row -mental-hospit-001-photo.html.
7. Gerald Grob, *From Asylum to Community: Mental Health Policy in Modern America* (Princeton, NJ: Princeton University Press, 2014), 91.

Index

Alisa Roth is a former staff reporter at *Marketplace* and frequent contributor to National Public Radio and other outlets. A Soros Justice Fellow, her work has also appeared in the *New York Review of Books* and *New York Times*. She lives in New York.